Theology and Literature

T. R. WRIGHT

Basil Blackwell

Basil Blackwell Ltd
108 Cowley Road, Oxford, OX4 1JF, UK

Basil Blackwell Inc.
432 Park Avenue South, Suite 1503
New York, NY 10016, USA

British Library Cataloguing in Publication Data

Wright, T. R
    Theology and literature.—(Signposts
    in theology).
    1. Christianity and literature
    2. Theology
    I. Title   II. Series
    230   PN49
    ISBN 0–631–14848–5
    ISBN 0–631–14849–3 Pbk

Library of Congress Cataloging in Publication Data

Wright, T. R (Terence R.), 1951–
    Theology and literature.

    (Signposts in theology).
    Bibliography: p.
    Includes index.
    1. Religion and literature.   2. Bible as literature.
    3. Theology in literature. I. Title. II. Series.
    PN49.W73   1988   809'.93382   87–21793
    ISBN 0–631–14848–5
    ISBN 0–631–14849–3 (pbk.)

Typeset in 10 on 12pt Century Schoolbook
by Opus, Oxford
Printed in Great Britain by Page Bros., Norwich

CONTENTS

vi   *Contents*

PREFACE

This book is *about* theology and literature but *by* a literary critic, which probably accounts both for its strengths and its weaknesses. Thank God, some might say, that it was not written by the sort of theologian who would have been tempted simply to use literature in order to 'illustrate' theological concepts. Others may detect what they would call a want of conceptual rigour in my approach. I ask them at least to postpone judgement until they have considered my arguments about the nature of language and entertained at least the possibility of literary forms conveying theological meaning.

It sometimes seems that there are two different ways of thinking: one that assumes literary forms, whether narrative, poetic, or dramatic, and another that argues 'systematically' in terms of concepts. Many theologians, certainly, have fallen into this second category but my thesis is that theology need not be confined to this; it is possible and even necessary to talk about God in the form of stories, poems and plays. This book is an attempt to continue a dialogue that has already begun between theologians and literary critics on the nature of their disciplines and the possibility of interaction between them.

If there is to be such a dialogue, of course, we must learn to use each other's languages. I have tried as far as possible both to understand theological terms and to explain the many new terms which modern critical theory has brought to bear upon literature. These terms can be annoying (as any new 'jargon' always is). But I ask readers who are unfamiliar with them to make the attempt to understand how they are used and to appreciate their power to describe literary effects which could not previously be observed for want of a vocabulary.

This book, I should explain, is systematic but not

comprehensive, attempting to cover the main areas of inter-action between theology and literature over a wide range of historical periods. Whole areas have been omitted, however, in order to focus in some depth on a few representative texts. My selection no doubt reflects my own personal enthusiasms. But I have tried to represent as fully as possible the range of work that has already been done in this area and to suggest lines along which future research can proceed.

I should, of course, acknowledge a deep indebtedness to the pioneers in this field, mostly in America, where religion and literature have been linked at university level for at least four decades. My notes, bulky though they may seem, reflect only a fraction of this debt. I am particularly grateful to the American Academy of Religion and to the National Conference of Literature and Religion in this country, whose conferences have sparked off much of my thinking. Among individuals who have helped me most David Jasper deserves the greatest thanks but I have also received encouragement and advice from Stephan Chambers, John Coulson, Robert Detweiler, John Frankis, Ernst Honigmann, Ann Loades, John Milbank, Judie Newman, Stephen Prickett, John Sawyer, Kenneth Surin, Stephen Sykes, Bill Telford and Kelsey Thornton. My deepest gratitude, however, goes to my wife, Gabriele, who has helped me in countless ways through each stage of this book's production.

CHAPTER 1

Towards a Poetics of Faith

THEOLOGY AND LITERATURE: A CREATIVE TENSION

Titles with 'and' are always ambiguous, for this small conjunction covers a multitude of possible connections. This short book, which cannot, of course, cover the whole of both subjects, will consider instead the relationship between them, those areas in which both theology and literature are involved. This, then, will be a study of what has become known as the 'interface' between theology and literature, a critical reading of texts in which these two disciplines meet and act upon each other.[1] These meetings are not always friendly since the assumptions of one discipline are often the heresies of another. Much theology, for example, tends towards unity and coherence, a systematic exploration of the content of faith which attempts to impose limits on the meaning of words, while literature, as Ezra Pound insisted, is often dangerous, subversive and chaotic, an anarchic celebration of the creative possibilities of language.[2] Yet language, which will be the main focus of this first chapter, is the medium both subjects hold in common and it is on the ability of language to express truths about life, however indirectly, that the importance of both disciplines rests.

Theology and literature also share a common enemy, a pervasive literalism which prevents many people from understanding the nature of Christian belief. As the House of Bishops of the Church of England complained,

> Western popular culture today has adopted a greatly oversimplified view of language. On this view only so-called 'factual' statements convey objective truths, while 'metaphor', 'poetry',

'symbolism' and suchlike refer solely to ideas existing in the mind. Thus, to call a story 'symbolic', for example, is thought to imply that it is fictional and that what it seeks to express is wholly within the human psyche. Neither assumption is correct.[3]

Poems, stories and plays, it is the purpose of this book to demonstrate, can express important theological truths. In some respects they provide a more acceptable means of talking about God than does systematic theology since they recognize more fully their own limitations as constructs of imagination and ideology. They claim merely to point towards a reality they cannot define.

Systematic theology often gives the impression of being too cut and dried, reducing the essential mystery of ultimate reality to a set of clearly defined concepts. But not all theology is systematic of the sort associated with Aquinas or Calvin, Tillich or Barth:

> There is a way to do theology, a way that runs from the gospels and Paul through Augustine and Luther to Teilhard and the Berrigans . . . which relies on various literary forms – parables, stories, poems, confessions.[4]

It is this alternative tradition which is the subject of this book, beginning with the Bible itself, the most obvious example of a text, or collection of texts, which relies on a variety of literary forms to express theological insight. Subsequent chapters sketch the outlines of a comprehensive 'poetics of faith', considering in turn the extent to which narrative, poetry and drama have been involved in the theological task of exploring the Christian faith.

Both theology and literature are better described, in fact, as procedures, in terms of what theologians and literary critics do, rather than as objects of study or bodies of knowledge. 'At the present', a recent introduction to the traditions and tasks of Christian theology disconcertingly begins, 'there is no general agreement even as to what theology is.'[5] The traditional definition, that it is faith seeking understanding, remains valid because it is so inclusive, comprehending all areas of God's creation. On this global map, von Balthasar has argued, 'theological aesthetics' should appear not merely as a 'little-travelled side-road' but a 'main artery' in the Catholic tradition. For truth, beauty and goodness are equally important aspects of God's grace as perceived by man.

In von Balthasar's view, theology should abandon 'the extra-theological categories of a worldly philosophical aesthetics (above all poetry)' and develop its own 'theory of beauty from the data of revelation itself', which he proceeds to do (in seven formidable volumes).[6] My own aim is more limited and also more liberal (and therefore open to the accusation of compromising with secular values): to work within the limits of 'worldly' criticism in order to explore some of the literary forms adopted by faith. It will be more a 'poetics of faith' than a 'theology of poetry', starting with the literary forms as they stand and attempting to assess their theological significance rather than developing theological principles with which to evaluate literary products.

If theology can only be described in the most general terms, literature seems altogether to defy definition. A recent introduction to *Literary Theory*, for example, begins with the question 'What is Literature?' only to abandon in despair the attempt to define the intrinsic qualities that comprise literariness, concluding that literature is not an 'object', certainly not an unchanging canon, but a reflection of how we read and value texts. Gibbon's *Decline and Fall of the Roman Empire* accordingly becomes literature when we read it not for information about ancient Rome but for its impressive style.[7] Literature, like theology, is more easily defined in functional rather than ontological terms, in terms of the effects for which readers and critics value certain texts. It is a matter of what they do for us and what we do to them. The content of a literature syllabus, as of a course in theology, can be expected to vary widely between different institutions but the students can still be said to be engaged in the study of literature and theology respectively.

Literature, then, should not be hypostasized (though the debates within literary criticism as to the nature of its object of study are every bit as violent as those between rival factions in theological controversy). But there are certain tasks which literary critics can be said to share, certain assumptions which they hold in common about the texts which they read. One of the most important of these, one of the few principles on which all critics agree, is the inseparability of form and content, a belief staunchly defended against the heresy of paraphrase. 'A literary work *is* its meaning'; its meaning cannot be 'abstracted' from it, cannot be paraphrased without loss.[8] Any interpretation, therefore, although it can analyse the various effects achieved by certain formal devices, cannot say precisely what the work means. The whole point of reading literature, its importance as a humane discipline, beyond that of giving pleasure (which is by no means unimportant), is that it says something about life which cannot be said in any other way. Literary devices, in other words, are not just ornamental, imparting additional eloquence to an otherwise bald and unconvincing statement or narrative. They have the capacity to generate new meaning by stretching language beyond its ordinary uses.

The dynamic capacity of literature to generate fresh meaning has its dangers, or at least poses a threat to the theologian who is struggling to impose order and system upon language. Writing, especially, is more versatile than speech. We can always ask a speaker what he or she means but having once committed his or her thoughts to paper an author loses any authority over their meaning: 'Once it has entered into the death of the text, the word . . . can be freed from the surface, resurrected, variously.' The meaning of *the* Word is therefore inexhaustible; the revelation of Christ has come, is present and is still to come, preventing any final closure of meaning.[9]

All this may be very exciting but seems to point towards a disruption of the theological project. 'The Death of the Author', in Roland Barthes' view at least, leads automatically to the death of God. Literature, or rather writing,

> by refusing to assign a 'secret', an ultimate meaning, to the text (and to the world as text), liberates what may be called an anti-theological activity, an activity that is truly revolutionary since to refuse to fix meaning is, in the end, to refuse God and his hypostases – reason, science, law.[10]

It is the fixation of meaning to which Barthes objects, as does Julia Kristeva, who claims that 'poetic language' is 'the enemy of religion', disrupting the constraints of 'transcendental rationality', reactivating libidinal drives suppressed by the reason.[11] For them there is no ultimate meaning to the text or to the world. Literature functions rather like striptease, to quote the fictional Morris Zapp, holding out the 'promise of an ultimate revelation which is infinitely postponed'. The text never allows itself to be possessed; the role of the reader is merely to 'take pleasure in its teasing'.[12]

This tension between theology and literature is not altogether new. The rise of English as an academic subject, with all the messianic fervour of its pioneers, can be interpreted as an ideological revolution, the 'saving' qualities of a finely tuned response to literature quite seriously being offered as a replacement religion, filling the vacuum of values created by the decline of orthodox Christianity. Looking on *Science and Literature* as alternative ways of organizing the world, I. A. Richards wrote of the need to throw off old religions, to turn instead to the values created by poetry, which 'is capable of saving us'; and such was the fervour with which Leavis and his disciples preached their new gospel that their enemies were soon calling them 'puritans' and religious fanatics.[13]

It may well be that there is a broad temperamental difference of the kind noted by Isaiah Berlin between hedgehogs, who are drawn towards holistic systems of belief, wanting to fit the universe into a single all-embracing pattern, and foxes, who prefer to take experience as it comes, in all its bewildering variety. The first type, the theory goes, is drawn towards theology, the second towards literature.[14] It would be absurd, however, to expect all theologians to behave like hedgehogs and all literary figures to be foxes. All it seems safe to say is that there is, in the modern period at least, a tension between the two subjects, a tension which has been exacerbated by the decline of belief in Christianity and the rise of literature as the provider of a new canon, a new set of scriptures enshrining an alternative set of liberal-humanist values.

A medievalist might express some surprise at the notion of literature as a rival to theology rather than its handmaiden. In the Renaissance too, as will become apparent later in the study of some of the great plays of the period, the tension between

Christianity and humanism was more implicit than openly avowed. Luther, for example, encouraged young people to study literature as the forerunner to revelation, a John the Baptist preparing the way for the Word of God. 'In almost all the classics of European literature written before the nineteenth century', John Coulson rightly reminds us, 'their authors assume the truth of the Christian faith.'[15] The onus of proof, he claims, then switched from the unbeliever to the believer. God, it has been claimed, disappeared from literature in the nineteenth century, which is, after all, when Nietzsche said that He had died.[16] Julian Huxley allowed him to linger on into our own century, calling the interest in Christianity still displayed by modern poets 'the last fading smile of a cosmic Cheshire Cat'.[17] That interest nevertheless persists among both poets and novelists, demanding a rather closer analysis than these dismissals would suggest.

In fact, if literature 'embodies what it indicates', as Auden believed, so that form and content, medium and message, are inseparable,[18] then it should fit very well into an incarnational theology. For Christ is the Word made flesh, a revelation recorded in language, in the story told by the gospels. His teaching too took the form of parables, of striking paradoxes and challenging metaphors. Jesus, as we shall see, is presented by Mark as forever admonishing his disciples for their narrowly literal understanding. The Bible itself, then, and much subsequent reflection on the meaning of faith, assumes literary form, employing narrative, metaphor, symbol and paradox in order to explore the truth. Christian poetics can therefore feel confident that it is not a peripheral part of theology.

Some explanation nevertheless needs to be found for the fact that much of modern literature has been either explicitly or implicitly hostile to the faith. Literature, Newman suggested, reflects 'the natural man' with all 'the leapings and the friskings, the plungings and the snortings, the sportings and the buffoonings' to be expected of 'the noble, lawless savage of God's intellectual creation' unenlightened by revelation.[19] A more universal theory suggests that an underlying pattern of life, death and resurrection can be found even in literature which is not overtly Christian.[20] Neither of these theories, which belong more to the theology of poetry than the poetics of faith, seems entirely satisfactory, partly because they attempt to embrace the whole of literature in their judgements. My own approach will be less holistic, focusing on particular texts as models of theological reflection in literary form.

One way of defining the area of overlap between theology and literature more precisely is to focus on the role of the imagination in both. 'Faith is a form of imagining and experiencing the world', writes one literary critic, elevating theology to 'a colleague imagination' rather than 'a desiccated beggar in search of help from the artist'.[21] Literary critics are often tempted to admonish theologians for their failure to exercise imagination. John Coulson, for example, sets out 'to show what the student and teacher of religion may gain from cultivating a properly imaginative response to literature'. Discussing Newman's distinction between notional or merely conceptual and real assent, he rebukes those theologians who ignore the role of the imagination, 'whose conceptions, by being thus "unlettered", are starved into "notions" and languish in seminary confinement'.[22] The split between theology and literature that he locates in the twentieth century is certainly to be deplored. But there are signs that it has not gone as far as he suggests. Many theologians are now aware of the importance of *The Theological Imagination* in constructing the symbols and concepts on which faith is fed. Theology, one of them claims, 'is (and always has been) essentially a constructive work of the human imagination . . . developing a symbolical "picture" of the world'.[23]

This kind of approach is sometimes suspected of being too Romantic, based too heavily upon a Kantian scepticism about the possibility of reason encompassing the absolute.[24] Schleiermacher's emphasis on feeling as the fundamental core of religion is perhaps the major theological strand of this tradition. It is certainly to the Romantic poets that Nathan Scott turns in his study of *The Poetics of Belief*, quoting Wordsworth on 'that highest candle that lights the dark', the imagination, which Blake calls 'the divine body of the Saviour, the True Vine of Eternity'.[25] What Coleridge is at pains to point out in the *Biographia Literaria*, however, is that the imagination is neither completely passive before an external object nor completely active in the construction of its images, as if unlimited by the constraints of the external world. The imagination is both 'the living power and prime agent of all human perception' and 'a repetition in the finite mind of the eternal act of creation in the infinite I AM'. It builds upon the material of sense-data which it 'dissolves, diffuses, dissipates, in order to recreate'.[26] Wordsworth is therefore praised for achieving 'the union of deep feeling with profound thought; the fine balance of truth in observing with the imaginative faculty in modifying the objects observed'.[27] The very distinction between subject and object, the integral Cartesian consciousness confronted with a mechanical external world, is broken down by the Romantics' insistence on an interchange between the two.

The recognition of the role of the imagination in theology was not, however, confined to the Romantics. Aquinas, as we shall see, stressed the importance of analogy in the theological enterprise, while Ignatius Loyola was forever exhorting the practitioners of his *Spiritual Exercises* to use their imaginations. At one point, for example, he instructs them, 'Imagining Christ our Lord before us and placed on the Cross, to make a colloquy with Him, asking Him how, being our Creator, He had come to this'.[28] Another exercise he sets them is 'to bring the five senses of the imagination' to bear upon the pains of hell and the delights of heaven, to gain an 'interior sense' of what these are like.[29] In this sense, the imagination has always been an integral part of Christian worship and reflection.

It should nevertheless be admitted that the tendency of scholarship in theology and literature in the United States, where the two subjects have been studied together most productively since the 1950s, has been towards theological liberalism, drawing on such thinkers as Bonhoeffer, Bultmann, Tillich, Heidegger, the Niebuhrs, Ricoeur and others, all of them working from human experience upwards rather than beginning with Barth from the absolute revealed Word of God. The focus throughout the 'first stage' of the joint enterprise, evident in the work of such pioneers as Amos Wilder, William Beardslee and Nathan Scott, was upon the existential significance of literature. Unlike the New Critics (to be discussed later), who tried to seal off literature from all contact with faith or history, they argued that the relevance of literature depended upon its relation to life, its capacity to illuminate the human condition.[30] British scholarship, it should be noted, has, until very recently and with a few exceptions, been rather suspicious of the whole business, preferring to keep theology and literature as discrete (and preferably discreet) disciplines.[31]

One of the strongest condemnations of the attempt to mix the two disciplines came from Samuel Johnson, who found the idea of 'poetical devotion' altogether repellent: 'The ideas of Christian Theology are too simple for eloquence, too sacred for fiction, and too majestick for ornament.'[32] Novelty was something altogether out of place in religion, as T. S. Eliot, writing in the same classical tradition, insisted. Those 'parasites' who praised sacred texts for their literary merits were merely erecting a monument over the grave of true religion. 'I could fulminate', he observed, 'against the men of letters who have gone into ecstasies over "the Bible as literature", the Bible as "the noblest monument of English prose".'[33] Helen Gardner, as we shall see, launched similar attacks on all attempts to discover literary qualities in the gospel of St Mark.[34] She also confessed to finding it difficult to 'criticise or evaluate' hymns because they were so 'intricately involved' with her religious life,[35] an inhibition which she implies should have prevented Lord David Cecil, in his introduction to the *Oxford Book of Christian Verse*, from dismissing most hymns as 'poor stuff', full of 'feeble sentiment' and 'flat conventional expression'.[36]

Helen Gardner specifically attacks the Romantic demand for originality, which finds it not enough that a poet 'make more vivid to us what we already know and feel' but insists he make us 'know and feel what without him we should never have known and felt'.[37] She appears to assume that 'truth' can be revealed in straightforward language without 'literary' distortion and that Christian doctrines and feelings require protection against the ravages of the intellect. These assumptions are examined in the following sections of this chapter, which consider in turn the dangers of literalism, the nature of language and the referentiality of literature. My main point will be that it is because no language is completely transparent upon reality, providing unambiguous 'names' for clear-cut 'things', that the indirect mode of reference employed in literature constitutes some of the most effective theology. The remainder of the book will illustrate in greater detail the ways in which theology uses language in literary, non-literal ways in order to generate meanings which could not be attained in any other way.

The study of 'The Bible as Literature' in the second chapter is certainly not parasitic in Eliot's sense. Attention is by no means directed towards its 'style' in isolation from its 'meaning'. Nor is the approach casual. For, in Austin Farrer's words, 'They say that the Bible makes good reading, but unless you are concerned for the salvation of mankind, you will prefer to look for your reading elsewhere.'[38] The Bible demands a response which alters our whole mode of being in the world. It provides an answer to the meaning of history but one which is couched in the form of myths, stories, chronicle, poetry, sermon and prophecy, a variety of literary forms which require literary interpretation. It is a religious classic, *the* religious classic, with the capacity to call from its variety of historical periods to that of the reader.[39] But it remains a classic only in the minds of its readers, which is why the gradual disappearance of familiarity with the King James Bible, one of 'the greatest literary achievements in the English language',[40] is a source of despair to so many people.

The Bible, then, is more or less literature. In some ways it is less, 'a spectacularly bad poem';[41] in other ways more, for it demands more in the way of response than other literature. The second chapter of this book will consider first the insights that can be gained from literary criticism of the Bible. Traditional biblical criticism has been primarily historical in orientation, using the texts as evidence for what actually happened and subordinating all 'literary criticism' to this end. In recent years, however, there has been a growing tendency to read the Bible as literature, taking the text as a whole and analysing the literary means by which it achieves its effects. This theoretical introduction to the principles involved in literary criticism of the Bible leads to a consideration of two particular texts, Genesis and Mark, asking to what extent they are readable as literature and attempting to draw out the theological significance of the literary forms they adopt.

The question of narrative, the subject of chapter 3, is one that has dominated both theology and literature in recent years. The telling of stories, which clearly fulfils basic human needs, is involved in the way we make sense of ourselves and of the world, whether in history, myth, or fiction. After discussing the development of narrative theology, the increasing emphasis on story as a mode of expressing the Christian faith, I turn to confessional writing or autobiography from Augustine through medieval mystics such as Margery Kempe and Calvinist soul-searchers such as Bunyan to that Victorian 'Father of the Second Vatican Council', John Henry Newman. By the nineteenth century, of course, the novel had become the dominant literary form, so it is not surprising that the last two centuries have seen a massive outpouring of religious fiction, some explicitly didactic, arguing openly for a particular point of view, others implicitly ideological, encapsulating their message in their form. The final section of this third chapter considers the abandonment of metaphysics by the great realist tradition represented in the nineteenth century by George Eliot and in the twentieth by Iris Murdoch. Resisted by defenders of Catholic orthodoxy such as Evelyn Waugh, Graham Greene and Flannery O'Connor, it has recently been undermined by metafiction, that post-modernist recognition not only of the illusory nature of realist fiction but of the fictive nature of the 'real world' as it is constructed by the bourgeois liberal-humanist ideology known as 'common sense'.

If narrative is the way we construct our sense of identity, metaphor is how we think, especially in areas in which we need to build our knowledge of the unknown by comparison with the known. The fourth chapter of this book therefore examines some of the basic figurative devices employed both by theologians and by poets. Metaphors abound as much in Tertullian and St Teresa as in metaphysical poets such as Donne, Herbert, Vaughan and Crashaw, whose violent yoking together of heterogeneous elements so scandalized a later age, concerned to impose more rigorous control upon language. Symbols too are of vital importance to poetic language, participating, as Tillich insisted, in the reality to which they point. The cross can be seen to have provided a central symbol of poetic meditation while the sacraments of the Church resound with natural symbols such as water, bread and wine. The Romantics and Symbolists in particular rebelled against the constraints of a rationalism which threatened to 'desacralize' the world, to empty it of all religious significance. Wordsworth's 'theology' sees nature itself as a sacrament, while T. S. Eliot rejuvenates the traditional symbols of Christianity. The third poetic device on which I will concentrate is paradox, which is at the heart of Christian doctrine. Pascal and Kierkegaard are perhaps the best-known writers who press Christian paradox to the limits of sense but Newman too belongs at least in part to this tradition. Paradox and its inevitable corollary, ambiguity, are particularly evident in the work of contemporary poets such as Geoffrey Hill and R.S. Thomas, with whom this chapter ends.

There is, finally, a sense in which liturgy can be seen as the drama of faith, enacting theological meaning in ritual. The concluding chapter will consider some of the ways in which a study of drama could contribute to a complete poetics of faith. Liturgy itself often assumes dramatic form, growing into fully-fledged liturgical drama in the medieval period. The Corpus Christi cycle of mystery plays 'enacts' the Christian view of the world, centred as it is on the body of Christ. Renaissance tragedies such as *Dr. Faustus* and *Macbeth* dramatize the conflicting ideologies of that period, while absurd drama, represented here by the work of Samuel Beckett, displays a continuing if desperate fascination with Christian theology. Drama, like other literary forms, does not necessarily resolve conceptual difficulties; it displays them, acting them out physically on stage and thereby coming to a fuller understanding.

The central tension between systematic theology and literature can be seen throughout this detailed analysis. In literature, meaning is never fixed; any 'complete' interpretation would render the literary 'work' redundant (both the artefact and the imaginative processes involved in its production, its writing and its reading). Interpretation of literature is always a temporary illumination, never, fortunately, a 'final solution'. There will always, therefore, be a tension between conceptual and creative discourse. Systematic theology will continue the necessary attempt to impose clarity and consistency upon language while literature will no doubt maintain its equally necessary task, to explore, to complicate and to enrich the apparent security of theological concepts.

LITERALISM: THE COMMON ENEMY

One of the main purposes of encouraging an interaction between theology and literature is to avoid the dangers of literalism. For anyone unacquainted with the devices by which meaning is achieved language often appears to be transparent, a clear window on to an external world of objects waiting simply to be given names. But language works not only in literature but in science as a rather special kind of window, organizing what is seen and even, some would argue, constructing its 'objects'. This is Max Black's analogy:

> Suppose I look at the night sky through a piece of heavily smoked glass on which certain lines have been left clear. Then I shall see only the stars that can be made to lie on the lines previously prepared upon the screen, and the stars I do see will be seen as organised by the screen's structure.

Metaphors function in this manner, allowing us to see something in the 'light' of a new 'lens', the optical metaphors here pointing to a mental process which is not itself visual but is 'like' what happens when we quite literally look at visible objects. Black uses the simple example, 'Man is a wolf', to illustrate the way in which the 'wolf-language' reorganizes our view of man. The new insight gained by the new point of view, the new properties of the object made open to our gaze, he accepts, can be explored further in straightforward 'plain language':

> But the set of literal statements so obtained will not have the same power to inform and enlighten as the original ... The literal paraphrase inevitably says too much – and with the wrong emphasis.

It is not just that it is 'boringly explicit', leaving too little to the imagination. It actually says something different.[42]

More complex theories of metaphor will be considered in chapter 4. My present concern, however, is the problem of literalism, which arises, according to Northrop Frye, from a 'cultural prejudice' produced by generations of common-sense empiricism which associates 'truth' with 'descriptive verbal structures', giving all words connected with literary devices, such as 'myth', 'fable', or 'fiction', the secondary meaning 'not really true'.[43] Frye has fun at the expense of the biblical fundamentalism so dominant in the United States, which misreads the literary as the literal. In Norse sagas, for example, which contain a mixture of chronicle and myth, history and fiction, not dissimilar to some parts of the Bible, readers remain undisturbed by insistent demands that the stories about the unipeds, who possess only one foot, should be taken literally. When it comes to the Bible, however, there are determined attempts to take every single detail as historically accurate, to read Ezekiel's chariot of fire in terms of spaceships, explain Moses bringing water out of the rock as a primitive form of dowsing and to rejoice at reports of boat-shaped structures on Mount Ararat, complete with animal cages, as vindicating a literal reading of the Book of Genesis.[44] To look for ancient records of extraordinary stars and lunar eclipses coinciding with the birth and death of Christ may seem a harmless enough hobby but points to a misreading of the gospels as literally true in every detail.

Aquinas attempted to escape this kind of problem by defining the Bible's *sensus literalis* as its intended meaning: 'When Scripture speaks of the arm of God, the literal sense is not that he has a physical limb, but that he has what it signifies, namely the power of doing and making'.[45] This certainly avoids the naïvety of literalism as normally understood but raises additional problems. For the intentional fallacy is as much anathema to literary critics as the heresy of paraphrase. The 'intended' meaning of an utterance clearly lies in the mind of the speaker but the mind of an author is often unattainable. Meaning is not, in any case, simply wrapped in language as in a parcel, waiting patiently to be unwrapped by the recipient. Nor does a reader behave like

Jack Horner, joyfully removing the plums placed in the text by the author. For meaning changes with context, and contexts, of course, are limitless. It has become a kind of parlour-game among modern schools of criticism to invent new contexts which produce ludic meanings, clearly unintended by their authors, as part of a campaign against lucidity, the belief that language is, or should be, transparent. Others would accept some degree of control over language, some 'rules' governing what is an appropriate reading of a given text. But all would agree that part of the excitement of literature lies in the unpredictability of language, its capacity for happy accidents, the 'grace' that attends creative writing.

Another attack on the common-sense belief, common since Descartes founded the modern Western philosophical tradition by separating the discerning consciousness from the perceived world, that language is the vehicle by which autonomous 'subjects' describe pre-given 'objects', comes from a Marxist source. What is overlooked in this naïvely empirical tradition, according to Althusser, is the role of ideology in the very formation of these clearly demarcated 'subjects' and 'objects'. Ideology, in this new sense, involves the 'interpellation' of individuals in their society, equipping them with an appropriate understanding of themselves and of their world, an understanding which becomes so familiar as to appear 'natural'. As Tony Bennett explains,

> Ideology might thus be said to consist of those myths through which individuals are reconciled to their given social positions by falsely representing to them those positions and the relationships between them as if they formed part of some inherently significant, intrinsically coherent plan or process.[46]

Some form of ideology is, of course, a necessary part of any individual's sense of belonging to any society but it can be more or less 'false', more or less aware of its 'fictive' elements, more or less self-critical. Any ideology inscribes individuals into their society by means of rituals, material practices which confirm the subject's self-understanding:

> The celebration of communion might thus be regarded as quintessentially ideological. It consists of a practice of signification which, inscribed in ritual form and housed within the

ideological apparatus of the church, produces the consciousness of the communicant.[47]

To be aware of the processes by which our thoughts are produced, to be aware of the materiality of language, which controls us as much as we control it, is to be guarded against the dangers of literalism.

Theology, then, could be called a form of ideology, a set of concepts and practices which form our understanding of ourselves and the world. This does not mean that the language of theology is non-referential but that its mode of reference is necessarily indirect, part of a whole system of perceiving and describing the universe which involves complex and even contradictory uses of language. It is possible, therefore, to maintain a belief in the external reality to which theological language points at the same time as accepting the limitations of that language. Simone Weil expresses this paradox neatly:

> There is a God. There is no God. Where is the problem? I am quite sure that there is a God in the sense that I am sure my love is no illusion. I am quite sure there is no God in the sense that I am sure there is nothing which resembles what I can conceive when I say that word.[48]

Some recognition of the gap between our language and the 'real' world helps to prevent too simple an identification of concepts and objects, words and things.

To call God 'Our Heavenly Father', for example, and to say that 'He is infinite' is not to ascribe 'a characteristic to a "thing" but to use models taken from ordinary experience to attempt a description of what is beyond that experience. These models, as Ian Ramsey has shown, are carefully qualified to emphasize their special status. God may be like a human father but He is also 'Heavenly', radically different.[49] Religious language often functions in this indirect way, stretching or even challenging habitual assumptions. It rarely uses words as 'labels for a group of hard, objective "facts" ', as if providing a 'verbal photograph' of God.[50] As Wittgenstein observed, 'God's eye sees everything' is a figurative comment upon His omniscience, not an encouragement for us to speculate whether He has shaggy eyebrows.[51]

It is scarcely surprising that philosophers who insist on 'literal' meaning find religious language unintelligible. In the revised version of A. J. Ayer's principle of verification, for example, 'a statement is held to be literally meaningful if and only if it is either analytic [which is to say tautological] or empirically verifiable'.[52] God clearly can't be proved empirically so becomes 'meaningless'. Mystics are forced to rely on 'non-literal' speech which 'on any literal interpretation, is obviously false'.[53] Ayer takes this argument to marginalize theological language as nonsense. But it can also serve to substantiate the need to go beyond literalism in theology. For theologians, in order to meet these objections, must acknowledge the value of figurative language as the necessary means of describing a God 'who cannot be named, except in tropes and figures'.[54]

The biblical tradition of talking about God is indeed indirect, allusive and figurative. He is described in terms of a series of metaphors: regal (He is King), legal (He is Judge) and domestic (He is Husband, Father, Lord, or Master). He is also a shepherd, a vine-keeper, a fountain, a mother hen and much more. To take these metaphors literally would clearly be absurd, while to place undue emphasis on any single model is to risk worshipping an idol. For feminist theologians, for example, the continued stress on God as Father is offensively one-sided,[55] while objections to altering the liturgical use of the male pronoun for God often reveal a refusal to accept the metaphorical status of these terms. The legal metaphor developed in patristic accounts of the atonement, making the merciful Son plead to the just Father, eventually offering himself as a sacrifice to appease paternal wrath and to pay the penalty for man's sin, the ransom owed to the devil for otherwise lost souls, paints a picture which seems excessively harsh and legalistic to most modern believers. The 'moral stop-card' which should have prevented this metaphor from being taken too literally was played too late in the development of this doctrine.[56]

The Old Testament tradition insists from the beginning that God cannot properly be named. When Moses asks before the burning bush what he should say to his people about their God, he is told, 'I AM THAT I AM . . . Thus shalt thou say unto the children of Israel, I AM hath sent me unto you' (Exodus 3:14). The name Yahweh, which He adopts in Exodus 6, is a scholarly reconstruction, filling out the unutterable tetragrammaton to compose a part of the verb 'to be'. This name is never to be taken in vain (20:7) nor can the reality to which it points ever be seen, 'for there shall no man see me and live' (33:20). Moses is, in fact, allowed a glimpse of His 'back parts' (33:23), but even the most rigid fundamentalist would find it difficult to take this literally. Job too wrestles with the problem of a God who cannot be seen (Job 9:11; 23:8–9) while the psalms celebrate a God who is seen only in his effects in nature and in history. He should be spoken of, they warn us, without anthropomorphism: 'thou thoughtest that I was altogether such an one as thyself: but I will reprove thee' (Psalm 50:21). The gap between man and God is emphasized by Isaiah: 'For my thoughts are not your thoughts, neither are your ways my ways, saith the Lord' (Isaiah 55:8). The Jewish practice of never presuming to utter or to write the sacred name maintains this reverent recognition of the limits of language.

The New Testament too recognizes these limits, continuing to teach that 'No man hath seen God at any time' (John 1:18). The name which Jesus clearly preferred, 'Son of Man', is 'beautifully problematical', preventing his being 'netted' by his disciples' preconceptions. The meaning of this term, as of the others used of Jesus in the New Testament, 'Christ', 'Messiah' and 'Son of God', are all radically altered by the events of his crucifixion and resurrection.[57] Context, once again, is seen to have determined meaning. Jesus' own teaching, of course, bristles with metaphors ('I am the door', 'I am the vine', 'I am the bread of life'), with extravagant hyperbole (He speaks of beams in people's eyes), and richly inventive parables.[58] His 'deliberately enigmatic and pretentious style of teaching', in fact, was one of the features to which the literal-minded Francis Newman most objected.[59] For literalism, as this example illustrates, fuels disbelief as much as belief.

It was Francis Newman's brother, the Cardinal, who pointed out that literalism can lead to heresy, as in the case of the Arians, who were over-anxious to distinguish between the

Father and the Son.[60] To say that Christ is God, that God is three persons in one, that the bread and wine celebrated in the eucharist are the body and blood of Christ, is to stretch language beyond the literal. 'His Majesty's Preface' to the Thirty-Nine Articles may insist that they be taken 'in the literal and grammatical sense', but Newman showed that they were susceptible to interpretations other than those intended by their compilers. The point, once more, is that meaning cannot be fixed. The language of doctrinal statements is riddled with 'literary' devices such as metaphor and paradox which defy literal interpretation. Theologians therefore find themselves constantly condemning 'immature and over-literal talk about God – talk which drags God down to some idolatrous fiction of our minds'.[61]

The language of our creeds and liturgy is also laden with figurative terms. The Nicene Creed, for instance, after a highly poetic evocation of Christ's divinity, full of repetition, imagery and conscious archaism ('Light of Light, Very God of Very God'), tells the story of his incarnation in mythical terms ('He came down from heaven'). His return to his mythical abode, where He is 'seated at the right hand of the Father', also defies literal interpretation. In addition to this, any recitation of the creed, as J.L. Austin has observed, has a performative force which is behabitive (expressing gratitude to God), verdictive (registering or re-registering a decision to embrace religion) and commissive (committing the speaker to certain courses of action).[62] It should not be regarded as a simple recitation of 'facts' about God.

The Lord's prayer performs similar functions. It too begins with a metaphor ('Our Father') followed by a myth ('Who art in heaven') which itself functions as one of Ramsey's qualifiers, making the limits of the metaphor abundantly clear. Taken literally, as a reference to the place where God actually lives, it would become heretical, since God cannot be confined within a single place. 'Hallowed be thy name' inculcates a properly respectful attitude not only towards the deity (His name acting as a metonymy for His person) but towards language. 'Thy kingdom come' involves one of the most complex metaphors of Jesus' teaching, while 'Give us this day our daily bread' uses part of our staple diet as a metaphor for the whole of God's creative and sustaining providence. The implied meaning, clearly, is not a request so much as an expression of gratitude, a recognition that we should not take the world for granted. The point need not be laboured. Our most basic liturgical practice involves the complex and indirect generation of meaning through richly suggestive language and a variety of literary devices. It was not created overnight but by generations of worship, writing, reading and reflection.[63]

A recognition of the literary, non-literal nature of liturgical language is a matter of vital importance. Ian Robinson, himself an unbeliever concerned for the survival of English rather than the Church of England, criticizes a more virulent atheist for her insistence that children be told 'in a factual way, the content of the myths and doctrines' of religion, for this would preclude any possibility of understanding them: 'For of course myths factually recounted, doctrines separate from their home in religious life, will be simple nonsense by the standards of the language of materialism'.[64] Robinson has been accused of aestheticism, of deploring new versions of the burial service on literary grounds, 'reviewing' the service like a literary critic. What he is actually attempting, however, is a defence of religious language against the literalism which sees style as a matter of ornament. To modernize the liturgy is not in itself to deprive it of poetic vigour. But to prefer the literal to the poetic is to impoverish the language.

THEOLOGY: A MATTER OF LANGUAGE

'The question of language,' it should now be clear, 'occupies a pivotal place in contemporary theology',[65] as it does in contemporary philosophy and literary theory. As Iris Murdoch said,

> We can no longer take language for granted as a medium of communication. Its transparency has gone. We are like people who for a long time looked out of a window without noticing the glass – and then one day began to notice this too.[66]

What for George Herbert was simply a matter of will,

A man that looks on glasse,
On it may stay his eye;
Or if he pleaseth through it passe,
And then the heav'n espy,[67]

has become for many modern schools of thought an impossibility. For they see language as an impenetrable barrier, a completely enclosed system without reference to any extralinguistic reality. I want to challenge this view, first in philosophy and then in theology. Literature, too, I will argue in the following section, while not directly describing 'real objects', can claim to depict 'reality' indirectly, by means of linguistic and literary conventions which are not merely self-referential. It is possible to advance from sense, an understanding of the 'internal organization' of a text, to reference, its capacity 'to refer to a reality' beyond itself.[68]

Language is too easily polarized into descriptive and expressive, cognitive and emotional, functional and aesthetic, objective and subjective. Two of Wittgenstein's Viennese contemporaries, for example, described the attempt to blur this distinction as mistaking urns for chamber-pots and vice versa.[69] The whole point about Keats's Grecian Urn, however, is that it does have something to 'say'. The whole poem has a meaning, unparaphrasable though it may be, a meaning which refers to the real world, in which beauty and truth should not be separated. The debate over language and its function in philosophy, and theology, summarized in the next few pages, all hinges on this same basic point. Wittgenstein himself, developing from a straightforward 'naming' view of words as pictures of things to a more complex theory of autonomous language-games relating (if only obliquely) to the real world, will be taken as a focal point in the development from the literalism of logical positivism to what has been called 'critical realism', an acceptance of the essentially figurative nature of language which does not undermine its potential referentiality.

This basic division between 'objective' views of the Word, which Barth is sometimes taken to represent, and the 'subjective' extreme exemplified by Heidegger and the New Hermeneutic, between the 'conservative' notion of doctrines as propositions containing information about the world and the 'liberal' understanding of them as symbols of inner experience, is a major problem in modern theology. Recent 'post-liberal' theories, fed by developments in anthropology and linguistics, have tried to solve this dilemma by seeing doctrines as 'merely' language, self-contained systems by which the Christian community constitutes its world. They appeal to literature as another example of a self-enclosed semiotic system. But to deny all referential function to these systems is, as I hope to show, an extremely dangerous move to make.

First, however, in the realm of philosophy, it should be noted that the empiricist or positivist assumptions criticized in the last section as a source of literalism have a long tradition which could be taken back to Aristotle and his rejection of Platonic speculation about ideal objects. In the Middle Ages, nominalists such as William of Ockham also strove to restrict language and knowledge to what could be observed, bringing his celebrated razor to bear upon the unnecessary multiplication of metaphysical entities, real though invisible essences lying behind phenomena. It was in the seventeenth century, however, that the scientific description of phenomena was seen to necessitate a rejection of all figurative language and the possibility of reference to unobservable spiritual truths. Knowledge was restricted entirely to observable 'objects' and their necessary causal relations.[70] Hobbes specified the use of metaphors, tropes and other rhetorical figures as one of the main causes of 'absurd conclusions', especially in theology, which was full of 'names that signifie nothing; but are taken up, and learned by rote from the Schooles, as *hypostatical, transubstantiation, consubstantiate, eternal*'.[71]

The Royal Society set out deliberately 'to shut off Fact and Judgement from Metaphor and Fancy', to achieve 'a close, naked, natural way of speaking', while David Hume denounced poets in particular as 'liars by profession'.[72] A section on 'The Abuse of Words' in Locke's *Essay Concerning Human Understanding* continued the onslaught on figurative words as 'cheats'. Rhetoric was all right for 'pleasure and delights' but not for 'information and improvement', 'truth and knowledge'.[73] The tradition was clearly established by which language was to be divided into the cognitive and the emotive, the functional and the aesthetic, closing the door on the possibility of imaginative, literary or theological language 'saying' something about the 'real' world.

Modern philosophy of science is more aware of the extent to which we 'make' our experiences by the questions we put to nature.[74] Models and metaphors are accepted as necessary devices to describe, albeit indirectly, phenomena which are not directly observable. We talk quite confidently of light waves, magnetic fields, electric currents and black holes, aware that these metaphors represent a manner of speaking about phenomena whose effects we can observe and utilize without knowing their essential nature. There is, of course, continuing disagreement about the status of these hypotheses, whether they are merely heuristic fictions whose usefulness is temporary, destined for oblivion as soon as even more useful paradigms appear (the nominalist position), or whether they refer to real entities or relations (the realist position). The question of figurative language divides 'naïve' from 'critical' realists, the latter stressing the necessary indirectness with which language describes reality.[75]

A similar debate takes place within linguistic philosophy. Logical positivism, as we have seen, continues the empirical, nominalist tradition in which language is seen to function analytically, confirming its own rules, or synthetically, giving names to observable phenomena. Statements can only be meaningful if they can be verified or falsified. In a much-publicized discussion of 'Theology and Falsification' Antony Flew complained about the lack of 'cash value', solid information about the world, human history, or experience, in such utterances as 'God has a plan', 'God created the world' and 'God loves us as a father loves his children.' If no evidence, no imaginable catastrophe or suffering would make a believer change his mind and say 'God does not exist', then these statements, according to Flew, are vacuous.[76]

One way of answering this charge is to admit with Hare and Braithwaite that religious statements are non-cognitive expressions of *bliks* or world-views, representing ways of living rather than empirical propositions.[77] Another is to argue with Ian Ramsey that theological statements refer, albeit indirectly, to real objects. Ramsey's 'Empirical Placing of Theological

Phrases', as we have seen, works within the tradition of philosophical linguistic analysis to discover the 'objective' reference lying behind seemingly 'subjective' statements about God.[78] Yet a third possibility, to be considered later, is to identify human experience as the 'real' reference of theological discourse. To dismiss all metaphorical and metaphysical language as meaningless is to limit language to one register, to neglect its potential to generate meaning in a variety of ways and to forget that 'one can be meaningful and imprecise'.[79] Blurred photographs can be more appropriate than clear pictures; Impressionist paintings, as Oscar Wilde insisted, teach us to appreciate real fog. Flew and his fellow philosophers themselves rely on stories and parables in order to dismiss metaphysics as 'fiction', clearly supposing that their stories relate in some way to the real world.

The question of reference is a key issue in the work of Ludwig Wittgenstein, who moved from a 'correspondence theory' of language as composed basically of names given to independent objects to place increasing emphasis on the involvement of language in the construction of the perceived world (the 'constitution theory' of language).[80] The *Tractatus* seems clear enough: 'A name means an object. The object is its meaning . . . A proposition is a picture of reality'.[81] Propositions must be negatable in order to be significant. So far this sounds sufficiently like the logical positivists for Wittgenstein to be taken as one of them (which he was, by them). But the relation between the picture and the reality, even in the early Wittgenstein, is more complex than this. He too makes Frege's distinction between *Sinn* and *Bedeutung*, sense and reference. A picture's sense is its meaning, its depiction of a possible situation; its reference is the actual situation to which it points. To make sense, to be intelligible, we need to use accepted public conventions. I cannot say 'bububu' and mean 'If it doesn't rain I shall go for a walk.' But for a painting to represent an object there must also be some internal correspondence between them, some common form or structure.[82] This, Wittgenstein believed, was how art functioned, poetry and novels being untranslatable into propositions because their truth was manifest in their form.

The famous injunction to silence at the end of the *Tractatus* need not therefore be interpreted as hostile to religion.

Wittgenstein did not believe with the positivists that what we can speak about is all that matters; on the contrary, 'all that matters is precisely . . . what we must be silent about'.[83] In fact, as Russell pointed out in his introduction to the *Tractatus*, Wittgenstein managed to say a good deal about what could not be said. His essay on 'Ethics' too, while recognizing the allegorical, anthropomorphic nature of all concepts of God and describing the attempt to talk about religion as a hopeless running against 'the walls of our cage', the boundaries of language, accepts the inevitability of making the attempt.[84] A tantalizing sentence in the *Philosophical Investigations* even holds out the possibility of theology functioning as a 'grammar', providing the rules by which the religious language-game is played.[85] For language in Wittgenstein's later writing is seen as something to be learnt in use, like inferring the rules of any game by watching it being played. As in chess, 'the meaning of a piece is its role in the game'.[86] Individual pieces have no meaning outside the whole system of which they are part.

This is clearly the case in liturgy where only a long familiarity with the formulations of a particular worshipping community allows us to understand how they work. More fundamentally still, as Wittgenstein explained in his 'Lectures on Religious Belief', we learn to use the word 'God' appropriately, as we learn to use other words, through a process of imitation, trial and error. He is a person who can be pictured but not in the same way as other people. To be a believer is to take these pictures seriously, to be prepared to risk commitment to a vision of life of which we cannot be certain.[87] The difference between believers and unbelievers is not a matter of disputed facts but of the pictures of the world which we hold in our minds.[88]

Wittgenstein's admission that philosophy cannot interfere with language but only describe it ('It leaves everything as it is'[89]), his recognition that the only way to understand religious language is to study how it is used, has been wrongly interpreted as evacuating such language of all reference. D.Z.Phillips, for example, sees the role of the philosopher in analysing prayer as not to ask whether any contact is made with a real God, or whether such a Being exists, but how this particular form of language works: 'to know how to use this religious language is to know God'.[90] It is a position rightly described as 'invulnerable but vacuous'.[91] For it clearly matters to believers that their language makes 'truth-claims', that their picture of the world corresponds to external reality. It matters so much that the loss of faith is a traumatic experience. Phillips claims that 'a religious picture loses its hold not because it is shown to be mistaken but because it is supplanted by a rival picture'.[92] But what causes a picture to lose its strength, its power to sustain, leading people to abandon their faith, has something at least to do with reference, with the correspondence of this picture with the 'facts' of the 'real' world.

The theological debate over the way in which language operates in religion reveals a similar spectrum, ranging from the 'objective' to the 'subjective' extreme. The conservative view, bolstered by literalist and positivist assumptions already discussed, considers doctrines to be cognitive propositions about objective realities. There is, however, a neo-orthodoxy, best represented by Barth, which has less confidence in the accuracy and objectivity of human language, relying on divine grace to provide its own special language. For Barth the language of theology is given by God, revealed in the Word:

> We have no reason not to take the concept of God's Word primarily in its literal sense. God's Word means God speaks. Speaking is not a 'symbol'.[93]

Yet the way in which God speaks is clearly different and the meaning of His Word is so complex that it requires volumes to unravel. It is, according to Barth, fundamentally personal, centred on the person of Christ, and spiritual, operating at a deeper level than ordinary language, yet it is also public, written in the scriptures and proclaimed by the Church, which is especially protected by God's grace. The task of theology is to criticize and to revise this language but it can never initiate meaning, never develop ideas from merely human experience (there is no natural theology in Barth). We can only speak of God in the language which He gives us.[94]

For liberal theologians such as Bultmann and Tillich, of course, there is no specially protected language and the original words of the early Christians incorporate patterns of thought which a modern Christian does not share. Bultmann distinguishes the Word of God, which men can never fully understand, from the kerygma, particular historical formulations of the faith, and from theology, which translates the kerygma into concepts.[95] The language of the New Testament is 'a mythological "objectification" of the experience of faith', describing this experience in terms of contemporary world-pictures.[96] Just as the story of the fall expresses man's consciousness of sin, the myth of the resurrection expresses the disciples' experience of reorientation as a result of communion with Christ. These existential interpretations of doctrine, like the various paraphrases Bultmann produced to convey his understanding of God, are necessarily relative. They point to a reality but one which can only be understood through culturally conditioned terms.

The demythologizing process, the recognition of the symbolic nature of religious language, is apparent also in the work of Paul Tillich, who is more aware of the limitations of conceptual language and the consequent need for symbols. He is careful to distinguish symbols from signs. Signs are entirely conventional (like traffic lights) whereas symbols 'point beyond themselves to something else', opening up new levels of understanding which could not otherwise be attained:

> All arts create symbols for a level of reality which cannot be reached in any other way. A picture and a poem reveal elements of reality which cannot be approached scientifically ... A great play gives us not only a new vision of the human scene, but it opens up hidden depths of our own being.

Religious symbols function in the same manner, rising from the unconscious, participating in the reality of what they represent but being transcended by it. Ultimate reality cannot be fully represented in finite terms: God necessarily transcends His own name, which is why 'the use of His name easily becomes an abuse or a blasphemy'. Concrete images become attached to the name which must also be allowed to remain indeterminate, the symbol for 'the fundamental and universal content of faith'. Myths and symbols cannot be abandoned or 'replaced by scientific substitutes'. They need, however, to be 'broken', that is, understood as symbolic and not literal.[97]

The language of 'Being' in both Bultmann and Tillich has its source in Heidegger as does their whole reorientation of hermeneutics. Man's relation to reality involves interpretation at every stage, bringing a frame of reference to objects which can only be perceived 'as something'. In his later work Heidegger emphasized the constitutive role of language in this whole process of interpreting reality, coming close to identifying Being and language.[98] For language creates possibilities of existence and understanding, it allows Being to speak. The tired logical forms of Western thought separate Being from thought and prevent authentic existence. But poetry can resurrect language allowing the gods to address us and us to claim them: 'The thinker speaks being. The poet names the holy.'[99] Heidegger repeatedly quotes Hölderlin:

> Full of merit, yet poetically, man
> Dwells on this earth.

For a 'destitute time', when the divine finds no place in ordinary language, Heidegger argues, poetry alone can enable men to 'dwell' and to 'build', to live authentically. God is called into being, for example, in prophetic Judaism and in the preaching of Jesus. But everyday language, 'a forgotten and used-up poem, from which there hardly resounds a call any longer', cannot find room for Him.[100]

Heidegger's insistence on the constitutive nature of language has given rise to a whole new hermeneutic which speaks of salvation in terms of 'language-events', not what language represents so much as what it effects or sets going. Jesus is the Word of God, not the 'object of faith but the founder of a new linguistic tradition', a gain in language which enables a new mode of being. Faith, according to Gerhard Ebeling and Ernst Fuchs, is not towards objects but experienced by subjects. The reference for theological language is not transcendental objects but human experience and the task of the theologian becomes that of translating words such as 'God' into terms which make sense to modern, secular man. For some this means divesting it of all supernatural significance.[101] Whereas the old hermeneutic, exemplified by Schleiermacher and Dilthey, was fundamentally historical, focusing on the past in order to discover what was 'meant' by the original authors and their original audience, the new hermeneutic centres on the present, what they can 'mean' for us now. The language of the New Testament is seen to provide not objective facts (as if history did not involve interpretation) but 'pictures' of what Christ was like. The language of theology functions therefore like a poem, creating a world of its own which refers only indirectly to the 'real' world.[102]

The question of reference is abandoned altogether by more recent 'post-liberal' theologians such as George Lindbeck, who draws on Wittgenstein and structuralist linguistics in viewing religious language as a coherent self-enclosed system whose 'grammar' theology articulates. 'Religions', he argues, 'resemble languages' and should be understood 'semiotically as reality and value systems – that is, as idioms for the construing of reality and the living of life'.[103] His approach is 'intratextual', finding the meaning of theological terms not by reference to anything outside the text or semiotic system but immanent in it: 'the proper way to determine what "God" signifies . . . is by examining how the word operates within a religion.' Just as the aim of linguistics is to spell out the system of competence underlying the actual performance of native speakers, so the task of theology is simply to 'give a normative explication of the meaning a religion has for its adherents'.[104]

Lindbeck's model for theology is quite clearly structuralist in origin, and since a similar model will feature prominently in my discussion of literary criticism, I should perhaps explain this term more fully. Structuralism was founded in linguistics, centring on Saussure's concept of the sign, which is comprised of signifier (spoken sound) and signified (mental concept). Deliberately ignoring the relation between the concepts signified and any real 'referents' in the external world, Saussure was concerned to study *how* language works as a system of arbitrary differences with no necessary relation between words and concepts. It is only familiarity with a native language which makes it appear 'natural', an illusion soon destroyed by foreign travel. Linguistic systems such as those developed by

Sapir and Whorf stress the 'unnatural' aspects of language, the arbitrariness with which 'we dissect nature' in language and 'organise it into concepts'.[105] The colour system is an obvious example of this process, different languages dividing the spectrum in different ways. According to Whorf, languages impose totally different conceptual systems on to the world, making communication between different cultures an impossibility. Structuralist linguistics, in other words, provides a systematic retelling of the legend of Babel.[106]

The dominance of language in the construction of the world as we perceive it lies at the heart of John Dominic Crossan's thought. 'Reality is language', he insists, 'and we live in language like the fish in the sea.'[107] It is only in language that we can create meaningful stories about ourselves and the world, although this, of course, creates a dilemma. For God is 'either *inside* my story and . . . merely an idol I have created, or, God is *outside* my story, and completely unknowable'.[108] The only way Crossan can overcome this dilemma is by locating God 'at the edges or limits of language or story. It is where our language-world does not extend, or where it breaks apart, that God can be found'.[109] He remains quite literally ineffable, beyond the reach of all discourse.

This new version of a 'God of the gaps' makes use of deconstructive modes of analysis which pick up precisely those places in a linguistic, literary or theological system where contradiction or inconsistency appears. Deconstruction attacks what it calls logocentrism, the metaphysical tendency of Western civilization to find coherence and unity in everything, world, self and sign. Saussure himself, privileging speech above writing, locating meaning within the mind of the speaker, (who says what he or she means) and attempting to create a stable sign, in which signifier and signified are united, is one of the main culprits. Yet his claim that the linguistic system contains differences without positive terms ('bat' means what it does because it differs from 'cat' and 'mat' not because of some intrinsic quality; the letter 'b' has no essential element but acquires meaning by differing from the letters 'c' and 'm') opens the way for the infinite play of meaning, the radical indeterminacy of language celebrated by Derrida, 'the Zen master of western philosophy, undertaking to shock us out of our habitual linguistic categories'.[110] Every signified, for Derrida and his disciples, is also a signifier, itself in need of interpretation, and so on without closure.[111]

'Deconstructing Theology', however, is a dangerous business, entailing the 'Death of God', the 'Disappearance of the Self', the 'End of History' and the 'Closure of the Book', to quote the chapter titles of a recent book on the subject, which argues that these 'essences' are composed of cultural codes, products of signifying practices rather than 'objects' existing independently of those codes. There is nothing beyond or behind them. The radical christology to which this leads, however, is 'thoroughly incarnational' since 'the divine *"is"* the incarnate word', forever embodied or inscribed in language: 'the word "God" refers to the word "word" and the word "word" refers to the word "God".' There can be no escape from the circle of signifiers: 'the sign is a sign of a sign.' The Word exists only as *scripture, writing* which 'is not *about* something; it is that something itself'.[112] The relationship between the word and the world, according to deconstructive critics, is not one of reference leading to the possibility of interpretation and even (dare I say) truth. It is one of power: 'Texts are in and of the world because they lend themselves to strategies of reading whose intent is always a struggle for interpretative power'.[113]

All this may be open to Christian interpretation. Michael Edwards, for example, feels that Derrida's onslaught on the 'transcendent signified' does not threaten Christianity itself but only 'a pseudo-Christian philosophy unaware of itself'. The Cartesian ego, 'blithely sinless' and full of confidence in its own full presence (and that of God), should not be allowed to forget the linguistic consequences of the fall.[114] Yet there is a real danger of creating a neo-literalism, worshipping the word and nothing but the word. For if language cannot refer but only defer (passing the buck on to another signifier), if Christianity can only be understood from inside its own circle of signifiers, the Church is in danger of becoming an intellectual ghetto, a sectarian community increasingly remote from the rest of the world. If all we can do is to tell the stories of our own community, why should we expect anyone to listen? It is a question, appropriate to literature as well as theology, which will be raised again in chapter 3. The answer involves a recognition of the cognitive value of literature, which demands attention because it has something to say about life. This is 'the point of reference' to which I will now turn.

LITERATURE: THE POINT OF REFERENCE

The way in which meaning is created in theology, then, is not through straightforward literal denotation, single words pointing to clearly defined 'objects'. The word 'God' operates within a complex linguistic system to refer to a reality which is not fully understood. But the belief that language does point to a 'real' referent, however indirectly, seems to me to be crucial to Christian faith. And one of the most powerful means of describing this reality, I want to suggest, is necessarily the most indirect: literature. It is through literary devices, narrative, metaphor, symbolism and so on, that we come closest to understanding the human predicament. Recent literary criticism, however, in a laudable attempt to clarify its own methodology and to define itself as an autonomous academic discipline, has tended to ignore and to deny this aspect of literature, upsetting a balance which I will attempt to restore. It may bring methodological purity to literary criticism to say that it is concerned solely with the processes of reading literature and not with the 'meaning' of literary works themselves. But it is an impotent purity that undermines the importance of literature as a means of expressing the 'truth' about the real world.

The retreat from reference, the creation of impenetrable barriers between literature and the world, is a relatively recent development within literary criticism, a product of the 'institutionalization' of English as an academic discipline and the resultant need to spell out its precise boundaries and 'scientific' principles. Matthew Arnold was able to distinguish between literary and scientific language (in order to characterize the Bible as an example of the former) without denying referentiality. 'The language of the Bible', he insisted, 'is literary . . . language *thrown out* at an object of consciousness not fully grasped, which inspired emotion.' Arnold's attempts to redefine this object became notorious for their vagueness ('the not ourselves that makes for righteousness' and so on)[115] but his point was that the 'object' of religious feeling did exist even if it could only be described indirectly, by means of literary devices.

The founders of 'Cambridge English', however, erected literature into a religion of their own. I.A. Richards, for example, made a similar distinction to Arnold's between 'the *scientific* use of language, which makes statements for the sake of *reference*', and 'the *emotive* use of language', which stresses 'the effects in emotion and attitude' produced by the text. Poetry is 'the supreme *emotive* language', subordinating as it does 'reference to attitude'.[116] Richards talks of a provisional, conditional kind of 'reference', 'objectless beliefs', which are a matter of feeling rather than fact.[117] The joy that comes from response to great tragedy 'is not an indication that "all's right with the world" or that "somewhere, somehow there is Justice". It is an indication that all is right here and now in the nervous system'.[118] But tragedy, as I hope to show in the final chapter of this book, does have something to say about the world as well as the nervous system. Much of Richards's argument, in fact, depends upon this, for otherwise the study of literature would not assume the importance he gives it. The keen enjoyment of bad poetry, he insists, leads to 'an acceptance of the mediocre in ordinary life ... a blurring and confusion of impulses and a very widespread loss of value'. Good poetry, however, lifts the 'film of familiarity' which, as Coleridge had complained, prevents 'ordinary' people from achieving 'an impartial awareness of the nature of the world in which we live'.[119]

In the work of another major figure in the creation of Cambridge English, F.R. Leavis, the link between literature and life is given even greater emphasis. The whole point of developing a discriminating response to literature, he argued, was that this involved judgements of value inseparable from those made in life.[120] The reason why Leavis was so concerned to preserve language from the tainting influences of journalism and the alternative 'scientific' culture of the technologico-Benthamite establishment was that he believed it to be a storehouse of values affecting the quality of a nation's life. 'Literature matters' because it represents the highest values of each age. Unless it is read widely it will become the property of an 'insulated minority ... without effect upon the powers that rule the world'.[121] It was in the attempt to prevent the 'scientific culture' represented by C.P. Snow from dominating education that Leavis spelt out the importance of literature for an understanding of 'human nature and human need'. Great novels ask basic questions, 'What for – what ultimately for? What do men live by?', questions which worked at 'a religious depth of thought and feeling'.[122] Leavis's later work continued to insist on the centrality of literature to an awareness of the significance of life. It was a 'discipline of thought', teaching ways of responding to a world of which 'science' remained ignorant.[123]

The current importance of English as a subject taught in schools and universities could be seen as a measure of the success of such claims. Much of the messianic fervour has been lost as the academic discipline has been more carefully defined. This narrowing process is observable in the movement known as New Criticism, associated with such American critics as W.K. Wimsatt, Cleanth Brooks and Yvor Winters, who presented literature as an entirely autonomous object, the exclusive subject of a new academic discipline whose aim was to demonstrate *how* the poem came to mean what it did. If Richards had sheltered literature from all direct reference to the external world, Wimsatt seemed to go even further, quoting Archibald MacLeish's line, 'A poem should not mean but be.' It was a *Verbal Icon* representing its meaning through its form. It was not *about* anything, it simply *was*.[124] Donne's poem 'The Canonization' *was* the *Well-Wrought Urn* discussed in the text, a suitable monument in which the lovers are made immortal – but only in the poem. The book which took its title from Donne's poem argues that a poem should be judged by its internal unity and coherence rather than by external considerations: 'To refer the structure of the poem ... to something outside the poem', whether a paraphrase, a real object or an authorial intention, is 'heresy' against New Critical doctrines.[125]

It is in Russian formalism and structuralism, however, that non-referentiality has been most systematically expounded, trapping language within a prison from which there is no escape to the outside world. Setting out 'to suspend the commonsense view of the work of art as *mimesis*', a number of Russian critics of the 1920s focused their attention upon form as the defining feature of 'literariness'.[126] Poetic language was not 'thinking in images'; it did not present the unknown in terms of the known; it made the familiar strange, foregrounding 'the process of perception' as 'an aesthetic end in itself': 'Art is a way of experiencing the artfulness of an object; the object is not important.' *Tristram Shandy* could be called 'the most typical novel' since it was all plot (playing with the conventions of the novel) and no story (or hardly any 'events' of any importance).[127] Like Wittgenstein, Shklovsky took the rules of chess as a model for the conventions of language and art, the peculiar restrictions upon the manner in which the knight is required to move having nothing to do with any 'reality' outside the game itself.[128]

Although the focus of criticism, according to Shklovsky, should be upon these conventions rather than interpretation, the whole point of his celebrated 'defamiliarization' is to shake off linguistic habits which make the world stale, to 'recover the sensation of life . . . to make the stone *stony*'. Tolstoy seems to describe an object 'as if he were seeing it for the first time', shaming readers into seeing the horrors of flogging which custom had made all too familiar.[129] So in some respects at least Shklovsky is saying no more than Coleridge, who described Wordsworth in the *Lyrical Ballads* as 'awakening the mind's attention from the lethargy of custom and directing it to the loveliness and the wonders of the world before us'.[130] Critics will want to explain *how* poets achieve this end, exploring how their language works, but they need not deny referentiality. An attention to literary and linguistic convention, to devices such as defamiliarization, can serve to clarify and enhance our observation of the external world.

Structuralism, which studies language and literature as entirely closed systems, concerned to spell out their internal rules rather than their relation to the external world, can also be welcomed as providing a useful tool within a complete hermeneutic. Its neglect of reference can be seen as a temporary limiting of the field of study rather than a doctrinal necessity. Structuralist methods need not entail structuralist ideology, the insistence that semiotic systems *cannot* refer to reality. The model of communication provided by Roman Jakobson, for example, recognizes that context (reference to the real world) is involved in most messages. The 'referential function' of language dominates when the main point of a message is to convey information about the external world, the 'poetic function' when attention is directed more towards the message for its own sake. The 'emotive' function dominates when the focus of the message is on the speaker, the 'conative' when it is on the receiver.[131] But these categories are relative, a matter of degree not of absolute demarcations. To place emphasis on one of the functions is not to deny the presence of the others.

Many structuralist critics discern a seemingly unbridgeable chasm between text and world. They take great care never to commit what Umberto Eco called the 'referential fallacy', which 'consists of construing the signifier alone as the sign and as referring directly to the real world'.[132] The signifiers that comprise the text itself refer to a conceptual signified, a narrative world which the reader is encouraged to enter. That signified, however, while not being identical with the real world becomes itself a signifier pointing to the real world:

> To appropriate the metaphor of a Zen Sutra, poetry is 'like a finger pointing to the moon'. It is a way to see the light that shines in darkness, a way to participate in a transcendent truth and to embrace reality. To equate the finger with the moon or to acknowledge the finger and not to perceive the moon is to miss the point.[133]

This, it seems to me, is the danger of structuralist warnings never to confuse the 'poetic' or 'narrative world', the world created by the literary text, with the 'real world'.

Structuralists insist, for example, that fictitious characters should not be treated as real people. 'We occasionally speak of Sarrasine as though he existed,' admits Roland Barthes of the eponymous hero of Balzac's short story, but he should really be read as 'an impersonal network of symbols combined under the proper name ... we are not searching for the truth of Sarrasine, but for the systematics of a (transitory) site of the text'.[134] If all Barthes is doing here is to alert readers to the fact that characters in fiction don't really exist and that flowers should not be sent to their funerals, this is unexceptionable if unexciting. But to prevent readers treating fictitious characters as constructed similarly to themselves is to miss a crucial point about the relation of literature to life, that 'identity' in fiction and in 'fact' is based upon similar conventions which are an essential feature of liberal humanist ideology. To understand something about the process of characterization in fiction is therefore relevant to an understanding of the same process in life.

Northrop Frye, a structuralist of his own independent sort and more sympathetic towards Christianity, is equally coy about referentiality in the Bible. The 'centripetal' structure of a verbal structure, he insists, its internal organization, can be much more precisely observed than its 'centrifugal' aspect, its description of the real world:

> The Bible means literally just what it says, but it can mean it only without primary reference to a correspondence of what it says to something outside what it says. When Jesus says (John 19:9), 'I am the door', . . . there are no doors outside the verse in John to be pointed to. And when the Book of Jonah says that the Lord prepared a great fish to swallow Jonah, there are no great fish outside the Book of Jonah that come into the story. We could almost say that even the existence of God is an inference from the existence of the Bible: in the *beginning* was the Word.[135]

The 'almost' here almost saves Frye from confusing ostensive reference (pointing to an object) with the more indirect kinds of reference characteristic of both literature and theology. Almost, but not quite. For he goes on to say that since the Bible 'deliberately subordinates its referential or centrifugal meaning to its primary, syntactical, centripetal meaning' our only 'real contact with the so-called "Jesus of history" can be in reading. Even more daringly, he suggests that the nearest we can get to God is by reading the Bible, which is 'not a book pointing to a historical presence outside it, but a book that identifies itself with that presence', bringing the reader to a similar identification. The heart of the reader, as Milton claimed, becomes that of the Holy Spirit.[136] This transformation marvellously undermines the culturally and linguistically imposed subject–object division but it also imprisons God within the written word.

Structuralist critics, as will become apparent when we consider their treatment of the Bible, have developed some powerful exegetical tools. But they refuse to go beyond exegesis to interpretation. For them, interpretation is not the goal but the enemy of criticism. Culler's *Structuralist Poetics*, which attempts to do for literature what linguistics does for language, to articulate the unspoken rules which comprise literary competence, insists throughout that the focus of critical attention should be on the code rather than the message, the grammar of narrative rather than the particular story.[137] The first chapter of his *Pursuit of Signs* goes 'Beyond Interpretation', denouncing 'the widespread and unquestioned acceptance of the notion that the critic's job is to interpret literary works'.[138] Yet even he admits that no reading can be indefinitely open and ambiguous. Readers make interpretations, otherwise it would be impossible to study the processes involved in these readings.[139] By making the processes themselves the focus of critical study, attempting to explain *how* these interpretations are reached, not whether they are true, he manages to seal the subject off from the real world but also to diminish its importance. For if criticism does not pursue the truth about texts, including their relation to the real world, it does not deserve to be taken seriously.

Truth, as we have seen, the notion of a transcendent signified, is the target of deconstruction. Nietzsche's mottoes are constantly quoted by deconstructive critics: 'truths are illusions of which we have forgotten that they are illusions', metaphors which have become fixed and therefore dead, and 'there are no facts, only interpretations.' The world thus becomes a text which is open to any kind of reading. There is no such thing as a misreading, only strong and weak ones, interesting and boring. Deconstructive critics argue that structuralism failed to go far enough. Just as New Critics and early structuralists assumed that the individual work had an inner meaning, an inherent unity and coherence, so later structuralists assumed that their whole systems had a similar intrinsic harmony. For deconstruction, however, nothing holds together. Every text, every code, every semiotic system which man creates in order to invest the world with significance, is inevitably flawed and the task of the critic is to find the fault in the system, the *aporia*, the point of internal contradiction and inconsistency, exposing in the process the impossibility of making sense of the world.

In literary criticism as in theology, the denial of the referential dimension of language leads to inevitable fragmentation, the complete abandonment of the catholic enterprise which Eliot called 'the common pursuit of true judgement'. Only by denying the protestant principle of private judgement, subjecting the 'inner voice' to the discipline of external tradition, Eliot insisted, could criticism be maintained as a 'co-operative activity with the further possibility of arriving at something outside of ourselves, which may provisionally be called truth . . . or fact or reality'.[140] It is this possibility which so many modern theorists deny, replacing it with a bewildering variety of descriptions of the reading process, ranging from the phenomenological (Iser's account of the structured gaps in any text into which predetermined shape the reader is made to fit his own consciousness), through the historically conditioned (Jauss's description of the different readings produced under different historical circumstances) to the psychoanalytic (Bloom's account of the poetic struggle against influence which celebrates the possibility of creative misreadings, Holland's description of *The Dynamics of Literary Response*, in which different readers explore their own personal 'identity themes' through the text, and Bleich's totally *Subjective Criticism*). The most that can be achieved is a collective subjectivity, a sharing of response by different interpretative communities.[141] Lacanian criticism is perhaps the most arcane, insisting as it does that language is built upon absence, the signifier being a mere substitute for the missing thing. The symbolic (public codes such as language) is thus a distortion of the imaginary (private pre-linguistic self-consciousness) which is itself a distorted perception of whatever the real might be.[142]

The concentration on reader-response, however, has led at least in some critics to a return to some form of reference, a recognition that something is learnt in the reading process apart from a knowledge of how to read. Hermeneutics in Gadamer has become a dialogue between text and reader, a 'merging of horizons' which involves the reader being 'interpreted' or changed by the text, learning to see 'in a different way'.[143] It is not enough for Ricoeur to explore the internal relations of a piece of writing: 'To understand a text is to follow its movement from sense to reference: from what it says to what it talks about'.[144] Ricoeur has shown how reference can be achieved through literary devices such as metaphor and narrative. Poems, parables and stories all project their own worlds in which their readers are invited to dwell. It is only by suspending disbelief, abandoning principles of verification and falsifiability, that we can experience the new mode of being to which they give access, the new meanings they create. But these meanings only become important if they are in some way 'true' to the 'real' world. To ignore this dimension of literature is necessarily to diminish the whole subject.

Ricoeur manages both to inject into theology a sense of the cognitive value of literary devices and to redeem literary criticism from formalism. Metaphor perceives resemblances where none appeared to exist while narrative organizes scattered events into significant plots, both achieving semantic innovation without sacrificing referentiality. Both can be said to 'redescribe reality', offering new ways of perceiving and living in the world.[145] Formal criticism of literary texts may help to explain *how* they work but Ricoeur repeatedly insists on the need to go beyond explanation to interpretation, which requires response and commitment from the reader: 'Beyond the desert of criticism, we wish to be called again.'[146] Immaculate structuralist analyses of the parables miss the whole point of this genre if they fail to ask what they mean in terms of living in the world. To read the Bible as literature, therefore, is not to reduce its referential dimension, not to enter a new non-existent world, but to see this world anew. This, at least, is the theory which the following chapter is designed to test.

CHAPTER 2

On Reading the Bible as Literature

LITERARY CRITICISM OF THE BIBLE

'The Bible as Literature' is in many ways an objectionable concept, 'a phrase to set the teeth on edge'.[1] It offends both believers, who see the sacred texts as more than literature, and lovers of 'high' literature, who look down on the primitive 'popular' forms of writing to be found in the Bible. It is a phrase fulminated against by T.S. Eliot, as we have seen, and sneered at by Robert Alter, who argues that it labours the obvious. No one, for example, would talk of 'Dante as Literature', although the *Divina Commedia* is much more explicitly theological than the Bible.[2] And yet it brings into focus a crucial area in which theology and literature intersect.

The Bible is, after all, the Christian classic, the canonical volume on which Christian faith is founded. It is an extremely complex text, the end product of centuries of oral tradition, editing and often anonymous authorship. It is the corner-stone of Western civilization, feeding in countless ways into our 'secular' literature. And yet those who continue to read the Bible often misread it, paying no attention to the critical problems it raises, to questions of genre and literary convention, while those who have been professionally trained in literary competence rarely open its pages. However obvious it may seem, it needs to be said that the Bible is worth reading and that it is worth reading properly, with due attention to the literary issues which this chapter will explore.

To read the Bible as literature is not to refuse to take it seriously as a revelation of God's action in history. That would be to miss the whole point of the book. The Bible, Auerbach argued, makes a claim to truth and demands a response which involves a reorientation of our whole view of life:

> Far from seeking, like Homer, merely to make us forget our reality for a few hours, it seeks to overcome our reality: we are to fit our life into its world, feel ourselves to be elements in its structure of universal history.[3]

To read the Bible as literature is not to overlook these massive claims but to appreciate *how* they are made, through a variety of literary means, narrative and poetic, through myth and legend as well as history, through poems which dramatize personal despair as well as hymns which celebrate divine achievement.

Most professional criticism of the Bible has so far been historical in orientation, treating the Bible as a source of information about historical figures such as Moses and Jesus, which it undoubtedly is, however indirectly. Literary criticism has been used mainly as a tool for identifying separate documentary levels within the text, which is what the term 'literary criticism' has come to mean within biblical scholarship. It has also contributed to 'form criticism', the attempt to isolate different units of the text as the product of oral traditions and to understand their function within these original contexts, and to 'redaction criticism', the identification of the main motives behind an editor's arrangement of this material. But the historical aim of all this research, to get at 'what really happened', though laudable in itself, diverted attention away from the finished literary products, the texts as they stand within the Bible. Striving for the 'historical Jesus' *behind* the text of the gospels, biblical scholarship has been accused of ignoring the magnificent portraits of him actually in the text, of 'disintegrating the text' as 'an end in itself',[4] and of being more concerned with reconstructing 'how a particular psalm might have been used in a hypothetically reconstructed temple ritual than how it works as an achieved piece of poetry'.[5]

To read the Bible as literature is to restore the balance, to focus attention once more on the finished product. A century of biblical scholarship cannot be ignored. But it is possible to 'go beyond criticism by means of criticism', to achieve a 'second naïveté', restoring to the biblical texts their integrity and their imaginative power.[6] A literary reading of the Bible will 'accept the form of the work', entering into its imaginative world,[7] attending to 'the words of the narrator, bracketing questions of authorship as extrinsic to the reading of the text itself'.[8] It may well be that the text turns out to be lacking in the New Critical virtues of 'wholeness' and 'harmony'. But this is where the process begins, with a reading of the text as it stands. Historical research into the background of the text, the process by which it reached its final form, should not be allowed to eclipse what literary power it possesses.[9]

This section of the book will consider first to what extent the traditional methods of biblical criticism can be called 'literary'. Although their main aim was historical the pioneering biblical critics of the nineteenth and early twentieth centuries can be shown to have asked important literary questions both from the standpoint of the literary criticism of their own time, which was predominantly Romantic, celebrating the way in which an individual genius realized his or her intentions, and from the more recent standpoint which sees literary competence as primarily a matter of genre-recognition, knowing what to read a text as, which conventions to bring to it.[10] Only in the last three decades, however, have these questions been seen as literary. This new kind of literary criticism can be divided into three broad phases, the 1960s being mainly New Critical in focus, the 1970s seeing the massive entry of structuralism into the field of biblical narrative, and the 1980s going beyond structuralism either into deconstruction, pointing to the inherent contradictions and tensions within so many biblical texts, or into less dogmatic positions informed by structuralist methods but uncommitted to its ideology.

Old-fashioned 'literary criticism' of the Bible, the 'separating out of historically different layers in composite works', was based upon assumptions of authorial consistency in style and ideology which few modern literary critics would share.[11] Jeremiah, for example, was found to contain too many internal contradictions to have been written 'according to a logical plan by one man' (a judgement that could equally well be made of Joyce).[12] Assuming, however, that literature was written by logical and lucid people for a definite purpose, 'literary criticism' came to mean looking for logical and thematic inconsistencies, repetition, variant versions of the same event, changes in style or in viewpoint as evidence of multiple authorship, on the assumption that no one in his right mind would willingly have introduced such confusion.[13] It was the discovery of duplications and inconsistencies of style within the Pentateuch by pioneering critics such as Wellhausen and von Rad which led them to the hypothesis that the texts they were studying were composed of other texts, a hypothesis which it soon became the dominant purpose of their enterprise to verify. Literary criticism was thus transformed into a hunt for sources, a change of aim without a change of name.[14] The problems, in other words, were thrown up by an attempt at a literary reading of the text as it stood. When this failed to make coherent sense, biblical critics provided their hypothetical solution to the problems in terms of separate sources. At this point the exercise ceased to be recognizable as literary criticism in the modern sense.

Much traditional biblical criticism, however, as John Barton has shown, involved questions of genre-recognition.[15] The unreadability of biblical texts as they stood forced 'literary critics' to break them down into separate sources and 'form critics' to dissolve them into even smaller coherent units. Form criticism, therefore, as its German title implies, (*formgeschichtliche Methode*, the scientific study of the history of literary forms), can be seen as a mode of literary criticism, concerned though it is with oral traditions and their historical contexts. Both Dibelius and Schmidt were concerned to identify what kind of literature the gospels were: 'Kleinliteratur, literature for popular consumption',[16] 'cult-books' for the community which did not conform to conventional classical models of high literature.

Some form critics may have overlooked some of the literary qualities possessed by the gospels as a whole but they were asking appropriate questions. In classifying Jesus' sayings into five main types, 'paradigms, short-stories, legends, edifying utterances and myths', Dibelius may be accused, like the structuralists, of 'excessive systematization',[17] but he provided a useful framework for critical discussion, just as his mentor,

Gunkel, performed a valuable service for students of the psalms by dividing them into five main types: hymns, community laments, individual laments, individual songs of thanksgiving and royal psalms.[18] For this clearly affects such basic matters in any reading of the psalms as the identification of the first person, the 'I' of the poem. Many of the psalms fail to make sense if read as the expression of individual feeling without regard to liturgical conventions.[19] Historians may have used Gunkel's insights to speculate on the temple rites to which the psalms point. Literary critics are merely grateful for guidance in reading them.

If form criticism was inclined to disintegrate the text, treating the narrative framework of the gospels as an unimportant string on which pearls of more reliable historical material were hung, redaction criticism redressed the balance, focusing attention on the text as a whole:

> It is, indeed, with redaction criticism that we come closest to what the student trained in other literatures would mean by 'literary criticism': the attempt to give what is sometimes called a 'close reading' of the text, analysing how the author/editor achieves his effects, why he arranges his material as he does, and above all what devices he uses to give unity and coherence to his work.[20]

The trouble with this description of the literary process is its emphasis on authorial intention. Redaction criticism is sometimes called *Tendenzkritik* because of its focus on the intentions of the editor responsible for the final form of the text. Yet it is only *bad* literature which reveals its intentions so blatantly. To call a novel a *Tendenzroman* is to imply that it has evident designs upon a reader which need to be identified and resisted. This, of course, is the historical aim of redaction criticism. Mark's 'plotting' of his narrative is taken as evidence of his intention and of the time of writing but evidence *against* the historicity of his account. From a literary critical point of view, however, the text loses in value and persuasive power the more obvious its aims appear. If the redactor were entirely successful, of course, he would be undetectable. It is only his incompetence, his failure actually to produce a consistent whole from the diverse material at his disposal, that enables him to be identified.

Traditional biblical criticism, then, has used literary-critical techniques but for historical purposes. The dominant principle of biblical hermeneutics has been to get back to the original meaning the text had for its original audience. Biblical theology may have stressed the relevance of this 'message' for modern man but it also emphasized the need for modern man to change his patterns of thought, to 'think Hebraically', rather than to read the Bible in the light of his own ideas. Biblical theology was fundamentally philological and linguistic rather than literary, focusing on individual words and concepts as in Kittel's famous *Theological Dictionary of the New Testament*. It did not provide a theory of reading whole texts.

Canon criticism, on the other hand, involves a departure from traditional historical methods, stressing the need to read the Bible as a whole. B.S.Childs argues that

> the canonical approach differs from a strictly literary approach by interpreting the biblical text in relation to a community of faith and practice for whom it served a particular theological role as possessing divine authority.[21]

But this sounds very much like the kind of reader-response criticism advocated by Stanley Fish in which all claims to objectivity are relinquished in favour of inter-subjective agreement on a particular set of values shared by an 'interpretive community'.[22] The Church, in other words, teaches its members *how* to read, in particular how to interpret the Old Testament in the light of the New.

There has in the last decade been a general recognition within biblical scholarship of the need to escape too narrowly historical an approach, especially if that involves disintegrating and destroying qualities inherent in the text as a whole. A recent introduction to 'Methods of Old Testament Study' stresses the importance of literary criticism in the sense of 'close reading' of the text 'considered as a whole' and 'for what it is in itself'.[23] Just how recent the biblical scholars' interest in literary criticism is can be seen by the manner in which Stephen Neill speculated in 1964 on what might happen '*if* a reader, trained in the art of literary criticism ... *were* to come fresh to the gospels' (my italics).[24] It clearly appeared to be a most unlikely eventuality. Until the mid-1970s, in fact, there was only one 'book-length study in English by a professional Bible scholar that made a sustained effort to use a literary perspective' on the Old Testament.[25] By 1976, however, even Norman Perrin, pupil of Jeremias, was admitting that the interpretation of the gospels required a much broader eclectic literary criticism than the historical approaches he had earlier employed.[26] It is time now to summarise some of the insights afforded by these recent literary approaches to the Bible.

It would be wrong, first, to claim that it is only in the last thirty years that the Bible has been read as literature. Frei's whole point was that before the advent of historical criticism that is how it *was* read, as a whole, responding to its narrative and poetic power. Robert Lowth delivered his *Lectures on the Sacred Poetry of the Hebrews*, analysing the principles of poetic parallelism, as early as 1741.[27] Coleridge too argued that the Bible's authority lay not in an extrinsic infallibility but in its intrinsic power: 'the words of the Bible find me at greater depths of my being.'[28] Individuals no doubt continued to read the Bible imaginatively whatever the critics said. But until thirty years ago the accepted position, even among literary critics who happened to be Christians, was that expressed by C. S. Lewis, that the Bible could only be read as literature 'by a *tour de force*'[29] or, as T. S. Eliot argued, by 'parasites' who had long ceased to believe it to be true.[30]

The first phase of the rebellion against this orthodoxy was primarily New Critical in emphasis, focusing attention on patterns and images to be found within the text. A chapter on 'Prophecy and Poetry' in Austin Farrer's 1948 study of biblical imagery, *The Glass of Vision*, spelt out the New Critical doctrine that poetry could not be paraphrased[31] while the final chapter insisted that the imagery involved in Mark's gospel needed to be savoured as poetry: 'If we try to go round behind the words we have nothing but theology.'[32] This, of course, was a limitation theologians were slow to recognise. And when Farrer followed these patterns of allusive imagery through the whole gospel in his *Study of St. Mark* in 1951 he was dismissed as fanciful even by literary critics such as Helen Gardner, who valued Mark's gospel 'precisely because of its lack of literary quality' as the product of honest uneducated sincerity.[33]

The notion that the Bible was too crude to be considered as literature received a direct challenge from Erich Auerbach's enormously influential *Mimesis*, published in German in 1946 but not translated into English until 1957. 'A Study of the Representation of Reality in Western Literature', *Mimesis* begins with a detailed comparison of biblical with classical narrative. The story of Abraham and Isaac, for example, although terse and economical in description, with little naturalistic detail, is found to be full of suspense and 'fraught with background', demanding interpretation to get at the hidden truth about a God 'hidden' in history.[34] Auerbach argues that the account of Peter's denial of Christ in Mark's gospel could not have been written by a classical author because it offends the convention of decorum, which insisted on the strict separation of the comic style suitable for everyday events and lower-class characters from the tragic status accorded to the grand exploits of noble heroes. Such weakness of character in a mere fisherman could not have been granted serious sympathetic treatment. It is a revolutionary piece of writing recording the birth of a revolutionary spiritual movement 'from the depths of the common people'.[35] Auerbach showed that a concern for literary form was not a fanciful activity for parasites but an essential element in understanding the radical nature of biblical narrative.

Auerbach's insights led a number of American scholars to produce exciting books on the gospels in the 1960s. Perhaps the best known is Amos Wilder's *Early Christian Rhetoric*, 'a study of the literary forms and genres of the Early Church', including the oral traditions behind the final form of the texts. Wilder accepts that the gospels are 'subliterary' in terms of the conventions of contemporary classical literature and that they do not fit into any of the genres recognized by that culture. They were new forms fashioned by the community out of its own liturgical practice, 'cult-legends' which proclaim 'the faith-story of Christ as a pattern of meaning or life-orientation'. This new genre represented by Mark is modified by Matthew into more of a manual, by Luke into something like history and by John into a meditative sacred drama.[36]

Like Auerbach, Wilder captures the excitement of this creative process, an excitement which comes over most clearly in his discussion of the parables in which Jesus himself spoke of his new 'kingdom'. He shows, for example, that their realistic setting is central to their meaning, demonstrating man's destiny to be at stake in the ordinary details of life. He also looks at the poetry in the New Testament, particularly the liturgical chants in Paul's letters, insisting along New Critical lines that the images, symbols and myths of the early church are fundamental to its beliefs, untranslatable into 'rationalized' or existential terminology.[37]

New Critical close reading of the text as it stands is combined with an awareness of traditional biblical criticism in the work of William Beardslee, whose *Literary Criticism of the New Testament* considers many of the different literary forms (gospel, proverb, history and apocalypse) in the context of contemporary Jewish forms such as the macarism, the parable and wisdom literature in general. He treats the Book of Revelation as a 'great poem' without denying its liturgical roots.[38] Robert Funk extends Wilder's notion of the parables as metaphors, drawing on details of ordinary life but arresting the hearer by their vividness: 'the parable "cracks" the shroud of everydayness lying over mundane reality in order to grant a radically new vision.'[39] Its meaning, accordingly, can never be closed by paraphrase or interpretation, never fixed to a single 'ideational point'. It must be left open to be understood afresh by each reader entering imaginatively into the world it creates.[40] This is the fundamental New Critical principle of untranslatability which even Dan Via, examining the parables as 'aesthetic objects' and entering their hypothetical world, contravenes as soon as he attempts to describe their 'understanding of existence' in abstract Bultmannian terms.[41]

Much of the literary criticism of the Bible written in the last two decades, especially that produced by recently converted biblical scholars, has been along New Critical lines, subjecting the text as it stands to close reading and paying particular attention to its formal devices. But the late 1960s saw the rise of a new phase of literary criticism which claimed to do this more systematically and even 'scientifically'. This, of course, was structuralism, which soon won over many of the critics,

notably Funk and Via, who had previously practised New
Criticism (now suddenly grown old). The structuralism which
dominated literary criticism of the Bible in the 1970s was not
the anthropological sort derived from Lévi-Strauss and his
analysis of myths. Lévi-Strauss in fact avoided the Bible as too
'literate' to provide evidence for the innate structures of the
human mind he believed to be discernible in the products of
primitive pre-literate societies, though some of his disciples
have been less disciplined in this respect.[42]

The structuralism that pervaded literary criticism of the
Bible, however, was concerned with specifically literary structures. It too claimed to penetrate beneath the surface structure
which had been the subject of New Critical close reading in
order, in Via's words, 'to articulate the larger implicit
structure which in some way generates the text under
consideration', to explore 'the relationship between the surface
structure and the "deep" structures which lie implicitly or
unconsciously beneath, around, or alongside of the text'.[43]
Via's vagueness about the exact location of these structures
and the relationship between deep and surface structure
reflects a problem with which structuralists still struggle,
disagreeing, for example, about the relationship between
innate structuring principles within the mind, culturally
conditioned structures such as genres and literary conventions, and structures of the 'enunciation', observable properties
of the text as it stands. There is also debate about the freedom
an author has to resist, modify, or control the 'laws' of literary
convention. But one of their central hypotheses, that there is a
'grammar of narrative' similar to the grammar of a language, a
set of rules governing the story-telling process which a critic
can spell out, has proved enormously productive particularly
in the study of the parables. The very least it can claim to have
achieved is a more precise and systematic vocabulary for the
analysis of biblical narrative.

There are, in fact, a number of competing 'grammars of
narrative'[44] but the one that has dominated analysis of the
parables is the model derived by A. J. Greimas from Vladimir
Propp's more complex system of functions and actions in the
Russian folk-tale. Any story, according to Greimas, comprises
five main functions (mandate, acceptance, confrontation,

success and consequence) and six 'actantial' relations, six main roles which can be played by any number of characters and/or qualities in three opposed pairs: sender and receiver, subject and object, helper and opponent. The structuralists argue not only that any parable can be read in this way, fitting the characters into their respective roles, but that it must be so read, that the process of interpretation involves the kind of decision schematically represented by Greimas' system. Taking the parable of the Unjust Judge (Luke 18:2–5) as an example, Dan Via shows that the whole point rests upon a switch in roles. The judge ought to be the subject sent by God to achieve justice for Israel the receiver. In fact what he seeks is disengagement, wanting not to be bothered. Through the process of confrontation, in which the widow becomes the subject seeking vindication, the judge is made to change goals, abandoning his false freedom for a truly engaged selfhood. The parable as Via reads it, with the help of Jungian notions of the alienated unrealized self, is not primarily about persistence in prayer, as it is traditionally interpreted, but about true selfhood.[45] The argument is a complex one, going beyond structuralist exegesis to reach its conclusion. But the analysis in terms of actantial relations at least helps Via to explain how he reads the parable.

Structuralist analysis can appear very mechanical, especially as practised by less able exponents than Roland Barthes, whose actantial analysis of Jacob's struggle with the angel (Genesis 32:22–32) at the Chantilly conference on the study of the Bible in 1969 remains one of the classic examples of structuralist exegesis. The surprising feature of Barthes' analysis of this passage is that God turns out to be both sender and opponent. For it is an angel not a devil with whom Jacob fights and by whom he is named and blessed. The stereotypical ordeal of folklore is transformed in its new monotheistic setting, which has no room for supernatural opposition. This creates one of the 'discontinuities of readability' in Genesis to be discussed in the second half of this chapter. Barthes, it should be remembered, is not aiming 'to reduce the text to a signified . . . but to hold its *signifiance* fully open', to explore the processes by which meaning is produced rather than to settle on any single interpretation of the passage.[46] Structuralists are more concerned to spell out these literary codes than to interpret the messages they produce, just as linguistics is more concerned to articulate the grammatical rules of a language than to understand particular utterances. The Bible could be called God's gift to structuralists because it provides them with 'so much self-generated polysemiousness', so many examples of multiple meanings developed from an initial germ of narrative.[47] 'Used as a sieve', Barthes irreverently admitted, a receptacle for catching codes, the biblical verse 'has an excellent size'.[48]

It is easy to grow impatient with structuralism because it is not itself concerned with interpretation. But it can be a useful exegetical tool in the larger hermeneutic process, as Paul Ricoeur argued at the same Chantilly conference.[49] Ricoeur accuses French structuralists in general and Louis Marin in particular of ignoring historical questions both about the transformations in the text itself, the accretions to the parables as spoken by Jesus, and about the events described as taking place, reducing the gospel to a message about messages.[50] Marin *is* concerned with the process of communication, messages as they are embedded in the text such as the nesting of narratives surrounding Peter's acceptance of the invitation to eat with the gentile Cornelius (Acts 10:1–11:18). But to eat together, as in the sharing of the eucharist, is a central part of the gospel.[51] Similarly, as Marin shows, the women approach the tomb in the synoptic accounts of the resurrection seeking the body of the crucified Jesus but find instead an angel bearing a message. The 'object', in terms of the actantial code, has changed from a body to a message, as it has for the whole Christian community.[52] In both of these cases, it seems to me, structuralist analysis sheds light not only on the form of the text but on its central meaning.

Two major contributions to the literary criticism of the Bible have benefited greatly from structuralist analysis: Frank Kermode's *The Genesis of Secrecy* and Northrop Frye's *The Great Code*. Kermode dismisses structuralist ideology but his analysis of the way narrative works not only in the text of Mark itself but in the development of character through the other gospels draws upon its methods. Structuralist analysis of the way in which narrative necessarily generates additional details in an original story finds corroboration in the case of the gospels in the contemporary practice of midrash, by which Old Testament narrative was probed for its inner meaning and gaps in the story imaginatively filled, and by the use of testimonies, details taken from the Old Testament to augment the gospel accounts.[53]

One example of this process of narrative expansion is the character of Judas, which develops from the basic function of betrayal, an integral part of the initial story. The very name 'Iscariot' may have derived from the Aramaic word for betrayal. The questions that immediately arise from the need for Jesus to be betrayed are 'By whom?', 'How?' and 'Why?', and it is in response to these questions, Kermode claims, that the character and actions of Judas develop. The kiss by which the betrayal takes place, for example, not only takes the action from the first to the second of the five 'acts' of the drama (Leavetaking, Arrest, Trial, Execution and Reunion) but also serves as an ironic inversion of the eucharistic kiss of peace. In order to supply Judas with motives, Kermode argues, the evangelists turned to the Old Testament and Apocrypha, 'a sort of seminary of narrative germs'. So Matthew finds the thirty pieces of silver in Zechariah while Achitophel, hanging himself out of remorse, provides the model for that grim episode. Additional details such as the potter's field and the bursting asunder derive in a similar manner from other Old Testament stories.

Matthew, Kermode claims, was quick to spot the gaps in Mark's narrative. Mark, for instance, has the disciples at the Last Supper, on hearing that one of them is to betray Jesus, ask, 'Is it I?' Matthew makes Judas alone ask the question, to which Jesus replies, 'Thou hast said so', a reply which he is also to give Pilate, asking whether he is the King of the Jews, and the High Priest, asking if he is the Christ. John adds a demonic theme, makes Jesus give Judas bread in order to signify that he is the betrayer and concludes the episode, as Judas leaves Jesus and the disciples to fulfil his role, with the symbolic words 'And it was night.' In this economical but highly significant phrase, Kermode exclaims, 'we feel close to the novel.' He goes on to consider later imaginative developments in the character of Judas, the hero of a Gnostic sect and the incestuous figure of medieval literature. The point is that the closing of the canon cannot change a necessary literary process observable within the gospels themselves.[54]

Northrop Frye sees the Bible as one big self-enclosed system which *The Great Code* sets out to decode, explaining how language, myth, metaphor and typology work within it to create a meaningful whole. Frye is not, we have seen, concerned with the 'truth' of this world, its correspondence with anything really there. He is, however, determined to undermine literalistic misreadings of the Bible, in particular the vulgar notion that 'mythical' means 'untrue'. To notice the mythical structure underlying a narrative, he insists, is not to proclaim it unhistorical but merely to recognize the formal devices by which meaning is achieved. The life of Jesus as narrated in the gospels clearly repeats the pattern of the history of Israel, that U-shaped descent into disaster and bondage leading to deliverance. But this patterning of the narrative in terms of the history of Israel (Jesus calling twelve disciples, wandering forty days in the wilderness and preaching a new law from a mountain)[55] should be recognized for what it is: a statement about his significance not an account of what actually happened.

Classic structuralists such as Frye work with a very controlled model of how literature and other semiotic systems function. They insist that reading is a rule-governed process, that communication occurs when a message which has been encoded by the sender is decoded by the receiver. In literary texts, therefore, 'the black spots on the pages' are 'authorially-issued instructions', signifiers for which readers, familiar with the conventions concerned, supply the signified.[56] Post-structuralists challenge this watertight model, seeing the 'black spots on the pages' as full of potential accidents, misprisions of meaning which make up the excitement of literature. Much of the pleasure of reading, they argue, comes from the play of signifiers, their refusal to be tied down to a single fixed meaning. Deconstruction, as we have seen, delights in the contradictions and inconsistencies that can be found in any semiotic system, whether theological or literary.

The Bible, as traditional biblical criticism discovered, is full of such inconsistencies, which is partly a product of its complex textual history. But only partly. A deconstructive critic such as

Herbert Schneidau claims that the Bible deliberately encourages a 'sacred discontent' with the conventions and myths that comprise our culture. Demythologizing, therefore, is not what we do to the Bible but what it does to us, undermining those comfortable mediating myths which transform our fears and desires into 'mental patterns that can be dealt with'. The Bible destroys such stabilizing myths, not only in the prophetic writings, which continually attack their society as blind, greedy and complacent, but also in the historical record of Israel needing perpetually to be destroyed and rebuilt. This process of 'alienation', of being 'decentred' and 'acutely conscious of the fictionality of things', begins with the fall, in which meaning is seen to reside not in human culture, the apple of self-knowledge, but in God, 'the agent of disillusionment'.[57]

Another critic to read the Bible deconstructively is John Dominic Crossan, who describes his work as an attempt to discover experimentally 'what a future theology might look like once the literary imagination has been unleashed on the Bible itself'.[58] Crossan presents the parables as fundamentally disorienting, undermining their hearers' expectations, for instance that a Samaritan could be a good neighbour, and turning their whole world 'upside down'.[59] 'Parables', he claims, 'give God room' by shattering 'the deep structure of our accepted world', removing our defences and so opening us to the transcendent.[60] Crossan is particularly alert to the subversive side of the Bible, enjoying the Book of Jonah because it undermines prophetic conventions so savagely. God calls and Jonah flees. God commands him to go east by land and he goes west by sea. When he does eventually deliver his prophetic call to repentance, after his ignominious experiences in the fish's belly, he suffers the unusual fate of being heard. This involves a 'double reversal of expectation' in which the prophet disobeys while the pagans for once obey.[61] Jesus too can be found parodying the Bible, reducing the symbolic cedar of Ezekiel and Daniel to a mere mustard tree, deliberately undermining messianic pretensions to power.[62] Crossan's later work presents a disturbingly modern portrait of a Derridean Jesus puzzling his listeners with self-reflexive parables and Zen-style koans, shocking them out of their habitual modes of thought.[63]

Some of the most exciting and original literary criticism of the Bible in recent years has come from critics of no particular dogmatic position. Robert Alter's analyses of the art of biblical narrative and poetry, for example, reveal an interest in human values as well as semiotic structures, celebrating conscious artistry as well as literary convention. He too sees a major difference between myth, which arranges its material in accordance with perceived similarities in a system of subordination and the Bible, which leaves its meaning indeterminate, implicit, unspelt out, emerging only gradually through a process of continual revision. He is particularly keen on the 'historicised fiction' of the David stories, marvelling at the 'studied effect of opacity' which brings out the 'abiding mystery' that resides in character.[64]

Alter is, of course, aware of the fragmentary nature of most biblical texts, the 'constant stitching together' of earlier sources. But this leads not only to the contradictions, repetitions and discrepancies with which earlier 'literary criticism' was concerned but to an 'elaborately layered' and 'composite artistry' which he compares with photographic montage and even post-Cubist painting, with its penchant for juxtaposed and superimposed images. Of the first two chapters of Genesis, for example, he claims that

> the Genesis author chose to combine these two versions of creation precisely because he understood that his subject was essentially contradictory, essentially resistant to linear formulation, and that this was his way of giving it the most adequate literary expression.

Similarly, in chapters 16 and 17 of the Book of Samuel, he argues that the redactor deliberately included both the theological and the folkloric accounts of David's meeting with Saul since they brought out different aspects of David's character, the private person whom Saul loved and the public figured he feared.[65] Alter is clearly working with a model of authorial intention with which many other modern critics would disagree but he is much more alive than the earlier 'literary critics' to the variety of ways in which an author might choose to arrange his or her material. He has also learnt from structuralism to appreciate the constraints of literary convention, tracing different versions of the annunciation-motif (from Sarah and Hannah to Mary) as well as variations on the 'type-scene' of the betrothal (in Ruth, Rebekah and Rachel). These scenes all illustrate 'the unceasing dialectic between the necessity to use established forms in order to be able to communicate coherently and the necessity to break and remake those forms' which literary creation involves.[66]

The Art of Biblical Poetry, according to Alter, involves a similar discovery of new possibilities within old forms, turning 'formal limitations . . . into an occasion for artistic expression'. Parallelism, as Shklovsky observed, works by introducing disharmony into a harmonious context, defamiliarizing habitual perceptions and introducing slight but significant semantic modifications. Far from being merely repetitious, tricking out the same idea in 'different stylistic finery', biblical parallelism involves various forms of intensification, moving from the literal to the figurative, from the general to the specific, becoming ever more vivid in its exploration of an idea. In the lines from Isaiah which celebrate God's action on behalf of Israel, for example,

> Water from a rock He made flow for them
> He split the rock and water gushed
> (48:20–1, Alter's own translation)

there is a clear increase in immediacy of detail.[67] Parallelism, Alter shows, is particularly at home with violence and destruction, the splitting not only of rocks but of skulls, as in the Song of Deborah (Judges 5:24–31). It also lends itself to the expression of alienation and bitter complaint, developing the intensity of feeling in many of the psalms. The effects of parallelism can also run on from individual lines to whole poems, magnificently illustrated in the Song of the Sea (Exodus 15:1–18), which telescopes the history of generations into a few powerful verses.

The central point, once again, is that form has meaning. The answer to the problem of suffering raised by Job, for example, is provided not by logic but by poetry, God's magnificent celebration of the terrible beauty of nature, which is necessarily beyond human reason but allows us to glimpse 'an immense world of power and beauty and awesome warring forces . . . a welter of contradictions, dizzying variety, energies and entities that man cannot take in'.[68] It cannot possibly be paraphrased, as one of Charles Williams' characters observes:

> As a mere argument there's something lacking perhaps, in saying to a man who's lost his money and his house and his family and is sitting on the dustbin, all over boils, 'Look at the hippopotamus.'[69]

Poetry, Alter explains, is 'a special way of imagining the world . . . a special mode of thinking' in which form is integral to meaning. This is universally accepted in the study of 'secular' poetry but the sacred status of the Bible has discouraged its appreciation as 'a body of literature that uses poetry to *realise* meanings'.[70] Alter and the other critics I have discussed have helped to restore this perception.

Literary criticism of the Bible, however, has not come to abolish historical criticism but to complement it. Just as historical criticism should not ignore the semantic significance of literary form so literary criticism needs to accept that the Bible makes historical claims which need to be tested. It also makes theological claims. It is fundamentally about God's action in history, however that is understood. Literary critics should not begin by treating God as a fiction and ignoring all theological elements in the text, though they may end up, as Dan Jacobson does, by disbelieving them and seeking alternative explanations of the choice of Israel in terms of Freudian analysis and Marxist economics (God's 'punishment' becomes a projection of Jewish guilt over the occupation of Canaan and an inevitable result of Israel's geographical location between powerful empires to the north and south).[71] The point, whether Jacobson is correct or not, is that any reader of the text must take its historical and theological claims seriously. To read the gospels without facing the claims they make about the person of Jesus is to misread them. Literary criticism can help to establish this, by identifying the nature of the biblical texts and exploring how they achieve their multiple meanings, as the following detailed studies of Genesis and Mark attempt to illustrate.

THE READABILITY OF GENESIS

It is at least arguable that the reason the Bible is so little read is that it is unreadable. Modern readers, having acquired their literary competence from texts very different from the Bible and likely to be labouring under all sorts of false expectations about its contents, may well be bewildered by the extraordinary nature of its first book, Genesis. To what genre, they will ask, does this mixture of prose and poetry, myth and history, legend and chronicle, belong? What sort of God is this, sometimes majestic and distant, as in the opening chapter, and at other times crudely human, subject to frequent fluctuations of mood and changes of mind? What are these seedy events, sodomy, rape, incest, adultery and bigamy, doing in a sacred text and how can these patriarchs, perpetually at enmity with their own brothers, whom they cheat and kill, be admired? These are some of the major questions raised by a reading of Genesis and there are many other minor irritations, constant duplications and discrepancies of detail and a general uncertainty of narrative voice, all of which add to a reader's difficulties.

It is unlikely that Genesis would feature in anyone's list of the most 'literary' books of the Bible. The dramatic verse of Job, the erotic Song of Solomon, the epic Books of Samuel, the celebratory Psalms, the Wisdom literature, especially the sceptical Ecclesiastes, Deutero-Isaiah among the prophets, St John's meditative gospel, St Paul's passionate letters and even the Book of Revelation are more likely to be included in such a list. But Genesis is where people begin (and often end). The major problems of readability in the Bible as a whole are encountered most obviously in this book. I will begin with some general difficulties of reading translations of ancient texts before passing on to the specific issues of genre-recognition, the portrait of God and the characterization of the patriarchs. As well as attempting to solve these 'problems', I will try to bring out some of the positive qualities to be found in this extraordinarily ambitious account of the origins of the world and of the 'chosen people'.

It should be recognized, of course, that some of the difficulties experienced in reading Genesis (for those, like myself, unfamiliar with Hebrew) lie in translation. Most English translations, for example, make no distinction between the different names of God to be explored later. Commentaries help to explain individual features of the original language, the complexity of the opening two verses for example, the associations of *tohu wa-bohu* ('without form and void') and the violence of the verbs rendered rather weakly as 'moving over the face of the waters'. They can also point out the word-play involved in Adam (man) being made of *adamah* (ground) and then condemned to return to it after the fall. They can explain the etymology of many of the proper names. But they can never make up for that sense of loss, that lack of confidence in gauging the precise tone of the original, which is the inevitable corollary of reading a translation.

Another difficulty experienced even by those readers familiar with what survives of the ancient literature of the near east relates to the question of genre-recognition, the ability to detect where Genesis is obeying and where it is departing from contemporary literary conventions. The polemical elements in the first chapter, for example, define the Jewish concept of the Creator by advertising its difference from other myths, in particular the *Enuma Elish*. The deities of sun and moon which that epic celebrates are conspicuously reduced to the greater and lesser lights of Genesis, while the monster of chaos against whom God is made to struggle in the earlier epic is divided in Genesis into less threatening sea-monsters which are part of His conscious creation (1:21).[72] The serpent is sometimes seen as a kind of Leviathan (the word *nahash* is used of both) but he too is a mere creature, much less of a threat than the monstrous opponent of the *Enuma Elish*.[73]

The tree of life in the garden of Eden, to take another example, seems similar to that in the Gilgamesh epic, whose loss by the hero involves humanity's loss of eternal youth. But, a reader will ask, is the fact that Adam and Eve ignore this tree in order to concentrate their attention on the other forbidden one, the tree of the knowledge of good and evil, deeply significant, a direct allusion to the earlier epic or is this tree merely an unimportant piece of realistic detail, just one of many plants in the garden? The flood story in Genesis also preserves elements of an earlier epic, a Mesopotamian flood story which itself survives in three different versions, including the details of the dove being sent on a search for dry land and the gods being pleased with the odour of the sacrifice offered by the survivors. Is a reader to assume a continuity not only of genre but of theology between these texts or to treat the account of Noah as primitive epic unsuccessfully integrated into the more sophisticated theology of other parts of Genesis? These are difficult questions which an informed reading of the text must take into account.

Readers are faced throughout Genesis with a text which is clearly fragmentary, some of the more obscure passages probably surviving from earlier Hebrew epics of which we no longer have the full text. One of the earliest snatches of verse in the Bible, for example, is put into the mouth of Lamech, who tells his wives,

> I have slain a man for wounding me,
> a young man for striking me.
> If Cain is avenged sevenfold,
> truly Lamech seventy-sevenfold. (4:23–4)

All that we have been told of him before this is that he was the son of Methusha-el and 'took two wives' (4:19). The prose narrative immediately resumes with Adam begetting another son, Seth (4:25). So what is a reader to make of this savage revenge exacted for some obscure injury? Another Lamech crops up at the end of chapter 5 as the father of Noah, living to the unlikely age of 777, having expressed a wish to retire at a mere 182! Is he the same person, a reader wants to know, and what is the significance of all these sevens? The passage cannot be read realistically, that is clear, and it is difficult to resist the conclusion that this particular bit of Genesis cannot be read at all. Any meaning that it may once have communicated has been irretrievably lost.

Jacob's wrestling with the angel (32:22–32) presents similar problems of genre-recognition, knowing what to read it *as*. The narrative is particularly obscure here, adding a further 'complication ... of readability' by its confusion of pronouns, the repeated 'he said ... And he said' requiring of the reader 'a retroactive reasoning of a syllogistic kind' to work out the speaker in each case.[74] It is also unclear on which side of the river they wrestle, which is an important factor in deciding whether to read the passage as a piece of folklore in which the hero undergoes a conventional 'ordeal', as a metaphorical representation of the extreme anguish of Jacob's private prayer or as an explanation of an ancient Jewish taboo, not elsewhere recorded, of not eating the part of the thigh which shrank after being touched (22:32). Most modern readers will tend towards a metaphorical reading of this passage as prototypical of Christ's agony in the garden of Gethsemane but it is difficult not to feel uneasy about the distance between such a modern reading and the alien structures of feeling and thought involved in the original production of the text.

This gap between the modes of thinking current in ancient Israel and those of our own time becomes even more apparent in reading about God. The final text of Genesis, of course, is the product of such a long period of time that it reveals within itself very different understandings of the divine, even different names. The use of the plural form *Elohim* by one source, which has God reveal His name as *Yahweh* only to Moses (Exodus 3:14–15), has supplied the clearest means by which to identify this later layer of the text from the earlier more anthropomorphic accounts of *Yahweh*'s actions beginning in the second chapter. The differences are obvious. The God of Genesis chapter 1 is majestic, transcendent, orderly and systematic. He issues a command and the results are immediate. He sees that His creation is good but it would clearly be unseemly for Him to express any emotion over it. He uses the 'royal we' ('Let us make'), which is possibly a relic of earlier plural notions of deity retained in His plural name or, for a Christian reader properly trained in the principles of canon criticism, an indication that He knows He is really three in one. He could also, of course, be addressing the angels. What is indisputable is His distance from mankind.

The God of chapter 2, on the other hand, is much more human, with something of an artistic temperament. He moulds man out of clay, breathes life into his nostrils, plants him a garden and tells him to look after it properly. When, on second thoughts, He realizes that this is likely to prove rather a lonely kind of life, He models a few animals to keep him company. When even they prove insufficient He moulds woman out of

Adam's rib. Far from being omniscient, this God assures Adam and Eve, incorrectly, that if they eat from the tree of the knowledge of good and evil they will die. He walks through the garden of Eden unaware that they have already eaten this fruit, only discovering this by inference from their knowledge of their nakedness. He then grows very angry, cursing them, the serpent and even the ground. Yet before expelling them from the garden He has the grace to make them coats and to clothe them (3:21). This God, theologically more 'primitive', is an altogether more sympathetic, more 'human' figure than the impassive creator of the first chapter.

Similarly contradictory portraits of God occur in the account of the flood, which can also be divided into separate sources because of blatant numerical discrepancies both about the number of animals Noah is instructed to take aboard the ark and about the duration of the flood. In the Yahwist version, God is hurt by the fact that his 'sons' mix with 'the daughters of men'. In the immortal words of the Good News Bible, these 'supernatural beings saw that these girls were beautiful, so they took the ones they liked' (6:2). God first of all limits his sons' lives to a mere 120 years and then, when their wickedness continues, repents altogether of creating them and decides on a flood as a means of extermination. It is difficult in translation to gauge God's tone of voice, but He appears by turns pompous and simple, injured and aggressive. In verse 3, for example, He announces, 'My spirit shall not abide in man for ever' (RSV). The authorized version reads 'strive with man' while the New Jerusalem Bible makes Him sound like a pompous bureaucrat or headmaster: 'My spirit cannot be indefinitely responsible for human beings.' In verse 6 we are told that He is 'sorry' and 'grieved' at man's wickedness. 'I will blot him out', He resolves. But his words to Noah are much more pompous, as He resumes His headmaster's hat: 'I have determined to make an end of all flesh . . . and behold I will annihilate them' (6:13).

There is, as has long been recognized, a splicing of sources at this juncture. The differences of tone continue throughout the flood story, the Priestly Writer making God give Noah pedantic instructions about the ark (6:14–16) while the Yahwist portrays Him deriving such satisfaction at the smell of Noah's sacrifice that He resolves never again to destroy the earth (8:21). There is a difference too between the Yahwist's portrait of Noah, who is only another sinful man but is fortunate to find God's 'grace' (6:8), and the Priestly Writer's presentation of him as 'a righteous man, perfect among his contemporaries' (6:9) who obeys God with almost offensive alacrity: 'So Noah did just as God had commanded him. So he did' (6:22). The text as it stands, in other words, is almost unreadable. We have either to attempt to break it down into 'coherent' elements or to accept its inner contradictions.

That God should speak at all, of course, is a literary convention, a narrative device which enables Him to express His intentions. It should not be taken as a realistic account of what actually happened, how the people of Israel in fact came to divine His will. That God should speak to Himself, as the Yahwist portrays Him, is a characteristically simple device which contributes to the altogether anthropomorphic nature of His characterization in this part of the text. In confounding the builders of the tower of Babel He is even made to appear jealous of man's architectural prowess, almost spitefully destructive, deliberately setting out to 'confuse their language, that they may not understand one another's speech' (11:7). He seems more open-minded about the people of Sodom and Gomorrah, insisting on checking at first hand the reports of their sinfulness (18:21). This visit, in the form of attractive young male angels who inflame the perverted lusts of the Sodomites, is combined with an annunciation to Sarah which appears to invite a comic reading.

We are told that 'the Lord appeared' to Abraham 'as he sat at the door of his tent in the heat of the day' (18:1). But what Abraham actually sees are three young men whom he treats with typical Eastern hospitality. The narrative alternates between 'the Lord' and 'they' when referring to these young men and goes on to speak of 'two angels' when they pass on to Sodom (19:1). It is possible therefore to read one of the three men as God and even to interpret this as yet another trinitarian reference. The comic elements in this version of the annunciation convention begin with Sarah's laughter on overhearing God's promise of a son. She denies having laughed, only for God to insist, like a pantomime dame, 'Oh yes you did' (18:15, New Jerusalem Bible). The comedy appears to continue with Abraham pleading to God not to destroy Sodom even if there are only fifty, then forty-five, then forty, then thirty, twenty and finally ten righteous men there. Lot offering his daughters to the Sodomites as a substitute for the beautiful angels seems like black comedy, as does Lot's escape from the devastated city into the incestuous embraces of his daughters. This final twist in an already tortuous tale should perhaps be read as an example of Jewish xenophobia, casting aspersions on the Moabites and Ammonites who were believed to be descended from Lot and his daughters.[75] But modern readers are bound to feel lost at this point, totally lacking in confidence about the 'tone' of the narrative and their appropriate response.

God's actions continue to veer between the transcendent, inexplicable by human standards, and the anthropomorphic. He connives in Sarah's cruel and jealous expulsion of Hagar and her son (21:12) only to relent on hearing Ishmael's cries (21:17). He subjects Abraham to the severe test of sacrificing his son, again to relent at the last moment. He appears to sympathize with the underdog, opening Leah's womb because she was hated while leaving the more fortunate Rachel barren (29:31). But he rewards Jacob for cheating his brother Esau of his inheritance and his father-in-law Laban of his cattle. He seems not to mind Judah treating his daughter-in-law Tamar as a harlot though he earlier slaughtered her first husband, Er, for unspecified 'wickedness' and her second, Onan, for practising *coitus interruptus* (38:7–10). These stories should perhaps be read as deliberately aporic, emphasizing the gap between God's thinking and man's, the futility of attempting to pierce His motives. Yet this is hardly consistent with His repeated assertions of His plan for Abraham and his descendants. In portraying God as both logical and beyond logic Genesis is necessarily brought into self-contradiction.

The stories surrounding Joseph, however, bring a change in the way God is depicted. He constantly appears to Abraham and Jacob face to face, whether as a man or an angel, but to Joseph he appears only in dreams. Joseph's dreams are much more complex than Jacob's ladder (the only dream-vision that Jacob enjoys) and, on one occasion at least, unreliable. For

Jacob interprets his son's dream of the sun, moon and stars bowing down before him as a reference to himself, his wife and their other sons paying homage to Joseph (37:9–10). But it is seen to have been as much a product of youthful ambition as divine inspiration when the mature Joseph prevents its fulfilment by riding to meet his father, falling on his neck and weeping 'a good while' (46:29).

The Joseph narratives also present a different notion of divine providence. In the earlier patriarchal stories God appears suddenly and miraculously 'out of the blue' in order to express his special interest in their welfare. The God of Joseph works behind the scenes to achieve His ends through men's free actions.[76] It is Joseph himself who makes all the important moves in the plot to bring his brothers to repentance and reconciliation. His prosperity is a sign of the Lord's favour, his ability to interpret dreams an indication of his inspired intuition. The same speech that assures his brothers that he has not taken 'the place of God', that it is God who has turned their evil into good, also promises, 'I will provide for you and your little ones' (50:20–1). The divine purpose, as the rest of the Bible will illustrate, is achieved through *human* agents and revealed through *human* history.

There are, then, contradictions and inconsistencies in the portrait of God in Genesis which a deconstructive critic might read as a sign of His transcendence of human understanding. An historian might interpret them as indications of a developing understanding. The anthropomorphic God presented in the earlier level of the text, it might be argued, makes for a more interesting character than His more distant successor but creates theological difficulties, for the modern reader at least, which the 'hidden' God of the Joseph narratives helps to resolve.

It is its delineation of human character, however, that makes Genesis most readable. The same ingredients, inconsistency and indeterminacy, leaving readers to explore the hidden depths of character, become extraordinarily effective in an area where readers are more confident in their ability to discern significance in the smallest details. Reticence and frugality are characteristic of much biblical narrative, as Dan Jacobson discovered in expanding a few verses of Samuel into his novel *The Rape of Tamar*: 'every phrase, virtually every word . . . was like a seed . . . capable of astonishing growth'.[77] Milton discovered the same thing, expanding a few verses of Genesis into an epic poem. It is, of course, a property of all narrative to generate additional detail. But biblical narrative seems particularly powerful in this respect, condensing deep insight into character into terse details full of potential meaning.

Genesis chapter 3 provides a classic example. It begins with the serpent probing Eve's understanding of God's commands. She resents his implication that they are not allowed to eat the fruit of any of the trees in the garden; it is only the one tree that is forbidden, though her suggestion that they cannot even touch it suggests that it is this one restriction which most rankles, precisely what is forbidden that becomes most attractive. One verse reveals that this attraction is intellectual ('to be desired to make one wise') as much as sensual ('good for food' and 'a delight to the eyes') and describes Eve taking the apple, eating it, giving it to Adam and watching him eat. One more verse captures their resultant guilt as they become aware of their nakedness. These first seven verses are expanded in *Paradise Lost* into over a thousand lines (Book XI). Milton, of course, puts the blame more firmly on Eve, making her insist on working alone and thereby becoming a target of the serpent's guile. Adam resolves to eat only out of 'vehemence of love to perish with her'. In Genesis itself they are equally despicable. When God reprimands him he blames her and when God turns to her she blames the serpent (1:11–13). There is a subtlety about the psychology here, 'a degree of morally problematic interiority one would hardly expect in a primitive folktale'.[78] Readers are positively encouraged to fill the psychological gaps imaginatively (as Milton does, in his own misogynistic manner), involving them in the process of exploring sinful human nature.[79]

The characterization of Cain and Abel is more 'problematic' because we are told so very little about them. Abel meets a violent death at the hands of his jealous brother because his sacrifice pleases God more than Cain's. God curses Cain, driving him into a fugitive wandering life, but also affords him special protection. The 'mark of Cain' is therefore ambiguous, a stigma of sinfulness but also a badge of belonging. It is difficult to accept that God may have been pleased with Cain's 'ironic sacrifice' of his brother but the metaphor of the ground 'opening its mouth' to receive Abel's blood (4:11) retains suggestions of just such a primitive deity.[80] The difficulties involved in gaining a coherent picture of Noah, as we have seen, stem from contradictory sources, one making him altogether 'perfect', 'righteous' and obedient (6:9, 22), the other enjoying his discomfiture in the eyes of his son, Ham, who catches him sprawled out and naked in a drunken stupor (9:20–5).

Abraham too creates problems for a modern reader since this supposed model of faith and obedience lies to his Egyptian protectors, passing his wife off as his sister (12:10–20), and ignores God's promise of a son, first setting up a slave as his heir and then giving in to his wife's suggestion that he should inseminate her maid (16:1–6). When God assures him that Sarah will indeed bear him a son he falls over with laughter (17:17) and when this event actually takes place he allows her to drive both maid and child into the wilderness (21:14). The moving account of his preparedness to sacrifice Isaac achieves its effects mainly through what it leaves unsaid. As Auerbach pointed out,[81] there is very little description either of the external landscape through which they pass or of the interior state of their minds. We are told (by God, in fact) that Abraham loves his son (22:2) but he makes absolutely no reply to the extraordinary command that he should offer him as a sacrifice. We have to read into the story the grim determination with which he must have risen 'early in the morning' (22:3). Similarly, Isaac's trusting affection lies 'behind' his exclamation, 'My father!', and his innocent, ignorant question about the victim for this particular sacrifice. Abraham's reply, 'God will provide himself the lamb for a burnt offering, my son' (22:8), could be read in a number of different ways. It could, for example, be a lie since Abraham does not know at this point that this is what God will do. In that case, 'lamb' and 'son' would be in sinister apposition. But it could also be an expression of faith. The suspense mounts as Abraham builds the altar, binds his son, places him upon the wood and even draws his knife. It is not until the last moment that the readers (and Isaac) are put out of their misery. Christian readers, of course, will see typological significance in this willingness of a father to sacrifice his son, a significance fully explored in the mystery cycles.

Isaac himself is a relatively unproblematic, even uninteresting character. Even his wooing is done for him. He repeats some of his father's mistakes, passing his wife off as his sister (26:6–11), but seems to lack his father's courage. He prefers to withdraw from opposition rather than confront it (26:12–33). Some of the tensions within his family, however, are revealed in one terse sentence: 'Isaac loved Esau, because he ate of his game; but Rebekah loved Jacob' (25:28). And on this simple conflict is built the whole complex story of the rival brothers. For Esau's appetite enables Jacob to cheat him of his birthright while Rebekah's partiality prompts her to suggest the trick by which Isaac is fooled into blessing the younger and smoother of his two sons.

Jacob, in fact, is to build his whole career on his ability to cheat his relatives. The way he fools the equally devious but less successful Laban, whose greed is economically captured in the moment that his eyes light up on seeing the ring and bracelets on his sister's arm (24:30), is full of burlesque scenes. He manages, for example, to make the stronger cattle produce the spotted and speckled offspring promised to him by Laban by placing rods before their eyes as they breed (29:41). And his wife Rachel, having stolen her father's 'household gods', calmly places them under her saddle while Laban rummages desperately through their tents, insisting that she cannot rise because 'the way of women is upon me' (31:35). Jacob himself becomes ridiculous, going frantic with fear at the prospect of the revenge his brother may exact when they meet again. Seeing Esau approach with 400 men he divides up his goods and family, bows obsequiously and offers generous recompense only to find that his brother has long forgiven him (33:1–17). The fact that it is Jacob rather than Esau who enjoys God's grace can only be taken as an index of the gap between men's thoughts and God's. For in human terms it is the elder brother who captures a reader's sympathy. But whatever their theological significance, it should be recognized that these scenes are richly comic, eminently readable.

Joseph, at least to begin with, is as unattractive as his father, whose spoilt favourite he is. The special gift of a long robe with sleeves is a clear mark of this favour, making work an impossibility. The third-person narrative, more intrusive in this part of Genesis than elsewhere, spells out the fact that 'his brothers saw that their father loved him more than all' and that they hate him for it (37:3–4). Joseph contributes to his unpopularity by telling tales on them and by recounting dreams which indicate the 'dominion' he hopes to have over them. And the robe which functioned as an index of favouritism serves also, stained with blood, as an instrument to convince Jacob that Joseph has been killed. In yet another ironic twist, the blood in which it is soaked is that of a kid, the same animal, in other words, that Jacob had used to cheat his brother of their father's blessing. The whole story resounds with ironic reversals, complex symbolism and subtle characterization.

The scene in which Joseph refuses to succumb to the seductions of Potiphar's wife reveals the economy with which this characterization is achieved. Joseph, we are told, 'was handsome and good-looking', making his master's wife 'cast her eyes' upon him with evident lust. The directness of her approach, 'Lie with me', contrasts with the flummoxed wordiness with which he lists all the reasons why he should not. She repeats her demand, catching hold of his garment, which is destined once again to play an important symbolic function in the narrative. In at least one midrashic development of the story, she is made to fondle and caress it suggestively.[82] In the text as it stands she merely uses it as a device to incriminate the too-innocent young man (39:7–18). Joseph now uses his ability to interpret dreams to better effect than before, escaping from the gaol and rising within Pharaoh's court, where he uses his position not to exact revenge upon his brothers but to bring about reconciliation with them through an ironic reversal of what they did to him.

There are two basic ironies, the first beyond Joseph's control: the brothers' action, abandoning him in a pit, the prey to any passer-by, turns out to have been instrumental in enabling him to fulfil his dreams, leading him eventually to Egypt. The second is directly designed by Joseph. He has them thrown into prison (as they threw him into the pit) and accuses them of spying, demanding that they send for their remaining brother Benjamin to 'test their words'. This test, of course, has nothing to do with the accusation of spying (they could have told the truth about their youngest brother and still be spies) but everything to do with true brotherhood.[83] Joseph's action produces the desired results, triggering the brothers' guilt over their earlier treatment of him and producing a confession on their part which Joseph, unknown to them, hears and weeps over (42:21–4). He allows them to return home, secretly replacing their money in their sacks. There are, in fact, two accounts of their discovery of this money, prompting source critics to complain of clumsy editing. In one, however, the stress is theological, for they recognize a divine hand at work, asking, 'What is this that God has done to us?' (42:28). The other explores what Alter calls the 'moral–psychological' axis of the story, their dismay being followed by Jacob's lamenting once more the loss of Joseph and refusing to countenance any parting with Benjamin. The inclusion of both versions of the discovery of the money keeps both axes, theological and psychological, firmly in view.[84]

A further famine gives Joseph the opportunity to complete the process of reconciliation with his brothers through more complex plotting (the planting of a silver cup in Benjamin's sack). Joseph, who weeps on meeting his mother's only other son, weeps even more on finally revealing himself to all his brothers. Again, source critics complain of the repetition of his words, 'I am Joseph' (45:3–4), earning Alter's condemnation for their refusal to recognize what is 'brilliantly effective' and 'obviously justified by the dramatic and psychological situation'.[85] Joseph finally abandons his position of dominance, his dreams of dominion, falling first upon Benjamin's neck and then kissing his brothers, weeping the while (45:15). The emotion is maintained when he meets his father (46:29), when Jacob gathers all his children together to bless them as the twelve tribes of Israel (49:1–28) and when Joseph himself, on his deathbed, passes on the patriarchal blessing (50:22–6). This is not merely 'a device to round off the Jacob–Joseph narration and bind it to a number of larger collections of tradition', as one redaction critic reductively complains.[86] In both closes the story in peaceful reconciliation and opens it up 'to a future which extends beyond the end of the narrative' to the whole history of Israel.[87]

To read Genesis as literature, then, is to pay close attention to the literary devices I have tried to explore, to its symbolism, irony and characterization, as well as its explicit theological commentary. There are passages, as we have seen, which are inconsistent and contradictory, and they should be acknowledged as such. Much of the book, however, retains the power to make its readers ask profound questions about God, creation, man and history, questions to which the narrative also supplies an answer. That answer is both theological and literary. Criticism can show how it is achieved but its full meaning and power is lost in any attempt at paraphrase.

THE MEANINGS OF MARK'S STORY

Perhaps the most difficult and important question in reading Mark involves a decision about its genre. The first verse, which may anyway have been added at a later stage, proclaims 'The beginning of the gospel of Jesus Christ, the Son of God'. But what is a 'gospel'? The word had been used before to refer to the 'good news' about Christ, the message of salvation which lies at the centre of Christianity, a meaning which it takes on later in the text (1:14, 13:10).[88] But this seems to have been the first use of the word for a written text, establishing in the process a new literary genre, 'the one unique literary form produced by early Christianity'.[89] It is not, fortunately, entirely original, otherwise it would indeed prove to be unreadable. It has elements of biography although it tells us nothing about the childhood of its subject, his physical appearance, personal preferences, habits, even whether he was married or not, none of those details which anyone interested in the development of personality would want to know.[90] Nevertheless, there are some similarities to other ancient lives, which also end with apotheosis, and it may well have been written to provide missionaries with material about Christ's early life with which to counteract the gnostic tendencies evident in St Paul, who seems to show no interest in the subject.[91]

Mark has been called an aretalogy, a cycle of miracle stories to illustrate the divine power of the hero.[92] It clearly draws on Old Testament histories, which also allowed for a much greater admixture of fiction than modern histories. It has strong apocalyptic elements, which take over in chapter 13. It actually meets most of the structural requirements of classical drama and employs many figures of classical rhetoric.[93] It can be seen as a sermon, using details of Christ's life in order to make theological and pastoral points.[94] It has also been described as theological polemic, attempting to counteract what was considered to be a false christology emanating from Jerusalem, insisting that Christ was not risen and already present in glory but still to appear with the parousia in Galilee.[95] But it is none of these things exactly. It is a gospel and readers must learn by experience what the conventions of this new form are.

Some knowledge of the context in which the book was written might help to illuminate this question of genre. If we could be sure, for example, that Mark was written for a Galilean church chastened by the disappointment of messianic expectations raised (and erased) in the Judaeo-Roman war or, alternatively, for a Roman church suffering from persecution and needing to underplay the Jewish elements in their faith, we would have a clearer notion of how to read the text. It is particularly exasperating to come across the contemporary reference to 'the abomination of desolation . . . standing where it ought not' combined with an authorial nudge, 'let the reader understand' (13:14), because this is precisely what the modern reader cannot do. Similarly, if the tradition quoted by Papias was right and Mark is mainly a record of St Peter's personal memories then this too would affect our strategies of reading. But these are questions of history, to be resolved, if ever, by historical research. I want now to focus on questions which can be answered by a consideration of the literary form of the gospel, drawing on some of the many recent studies of Mark as narrative, a story which necessarily employs literary devices in order to achieve theological meaning. Form-critics, as we have seen, denied that there was 'a developing story'. For them there was just a group of 'isolated stories', pericopes which a redactor provided with a wider framework.[96] Literary critics, however, consider 'the story as a whole', which one translation sets out in paragraphs rather than verses in order to bring out the shape of the whole narrative.[97] It is at least arguable that the gospel was first received in this way, read aloud at a sitting, as Paul's letters were, perhaps as part of the Easter liturgy.[98]

Such a reading of St Mark brings out the larger literary forms which constitute major elements in its overall meaning, elements which are destroyed by the historical disintegration of the text. Episodes which appear problematic when taken in isolation, such as the cursing of the fig-tree, make more sense when seen as part of a larger narrative sequence involving Christ's rejection of the temple. The duplication of feeding miracles, baffling not only to the disciples but to many later critics, can also be seen as part of a larger literary structure which places Christ's redemptive activity for the Jews and Gentiles in parallel. Some problems remain, such as the function of the young man in the linen garment who flees from the garden of Gethsemane and the shockingly abrupt and seemingly inconclusive ending. I will return to these in a moment. But I want to explore first the kind of story that Mark tells, to bring out some of the dominant features of the narrative. I will then consider three literary questions which are crucial to a theological understanding of the book: the narrative structure, which involves the opening of the kingdom to the Gentiles, the characterization of Jesus and his disciples, which raises critical questions of christology and discipleship, and the vexed question of the abrupt ending, which is vital to an understanding of the resurrection.

Technically, in terms of the rhetoric of fiction, Mark's is an intrusive omniscient third-person narrative. The story is told mainly in the past tense but switches quite frequently into the vivid present and also alludes fairly often to what is later to happen, either through direct prophecy on the part of Jesus, who makes four clear predictions of his death, or through indirect means such as the fate of John the Baptist, which clearly foreshadows that of Jesus. The seeds of conflict with the Jewish religious authorities which are to find their tragic outcome in the crucifixion are sown as early as the second chapter, when they take exception to his forgiving sins, breaking fasting laws and healing on the Sabbath. The plot, in other words, is structured in such a way as to lead inexorably to its violent climax.

Throughout the story the omniscient narrator moves from one scene to another as if invisibly present, having privileged access to the motives of all the characters, including Jesus. To suppose otherwise, to insist, for example, that the Marcan apocalypse consists of a verbatim report of what Jesus actually said to his disciples or that his tormented words in the garden of Gethsemane were 'overheard' by companions whom he thought to be asleep, is to resist necessary features of narrative which were common to all forms of ancient history.[99] Mark's narrator does not, of course, enter his characters' minds in the manner of a modern novelist, reporting their 'stream of consciousness' in characteristic patterns of free indirect speech. He uses direct speech and that quite sparingly, allowing Jesus only three utterances in the whole course of the passion narrative. In the account of Jesus' baptism he oscillates between a subjective perspective ('he saw the heavens opened and the Spirit descending upon him like a dove') and the more objective statement, 'and a voice came from heaven' (1:10–11). Mark tells us simply that Jesus was tempted in the wilderness in the company of wild beasts and angels (1:13), the psychological possibilities of this scene being explored more fully in Matthew and Luke.[100]

To say that a narrator is omniscient, then, is merely a manner of describing his freedom, if he chooses, to follow any of the characters, to move from Peter warming himself before the fire in the courtyard to Jesus confronting the high priests and back again to Peter denying his Lord three times (14:53–72). This does not require a tremendously sophisticated author, 'organising, alluding, suggesting, like a sort of ancient Henry James'. According to Kermode, Flaubert 'might have done more' with the basic idea of intercalating the accounts of Jesus' trial and Peter's denial, 'cutting back and forth, interspersing the cockcrows with the dialogue of the trial'.[101] But the telling of any story requires the use of fairly complex narrative devices, conventions which are employed in Mark to significant theological effect.

The intercalation or framing of scenes, placing one episode in the framework of another, is one of Mark's favourite ploys. He separates, for example, the sending out of the apostles from their return with an account of John the Baptist's death, which is therefore made to serve not only as an anticipation of the fate which awaits Jesus but also as a gruesome reminder of the dangers of discipleship. There are at least nine examples of this kind of construction in Mark,[102] one of the most significant being the cursing of the fig-tree. In one of three visits to the temple at Jerusalem (and it is another habit of Mark's to arrange things in threes[103]), a hungry Jesus seems unreasonably to vent his anger on the unfortunate tree for failing to provide him with fruit in spite of the fact, which the narrator makes explicit, that 'it was not the season for figs'. He curses it and proceeds into the city, where he drives the moneylenders and tradesmen out of the temple, returning to Bethany to find the fig-tree 'withered away to its roots' and to tell his astonished disciples that they should have more faith (11:12–24). Read literally, this appears to portray Jesus in a particularly bad mood. But the narrative form, by connecting the cursing of the fig-tree with the cleansing of the temple, requires a symbolic reading of the episode as indicating the deadness of the Jewish traditions which were about to be destroyed. The placing of the parable of the disobedient husbandmen of the vineyard in the following chapter underlines this meaning.

Another example of narrative form determining theological meaning is the geographical setting of the gospel. There is clearly a contrast between Galilee, where Jesus reveals his divine power in the first half of the book, and Jerusalem, the goal and setting for the second half, in which messianic fulfilment is found to involve suffering and death. In the first half Jesus is constantly being rushed from place to place by a breathless narrator whose favourite linking words are 'and straightway'. But in the progression from the river Jordan through the Sea of Galilee to the mountain on which he is transfigured there seems to be an underlying reference to the history of Israel.[104] And in crossing the Sea of Galilee repeatedly, performing parallel actions on either side, Jesus can be seen to preach the kingdom of God to both Jews and Gentiles. His first action on crossing the sea to the country of the Gadarenes (5:1) is to perform an exorcism, cleansing the unclean, which can also be interpreted symbolically as an indication that the Gentiles are included in the divine plan. Exorcism is followed by healing at Gennesaret on the Gentile side of the lake (6:53–6) just as it had been at Capernaum on the Jewish side (1:21–31).

This helps to make sense of the fact that there are two miraculous feedings of the multitude, one in a Jewish setting after which twelve baskets are collected (6:43) and the other, following a prolonged attack on Jewish ritual practices and the encounter with the Syrophoenician woman who persuades him to cast the children's crumbs to the dogs (7:27–8), after which seven baskets are collected (8:5–8). Twelve, of course, alludes to the tribes of Israel, while seven signifies wholeness, completion, universality. It is the number of 'honest men' added to the original twelve disciples in order to quell the 'murmuring' of the Hellenistic Christians against the Hebrews (Acts 6:1–6). Reluctant though modern readers are to respond to number symbolism (one of the most unpopular features of Farrer's *Study in St Mark*), it is difficult to resist the prominence Mark gives it. 'How many baskets full of broken pieces did you take up' after the first feeding, asks Jesus of the disciples, and they reply, 'Twelve'. And how many after the second: 'And they said to him, "Seven". And he said to them, "Do you not yet understand?" ' (8:19–21).[105] The symbolism here supports the narrative structure, forcing the reader to accept that the kingdom belongs to the Gentiles as well as the Jews.

It would be wrong to suggest that Mark is always tightly structured in this symbolic way. There are plenty of loose ends, vivid and seemingly insignificant details which may (or may not) be a product of Peter's actual memories. One of these is the minor mystery of the 'young man . . . with nothing but a linen cloth about his body' who flees from the garden of Gethsemane (14:51–2). This may be a signature on St Mark's part, placing himself unobtrusively in the text after (or somewhat before) the manner of Hitchcock. It may be a piece of insignificant detail designed to give the effect of realism. It may, as Morton Smith argues, be left over from *The Secret Gospel of St Mark*, a variant version which apparently circulated among a libertine Gnostic sect, in which a similarly clad young man spent the night with Jesus. The same young man, it is claimed, reappears 'dressed in a white robe', in the empty tomb (16:5). The young man in the garden may, on the other hand, be merely part of a wider pattern of responses to Jesus' arrest: others betray him like Judas or deny him like Peter. This man flees; his linen cloth may allude to the garment which played such an important part in Joseph's story.[106] All this must remain a matter of speculation since the text retains an element of indeterminacy of the kind enjoyed more by literary critics than theologians. It is a part of Mark's story whose meaning is by no means clear.

The question of characterization is rather more central to a book which announces itself as 'the gospel of Jesus Christ, the Son of God' (1:1). In many ways, of course, Jesus is presented as a very human figure. He is 'moved with pity', an emotion which in the Greek has connotations of anger (translated 'compassion' in the AV, 'warm indignation' in the NEB), by the suffering of the leper whom he cures in the first chapter (1:41). His anger is soon directed against the pharisees when they oppose his healing on the sabbath (3:5). It is also channelled against those 'friends' of his who think his messianic pretensions a sign of madness (3:21) and even against his own family, whom he disowns (3:31–5). The harshness with which Jesus is made to treat his family has been read as an indication of Mark's polemic intention to discredit the Jerusalem church, where they were held in high esteem.[107] It has even fuelled speculation that Jesus was ashamed of being illegitimate, a stigma which caused him to invent a heavenly father.[108] Mark, of course, suggests nothing of the kind. But he does present Jesus as perpetually impatient, smouldering at his disciples' denseness and bewailing their lack of faith.

The disciples in turn treat Jesus with surprising irreverence. They mock him for asking, 'Who touched me?' in the middle of a crowd (5:31) and laugh at him for claiming that Jairus' daughter is not dead (5:40). The accounts of the feeding miracles crackle with tension. In the first, Jesus is once more moved with 'compassion' towards the multitudes who come to hear him. He preaches, it would seem, at great length until the disciples remind him that it is getting late and they are in the middle of the desert. Shouldn't the crowd be sent away to 'buy themselves something to eat'? Jesus insists that they be *given* food. When the disciples, still economically minded, point out the likely cost of this Jesus orders them to check how many loaves they already have. 'Go and see', he thunders, and they return almost immediately with the answer, 'Five', adding 'and two fishes', it has been suggested 'out of sheer impertinence'.[109]

The disciples are presumably impressed by the miracle itself (they spend much of the time being 'astonished') but they still need to be 'made' to 'get into the boat' for Bethsaida while Jesus remains alone in prayer, reappearing to astound them even more by walking on the water (6:34–52). They seem not to have learnt anything from the first feeding miracle, however, since they make exactly the same complaints about feeding so many in the wilderness in chapter 8 (8:4). They continue to worry about their lack of supplies even after the second miracle, causing Jesus to rebuke them for their blindness and hardness of heart (8:17–18). He positively grills them on the significance of the number symbolism, as we have seen, and complains yet again about their stupidity (8:21).

Jesus is even harsher to Peter later in the same chapter when he identifies him as 'the Christ' but fails to recognize the need for suffering. It is Peter, of course, who first 'began to rebuke' Jesus, but Jesus by no means holds back, calling him Satan for being 'not on the side of God, but of men' (8:29–33). Jesus rebukes the other disciples for continuing to care about power and success, disputing 'with one another who was the greatest' (9:34), James and John being singled out for wanting to share his glory without his suffering (10:37–9). He is quite brutal with the young man who kneels at his feet and asks how to inherit eternal life, first objecting to being called 'good' and then insisting that he give away all his possessions (10:17–21).

The disciples themselves continue to misunderstand almost everything he says. Even after he has attacked Jewish traditions mercilessly and driven the money lenders from the temple, they point innocently to its architectural magnificence (13:1), eliciting in response his longest and most savage apocalyptic speech. In spite of his repeated prediction of his suffering and death, they fail utterly to understand the significance of his being anointed, complaining instead of the waste of ointment involved in what they see as a flamboyant gesture (14:3–5). They sleep through his torment in Gethsemane and abandon him on his arrest. They miss the crucifixion altogether. Whether after the resurrection they would have responded to the message the women fail to pass on is a question to which the text itself (as it stood in the first century) gives no answer.

The 'meaning' of this characterization of the disciples is hard to establish. Mark seems to go out of his way to discredit them, perhaps in order to undermine the authority of the Jerusalem church which, as Paul found, was reluctant to abandon Jewish traditions, perhaps to encourage persecuted Christians of his own time by showing how even the disciples found it hard to understand and remain loyal to Jesus.[110] It has been argued that we necessarily identify with the disciples, especially in the early chapters of the gospel, where they are presented more favourably as eager followers of the Lord. Their later failures then cause us to examine ourselves and to recognize similar failings. The characterization of the disciples can therefore be read as an implicit call to repentance.

The characterization of Jesus, as I have presented it, emphasizes his humanity. He is certainly no 'paragon of purity' but 'a fallible man; sometimes tired, hungry, irritable. Sometimes humorous, cynical, sarcastic. Often compassionate, often unreasonable.' From the 'many human touches' which Mark includes but the later gospels omit, a picture emerges of a 'moody' and 'passionate' man.[111] But there is another side to the characterization of Jesus in Mark. He is from the beginning a divine figure, 'the Son of God' (1:1), whose identity is recognized by John the Baptist (1:7–8), confirmed by 'a voice . . . from heaven' (1:11) and reiterated by the 'unclean spirit' who is the subject of his first miracle (1:24). He proclaims his divinity in the second chapter by forgiving sins (2:10) and by claiming authority over the law (2:28). The first half of the book is full of awe-inspiring acts of divine power from exorcism to miracles of feeding and healing, culminating in the transfiguration, at which a voice from the clouds once more confirms who he is (9:7). He calls the temple 'my house' (11:17) and reminds the scribes that even David called him 'Lord' (12:35). It is because of this 'blasphemy' that the chief priests and scribes arrest him and during the trial he admits openly to being 'the Christ' (14:61–2). His identity is underlined at the climax of the narrative, when he dies on the cross. 'Truly', says the centurion, 'this man was a son of God' (15:39). Finally, as he predicted, he rises from the dead (16:6).

Such is the discrepancy between these two sides of Jesus' character as presented by Mark that a deconstructive reading divides what it calls the 'mythological code', which is responsible for such miraculous scenes as the transfiguration, from the 'materialist' presentation of the revolutionary human being who associates with the outcast in order to subvert the dominant class structures of his time. His three predictions of the passion are seen to conflict with the 'narrative logic' of the rest of the book, which 'relies on contingencies'. There are thus two opposing discourses in the text, one working in human terms to present a human Jesus and the other 'remythologizing' this story in terms of a Pauline christology which appears openly at the point at which Jesus addresses God as 'Abba'.[112] The tension between these two ways of looking at Jesus, of course, remains within the doctrine of the Incarnation, which is not so much a resolution as a recognition of what is a literary as well as a theological paradox.

It is the ending, however, which presents the gravest difficulty in reading St Mark's gospel, 'the greatest of all literary mysteries'.[113] For the gospel which began with such a tremendous bang seems to end with a terrible whimper: three frightened women confronted with an empty tomb and the amazing message that Christ is risen. The final verse reads:

> And they went out and fled from the tomb; for trembling and astonishment had come upon them; and they said nothing to any one, for they were afraid. (16:8)

This, Kermode argues, is either 'intolerably clumsy' or 'incredibly subtle', far too subtle for the second-century Church, which added an appendix enumerating further resurrection appearances and taking the story up to the ascension. Among the less plausible explanations of the original ending are

> that Mark died suddenly after writing 16:8, or that the last page of his manuscript fell off, or that there is only one missing verse

which ties everything up . . . or that Mark intended to write a
sequel, as Luke did, but was prevented.[114]

Anything but such an anticlimax. For to give full weight to the
final verse as it stands, to accept that the women failed to pass
on the message and that the disciples therefore never met the
risen Lord in order to correct their previous misconceptions
about him, is unthinkable. It upsets all the readers' expectations that the disciples will come round in the end and that
Jesus wasn't entirely deluded in choosing them. It would make
the narrator 'a very nasty ironist' who has allowed all Jesus'
predictions to be fulfilled but to no purpose, everything being
put in jeopardy by the final verse.[115] Even Hardy would
hesitate before torturing his readers so cruelly.

What happens, of course, is that readers supply their own
ending. Mark's original readers, it is argued, must have been
familiar with the tradition of resurrection appearances as it is
found in Paul's first letter to the Corinthians.[116] But any
reader is forced at this point to leave the world of the story for
the 'real' world of history. Nor is this the first time that this
happens, for there is a reference to Pentecost in the very first
chapter (1:8) while the Marcan apocalypse, as we have seen,
brings contemporary events into the text. So Mark's gospel,
along with Genesis, can be called a self-consuming artefact, a
story which encourages its readers, especially at the abrupt
ending, to break out of the story world, to return themselves to
Galilee, the place where the kingdom was first preached and
where the parousia is expected, to follow for themselves the
difficult road of discipleship.

Mark's gospel, then, has many meanings not all of which can
have been 'intended' by the person or persons responsible for
the final version of the text. To interpret the story is to attempt
a description of the way in which these meanings are achieved
in the text. This need not, indeed should not, involve reducing
narrative effects to theological concepts. For these meanings,
as I keep insisting, are not paraphrasable. The gospel itself
should be seen as a form of theology, an interpretation of the
significance of the raw material it has transformed. Mark's
gospel, in other words, is a prime example of narrative
theology.

CHAPTER 3

Narrative Theology: The Stories of Faith

NARRATIVE, MYTH AND HISTORY

A recognition of the narrative form in which the Christian faith is often proclaimed, most notably in the gospels, is one of the component elements of what has become known as narrative theology. Much narrative theology is openly hostile to conceptual thought, born of deep frustration with the 'tyranny of definitions and dogma'.[1] By making faith a matter of story, the discovery of individual and communal identity through the intersection of our personal stories with the 'master-story' of Christian revelation, some narrative theologians at least seek to combine confessional commitment with philosophical relativism.[2] Stories, they argue, express the 'truth' about life more convincingly if less confidently than doctrinal propositions, offering a description of life rather than a definition of reality. The central claim of narrative theology, whether complementary or antagonistic to systematic theology, is that 'virtually all our basic convictions about the nature and meaning of our lives find their ground and intelligibility in some form of overarching, paradigmatic story.'[3]

Stories, it has long been recognized, have a power to entertain. 'Such is the universal charm of narrative', wrote Sir Walter Scott, 'that the worst novel ever written will find some gentle reader content to yawn over it, rather than to open the pages of the historian, moralist or poet.'[4] Sir Philip Sidney, following Aristotle and Horace, emphasized the power of fiction not only to please but to instruct by example. For poetry is free to invent perfect plots in which poetic justice is always observed, unlike history, the slave of contingency, which remains 'captived to the truth of a foolish world'.[5] Fiction, as Aristotle observed, is concerned with 'universal truths' rather than 'particular facts'.[6] But history too involves the telling of a story, the gathering of data into significant plots. And the Christian claim is that one particular story, centred upon Christ, tells the universal truth about history.

All narrative, the telling of any story, involves the organization of otherwise isolated 'facts' into a meaningful whole. 'Stories would not even exist', claims Amos Wilder, 'if human nature did not look to them avidly for illumination of its homelessness in time and circumstance.' Our interest in these stories involves more than curiosity, the desire to know 'what happened next'; it includes the demand that they should be 'true to life', expressing 'the way things are . . . the way things happen'.[7] All fiction is to this extent mimetic, an imitation of life. Realism, to be explored further in the third section of this chapter, requires not only the mirroring of superficial details from everyday experience (which is better labelled naturalism) but a representation of underlying 'laws', an exploration of what life is 'really' like.

Modern literary theory, however, has emphasized the illusory nature of realism while recent historiography has stressed the fictiveness of history. Derrida mocks our desire for origins and ends while Foucault pokes fun at our faith in a significant reality beyond discourse:

> We want historians to confirm our belief that the present rests upon profound intentions and immutable necessities. But the true historical sense confirms our existence among countless lost events, without a landmark or a point of reference.[8]

Whether ultimate reality has a 'plot', whether the world contains a meaningful history, is, of course, a matter of faith. What I want to illustrate in this chapter is that Christian faith necessarily involves the telling of stories, both of the self and of the world. I will consider first the light that literary theory can shed on the role played by 'story' and 'narrative' in theology before considering the narrative element in history. The following two sections will consider autobiography and the novel as literary forms of theological exploration.

It would, of course, be impossible to tell the whole story of the development of narrative theology. George Stroup, who attempted the task, complained of the 'bewilderingly diverse' proposals which invoke the term 'narrative'.[9] It is nevertheless possible to divide the subject into two main areas, the discussion of narrative in terms of its organization of religious experience and the consideration of revelation as taking narrative form, whether in the Bible or in the continuing history of the Church. It was in his book on *The Meaning of Revelation* that H. Richard Niebuhr first discussed 'The Story of Our Life', arguing that revelation took narrative form not only in the gospels themselves but in the ways in which individuals and communities appropriated them. The Church, for example, explains 'what it stands for . . . by telling the story of its life' in the creeds and in the sacraments.[10] Revelation becomes redemptive when it is 'appropriated at the level of personal identity and existence', when the story of God's action in history intersects with the stories which comprise the identities of individuals and communities.[11]

The 'sacred stories' of revelation, to use Stephen Crites' terms, function as 'myths', shaping the meaning of experience for whole cultures and providing the framework within which the 'mundane' stories of our individual lives can develop. Mundane stories also contribute to the way in which 'people articulate and clarify their sense of the world' but they are more flexible, more subject to change:

> Sacred stories, too, are subject to change, but not by conscious reflection. People do not sit down on a cool afternoon and think themselves up a sacred story. They awaken to a sacred story, and their most significant mundane stories are told in the effort, never fully successful, to articulate it.[12]

This awakening, of course, is traditionally described as 'conversion', that key moment in any Christian life when his or her personal story is found to have significance as part of a wider historical plot. It lies at the centre of many of the autobiographies to be explored in the following section.

These sacred stories or myths may develop as doctrines develop; their interpretation will certainly change in different cultures. But they are essentially enduring, their basic narrative structure remains resistant to change, as opposed to fictions, which are experimental and exploratory. In Kermode's words,

> Fictions are for finding things out, and they change as the needs of sense-making change. Myths are the agents of stability, fictions the agents of change.

History, Kermode continues, 'the imposition of a plot on time, is a substitute for myth'. He overemphasizes, I think, the absolute claims of myth to provide 'total and adequate explanations of things as they are'.[13] For it is their openness to different interpretations in different historical conditions which helps myths to survive, adapting, in evolutionary terms, to the demands of the times.

Crossan too places myth at the static pole of the narrative spectrum, referring to stories which claim to give 'the final word about "reality"' with parable at the opposite pole, 'subverting that "reality" and thereby introducing the possibility of transcendence'. In between, in his 'Theology of Story', come 'apologues', which defend the mythical world established by a particular culture, 'actions', which discuss and describe this world, and 'satires', which attack it.[14] Such is Crossan's distrust of story, however, his insistence that any God who can be contained within our stories must be an idol, a product of the human imagination, that his theology of story might better be called 'a theology of the limits of story'.[15] For it is only when our stories are shattered, according to Crossan, that the transcendent is allowed to break through.

The word 'myth', in ordinary usage, has unfortunate connotations, being taken to reduce what was held to be history to the status of fiction.[16] But what holds all types of story together is their narrative form. Aristotle, in fact, used the word *mythos* to mean plot, the organization of events into a significant whole with a beginning, a middle and an end.[17] It is the imposition of an order on events, departing from straightforward chronicity by selection, omission and other narrative devices, which distinguishes 'plot' from the raw material of 'story' in modern narrative theory. The same distinction between the bare facts of what actually or purportedly happened (the story) and the manner in which the story is told (the plot) is common to Russian formalists, who talk of *fabula* and *sjuzet*, and French narratologists, who distinguish *histoire* from *discours*, analysing in great detail the differences between story-time, the reconstructable order of events, and discourse-time, how a reader learns of these events. There can be changes of order (flashing forward or back), of duration (expanding or contracting the time an event could possibly take), and of frequency (telling the same event more than once from different points of view).[18]

All this, along with many other ways in which narrative discourse 'distorts' the straightforward story, has a profound effect on the meaning of a narrative. It is clearly a way of playing with a reader's desire to know what will happen, a desire which in a 'traditional narrative of resolution' is always eventually satisfied. In what has been called a 'plot of revelation', however, the emphasis is not so much on the answer to this question as on the 'state of affairs' which the discourse reveals, as Jane Austen's heroines, for example, come to a fuller awareness of themselves and of their world.[19] Nothing remarkable happens in the way of story; the development is entirely at the level of plot.

Narrative, then, is a product of human consciousness imposing order on to experience. Time itself, as St Augustine recognized, has no meaning apart from memory, which organizes it in the mind. Past, present and future are not independent metaphysical entities but categories of the organizing consciousness, categories which are crucial to the creation of personal identity.[20] Identity, in other words, is a matter of organizing past experience into a coherent plot.

One branch of narrative theology accordingly focuses on these stories, on *Theology as Biography*[21] or *Telling Your Story*,[22] encouraging individuals to celebrate what is unique to their experience. 'Telling stories', according to the most enthusiastic practitioners of this mode of theology, 'is functionally equivalent to believing in God', since both involve finding meaning and order in experience.[23] Within the Christian tradition, the function of personal testimony clearly plays a major role, especially in revivalist, evangelical circles.[24] It is

particularly important for oppressed individuals and communities to develop their own models of identity in order to
maintain their dignity in the face of suffering and to keep their
hope alive. The black community in the United States, for
example, has been shown to have 'lived its narrative theology
in song and sermon',[25] literary modes of expression which call
for close theological attention.

Another strand of narrative theology focuses on story as the
mode in which the Church as a whole preserves its identity.
Stephen Sykes sees liturgy, the routine ritual repetition of the
Christian story, as a more fundamental element in the
preservation of Christian identity than systematic theology,
which he nevertheless finds necessary in order to control
appropriate interpretations of these narratives. Support for his
understanding of the role of narrative in ritual can be found as
much in sociological explorations of the 'institutionalization' of
religious stories and psychological experiments on the memo-
rability of stories as in literary theory. The fact that 'narrative
is international, transhistorical, transcultural', a mode of
organizing experience which is *translatable* without
fundamental damage',[26] certainly helps the Church to remain
catholic. But, from a sociological perspective, the founding
events of a religion,

> what the prophet and his followers actually did becomes a
> behavioral model to be represented in stereotyped and selected
> liturgical form ... a sacred history, impregnated with the
> mythical elements so typical of liminality, that becomes
> resistant to criticism and revision and consolidated into a
> structure.[27]

This structure organizes the events into a plot which comprises
the significant order common to all narrative.

The stories which are best remembered, according to
evidence produced by experimental psychology, follow a definite pattern, first providing a setting, then a theme, then the
plot itself and finally the resolution. This is the order which
has been found to produce maximum recall, to be most easily
remembered.[28] These four requirements are certainly fulfilled
by the Nicene Creed, whose opening statement of belief in God,

'Maker of heaven and earth', sets the scene preparatory to an outline of the theme of redemption, a summary of the plot of Christ's life and a climax in the last judgement, which provides a resolution to the whole of human history.

Sacraments such as baptism can also be seen to involve a narrative element, endowing upon the baptised a new personal identity in a larger plot whose 'end is assured' and whose 'resolution is embraced in hope'.[29] The eucharist too requires the 'performance of a public narrative memorial' whose meaning is embodied in its structure. Its setting involves thanksgiving to the Father, the source of our daily bread and wine, its main theme is the memory of the last supper, and its basic plot involves the communion of the faithful in the kingdom of God, which provides the eschatological resolution. Sykes is careful to insist that narrative is not the only semiotic system to be found in the eucharist, a realization of whose total significance requires poetic symbols and theological concepts, especially that of sacrifice.[30] Drama, as we shall see in chapter 5, is another important element in the mass (or was in the Middle Ages). But narrative is undoubtedly there.

Story is sometimes presented as simply the raw material of theology. Revelation, according to Sykes, takes narrative form but requires theologians to pose the 'right' questions:

> The Creed contains a narrative sequence which does not itself instruct you whether or not it is appropriate to ask who was Jesus' human father, whether his bones were left in the grave, and upon what the throne on which the ascended Christ is seated rests in heaven.[31]

Theological competence, like literary competence, is a matter of learning to ask the right questions, which is particularly important in theology, where the wrong questions often lead to heretical answers. Yet narrative (the 'cooked' plot) as opposed to story (the 'raw' material, to use one of Lévi-Strauss's best-known binary oppositions) already involves inter-pretation. Literary analysis of the grammar of narrative is founded upon the assumption that the reading of a narrative follows certain rules, that readers agree in practice on plot synopses since they obey articulable principles about the main points of a particular story.[32] No narrative, however, is so completely determinate of its meaning that it does not allow for disagreement over its interpretation. So there is certainly a need for the Church to provide careful and authoritative interpretation of the major Christian stories.

In this sense even a major 'systematic' theologian such as Karl Barth can be called a 'narrative theologian'. For his exploration of the central doctrines of Christianity proceeds from a careful reading and retelling of the gospel narratives.[33] Barth points out that 'when the Bible speaks of revelation it does so in the form of narrating a story or a series of stories.' Dogmatics, therefore, becomes 'much less of a system than the narrative of an event'.[34] Unworried by the 'scandal of particularity' inherent in his focus on the one story (as it is told in the gospels, not as reconstructed by historical scholarship), Barth insists that it is this story which defines the 'world of meaning' within which theology operates, not the other way round. For this would be to fit Christ into our story. On the contrary, we must enter His story, encountering the living Christ through our reading of the gospels.[35]

Other forms of 'narrative theology' recognize the narrative modes assumed by revelation without sacrificing the concept of history. Biblical theologians such as James Barr acknowledge the variety of stories told in the Bible, some of which (but not all) come into the category of history.[36] Continental biblical scholars coined a new term, *Heilsgeschichte*, 'salvation history', for the whole continuous story of God's redemptive action as recorded in scripture.[37] But this still distinguishes 'sacred' from 'secular' history, *Geschichte* from *Historie*, as Pannenberg complained. For him revelation should not be limited to a special series of events cut off from the rest of history but include *all* history, which is not so much Hegel's 'self-revelation of the absolute' as a narrative interpretation of the significance of world-events.[38] Revelation, in this sense, is necessarily 'subjective', an inner conviction about the meaning of external events which remain open to 'objective' investigation.[39]

The narrative form adopted by history has become a matter of intense debate.[40] Robert Scholes, who was once happy to distinguish history from chronicle or annals because it selected, interpreted and organized its material into signifi-cant form,[41] now attacks narrative as a religious opiate providing believers with a false sense of order and coherence.[42] The *Annales* school of French historiography distrusts the whole understanding of history as composed of 'events' which 'individuals make happen'. For them there is no such thing as an 'event', no such thing as ready-made 'historical reality'. The focus of historical investigation, they insist, should be social history, 'the total social fact', the *mentalité* of a whole period.[43]

Narrative in history has its defenders, who claim that we can only talk about the past in 'irreducibly narrative statements', conferring meaning on events 'only in the context of a *story*'.[44] History has to be 'followable', has to satisfy the expectations of sequential narrative which any reader brings to it. History is to this extent a 'species of the genus story',[45] a literary artefact involving a shared competence in the telling and following of stories. Historical narratives can therefore be called

> verbal fictions the contents of which are as much *invented as found and the forms of which have more in common with their counterparts in literature than they have with those in the sciences.*[46]

In spite of these formal similarities, however, in spite of the fact that 'to narrate is already to explain', it is important to recognize that the stories told by historians have a basic epistemological difference from literary fictions. There is a specific external reference, an 'objectivity' which can be investigated, checked, challenged and modified. Historical accounts interlock like maps; the discoveries of separate investigators can be combined.[47] There is a fundamental similarity in narrative mode but a fundamental difference in the object of 'reference' between the stories we call 'history' and those we call 'fiction'.

The history of the world, however, can no longer be told with the same confidence as it was in the nineteenth century, when secular versions of biblical history abounded. 'To write the history of England as a kind of Bible', for example, to bring out its eternal significance, was Carlyle's aim.[48] Macaulay's myth of progress, Comte's three stages towards positivist utopia, Marx's model of class struggle and Darwin's complicated and seemingly pointless evolutionary plot competed with Christianity, the grand design of God, as the overriding explanation of world history.[49] Teilhard de Chardin has, of course, produced a Christian version of the evolutionary myth[50] while 'process theology' provides yet another teleological model of God's action in the world. None of these grand stories, however, can command more than conditional assent. People have become 'bored with stories of universal history', anyway, because they are so grand and so unprovable. The most they can accept is a

> story that establishes world without claim to finality, a story that asserts its own limits but nevertheless provides the best organisation of life that it can.[51]

For this reason, I would argue, stories of the world play a less important role in narrative theology than stories of the Church and stories of the self.

RELIGIOUS AUTOBIOGRAPHY: WRITING GOD AND THE SELF

To write an autobiography, to construct a coherent narrative out of the scattered events of one's life, is to interpret those events as part of a significant plot with an overall meaning. In this sense, autobiography has been seen to meet the religious needs of those 'looking for an order and meaning in life'.[52] For this meaning emerges with the perception of a pattern in events, the connection of one thing with another. It involves discovering not only a 'metaphor of the self', a focal point on which to build a sense of the subject's identity, but also a 'mythic statement' of the world, the creation of a 'symbolic universe' which enables the individual 'to understand and interpret, to articulate and organise, to synthesise and universalise his human experience'.[53] No individual exists in isolation; he or she develops in relationship with the world, with other people and, in the case of religious autobiography, with God. Autobiography therefore becomes a good place to look for literary constructs of the self and of God.

The 'subject' of an autobiography, the character created in the world of the narrative, needs to be recognized as a literary fiction, an 'autograph', a written version or interpretation of the self constructed by memory gathering together or 're-collecting' the disparate elements of experience.[54] Roland Barthes writes self-consciously about the fictiveness of his own autobiography: 'I do not say "I am going to describe myself", but "I am writing a text and I call it R.B." . . . I myself am my own symbol.'[55] The style of an autobiography is quite literally the man or woman, offering 'a system of revealing indices, of symptomatic traits . . . a system of original metaphors, according to which expression proceeds from experience'.[56]

Metaphor, to be explored more fully in the following chapter, has been seen as one of two axes, two aspects of language, by which we organize experience. Metaphor functions by perceiving similarities and making thematic connections while metonymy merely combines words or events in accordance with spatial or temporal contiguity. Metaphor requires imagination, in Coleridge's active sense of the word, 'emancipated from the order of time and space', while metonymy 'must receive all its materials ready made from the law of association'.[57] Naturalism, as we shall see, attempts to remain as much as possible on the metonymic axis of discourse but as soon as it begins to impose meaning upon the events it describes by selection and emphasis it becomes metaphoric narration.[58]

In telling the story of the 'Wolf-Man', for example, Freud apologizes for giving neither a 'purely historical' nor a 'purely thematic account of my patient's story'.[59] But all narrative does this, in different proportions and with differing degrees of distortion. For the process of selection and interpretation, especially in autobiography, where narrative design and historical truth very soon come into conflict, necessarily involves 'the unconscious polemics of memory'.[60] Freud's own autobiography, passing over his childhood with a revealing joke about his later interest in religion being a 'regressive development' towards those early days and presenting his life as a stately process of finding the solutions to a variety of scientific problems, provides a particularly good example of narrative distortion.[61]

All this may sound very modern but can be found in Augustine, the first autobiographer. His meditation on memory in Book Ten of the *Confessions* plays on the connection between *cogo* (I gather) and *cogito* (I think). For to think is to re-collect, to gather together the fragments of experience. In 'the vast cloisters of my memory', Augustine claims, lies the whole world, everything that he has ever experienced:

> In it I meet myself as well. I remember myself and what I have done, when and where I did it, and the state of my mind at the time . . . And yet . . . I cannot understand all that I am.

The power of memory and the problem of identity bewilder Augustine, who finds both more 'marvellous' than any prodigies of nature.[62] He realizes that it is by selecting the key moment of his conversion as the metaphor for his whole life, 'the intelligible event which makes all other events intelligible',[63] that he is able to make sense of himself and of the world. His conversion provides him with an answer to the many questions he asks about himself and about God.

Conversion, of course, is the key to most religious autobiographies, not only to Augustine's fourth-century *Confessions* but also to the other examples of the genre which I will discuss: *The Book of Margery Kempe*, the medieval English mystic, Bunyan's *Grace Abounding*, which I take to be typical of seventeenth-century Calvinist soul-searching, and Newman's mid-Victorian *Apologia pro Vita Sua*. None of these figures could be called 'normal'; they all suffered from the 'emotional susceptibility' or 'neurotic temperament' which William James found to be 'the chief condition of the requisite receptivity' to religious experience.[64] But some at least were normative, providing models upon which so many of their readers could structure their understanding of themselves and of their religious experience. They were not, of course, entirely 'original' since they moulded their own 'lives' in accordance with earlier literary models, particularly the Bible. These autobiographies, then, like other texts, will be found to be at least in part the products of 'intertextuality, a weaving together of what has already been produced elsewhere'. Their authors can only 'find' themselves and God in the literary forms which have been evolved for self-discovery and theological understanding.[65]

Augustine is generally taken to have initiated the whole genre of autobiography. But he too was drawing on earlier literary traditions: classical philosophical meditations such as those of Marcus Aurelius and Christian hagiography, which tended to focus on martyrdom. By fusing neo-platonic philosophy and classical rhetoric with biblical urgency, Augustine transformed both these traditions.[66] His extended neo-platonic meditations, for instance, are addressed not to an unknown mystery but to the God of Abraham, of Isaac and of Jacob, the God revealed in Christ. *The Confessions* are 'studded with' quotations from the Bible, particularly the psalms and St Paul, whose letters themselves tended towards autobiography, often relating his own experiences, telling his own story, as a means of answering theological questions.[67]

The *Confessions* are certainly very literary, exploring a life which has revolved around books. The autobiography, in fact, becomes in the end a commentary on the beginning of Genesis and even the earlier narrative can be seen as an illustration of how to become a good reader of the Bible. Augustine's account of his conversion is particularly 'literary', such symbolic details as the fig-tree in the garden being taken from St John's gospel. Whether there really was such a tree, whether Augustine really heard children's voices in a neighbouring garden saying 'tolle, lege' and if so whether they were practising their third-conjugation imperatives or reading a bibliographical instruction at the end of a returned essay, are not my present concern.[68] I want to bring out its intertextuality, its reliance upon other texts and upon literary conventions.

The story of Augustine's conversion, it should be noticed, involves a complex chain of conversion-narratives. To begin with, Augustine and his pupil Alypius are visited by a Roman official named Ponticianus who tells the story of his own conversion, which was a result of reading the life of St Antony, who was himself converted by a passage from the gospels heard in a church. Ponticianus claims to have been converted even 'while he was reading, his heart leaping and turning in his breast'. And while he is explaining all this, Augustine in turn begins to look at his own life, tainted as it is with 'ulcers and sores'. He turns to Alypius and asks, 'What is the meaning of this story?', that unlettered men can 'storm the gates of heaven' while the learned 'lie here grovelling in this world of flesh and blood'. It is in apparent answer to these inner torments that he hears the children's voices which he interprets as a divine command to read the Bible. The passage he finds, of course, is St Paul's attack on incontinence which dispels all 'darkness of doubt' from his mind.[69]

This, then, is an extremely intertextual conversion, the product of hearing a story about another conversion (that of Ponticianus) which itself was effected by another story (that of St Antony) whose conversion involved exactly the same personal appropriation of a biblical text. It is like the awakening of poetic awareness described by Harold Bloom, when a poet struggles to emulate, to repeat and even to improve upon his or her 'precursor'.[70] In this case, of course, Augustine is quite open about the 'influences' upon him, unlike most of the poets Bloom discusses, who resent any limitation of their 'original genius'. Augustine, whose conversion brought about his resignation as a professor of rhetoric on the ground of ill health, celebrates not only his new-found freedom to serve God with his pen but a new creativity which went with it, a release of psychic energy enabling him to become more creative both as a reader and as a writer.

One of the most important fruits of Augustine's conversion is his new-found ability to read and respond emotionally to the psalms:

> How I cried out to you, my God, when I read the Psalms of David ... How they set me on fire with love of you! I was burning to echo them to all the world, if only I could, so that they might vanquish man's pride.

He wishes in particular that the Manichees

> could have been somewhere at hand, unknown to me, to watch my face and hear my voice as I read the fourth Psalm. They

would have seen how deeply it moved me ... I quivered with
fear, yet at the same time I was aglow with hope ... All these
emotions were revealed in the light of my eyes and the tremor of
my voice.[71]

Augustine obviously enjoys the sight and sound of his own
rapture but the point is not to accuse him of self-dramatization
but to substantiate the argument that it is through reading
that he achieves his most intense awareness of himself and of
God. There is a clear lesson here for the reader of the
Confessions, who is expected to be equally responsive to this
text. 'Why', asks Augustine, characteristically probing his own
motives, 'does it matter to me whether men should hear what I
have to confess?' He has no particular desire to gratify their
curiosity and he cannot prove that his confessions are true. But
he wants to rouse them too to faith, to stir their hearts, to
inspire in them the emotions which brought about his own
conversion.[72]

Both 'Augustine' the narrator of the *Confessions* and the
'God' he addresses are, of course, literary constructs, which is
not to say that they do not refer to the 'real' persons 'behind'
those names but that they belong to a narrative world created
by the text. In fact, there are two 'Augustines' in the text, the
wise narrator and the foolish protagonist, the stealer of plums
and of forbidden sexual fruit. The first-person pronoun is
therefore ambiguous, concealing differences as well as proclaiming similarities, repudiating past errors but not refusing
'a responsibility assumed forever by the subject'.[73] Augustine
is fully aware that the past 'persona' he creates for himself is a
literary construct: 'it is not past facts which are drawn out of
our memories but only words based on our memory-pictures of
those facts'.[74] These words, however, 'signify a higher signifier,
the *logos* of human consciousness, which in turn signifies what
cannot become signified, the eternal *Logos*'.[75] Augustine's
fictional persona, in other words, is an image which describes,
in narrative form, the mystery of his inner self and its
experience of God.

The *Confessions* have been taken as a classic expression of
the 'divided self'.[76] Augustine certainly provides enough
insight into his relationship with his mother to have provoked

numerous psychoanalytic readings.[77] Another conversion-narrative, the story of the learned Victorinus, causes him to meditate upon the struggles between his old perverse will, still chained to the flesh, and his new desire for God:

> So these two wills within me, one old, one new, one the servant of the flesh, the other of the spirit, were in conflict and between them they tore my soul apart.

He talks of his 'true self . . . no longer on the side of which I disapproved', and that 'other part' which is still 'part' of himself. He is like a man half asleep, part of him keen to wake up, the other struggling to remain unconscious. For sin has become a habit which he has to fight to escape.[78]

This struggle is particularly violent in the moments before his conversion, when his 'inner self was a house divided against itself'. He longs to make a commitment but holds back, 'at odds with myself'. He approaches ever closer to the leap of faith but hangs back 'on the brink of resolution'.[79] It is grace alone which finally effects his conversion. He continues, however, to dwell on the 'problem' he is to himself, the question of identity.[80] He worries, for example, about the subconscious desires which plague him in dreams: 'Surely it cannot be that when I am asleep I am not myself?'[81] But the 'inner workings' of his mind remain 'veiled in darkness'; only God can save him from being 'dismembered and deformed', supplying him with a 'new form and new strength'.[82]

But what of God (to ask the kind of rhetorical question typical of Augustine)? He is, of course, 'the direct addressee of the discourse',[83] the divine analyst to whom Augustine pours out his soul. But that is by no means His sole function. It is at least arguable that Augustine's choice of an autobiographical format involves a recognition that 'a person's understanding of God is interwoven with his personal development', part of his self-understanding.[84] Autobiography, in other words, is a form of talking about God which recognizes the limitations of human understanding. The *Confessions* begin with a series of questions which emphasize the distance between the infinite and the finite. How, Augustine asks, can a man pray to a God he does not know, or how can God enter into one of his creatures? If heaven and earth cannot contain Him, then how can a human soul do so? Or does 'whatever exists' contain Him only in the sense that it could not exist without Him? Augustine baffles the reader with a whole series of questions of this kind, followed by a number of paradoxes which reveal the inadequacy of human concepts of the divine: He is hidden and yet present, changing and yet unchangeable, 'ever active, yet always at rest', grieving and loving yet 'without apprehension' or suffering. It is impossible to 'say enough' about Him and yet it is even worse to keep silent.[85]

The attempt to understand God as a substance, as a body, is presented in the *Confessions* as one of Augustine's major stumbling blocks, leading him to a 'conception' of God which is 'quite untrue, a mere falsehood . . . a fiction based on my own wretched state'.[86] Neo-platonic philosophy teaches him to abandon this concept without providing a satisfactory replacement: 'I did not know how else to think of you.'[87] No human concept, it turns out, is adequate to explain God. Even the Bible, read literally, gives a false impression:

> Some people, when they read or hear what Moses wrote, imagine God as a kind of man or as a vast bodily substance endowed with power, who by some new and sudden decision created heaven and earth.

They think of Him actually speaking, as human beings do, and their other ideas about Him are 'limited in the same way by their attachment to the familiar world about them'.[88] The only way to understand God, according to Augustine, is by probing the depths of the self. The *Confessions* show him learning this lesson, turning his gaze increasingly inward, no longer 'looking for you outside myself' but finding 'the God of my own heart'.[89]

The *Confessions* have been called 'a manifesto of the inner world'[90] for Augustine repeatedly insists that it is only in the 'inmost heart' that God can be known.[91] Following another of his rhetorical questions, 'What do I love when I love my God?', he launches into one of his most moving celebrations of God as beyond anything experienced by the senses, brighter than the most brilliant earthly light, sweeter than the most melodious music, superior to the fragrance of flowers, the taste of honey, or any imaginable beauty. Augustine asks the earth, the sea, the sky and the stars in turn, 'What is my God?', and they reply, 'God is He who made us'. He is *in* all these but He is not them alone. Similarly, He is in the soul, discovered through the inner self, but He is not identical with that self.[92]

It is of crucial importance that Augustine balances his inward spirituality with an awareness of God as creator for without this the *Confessions* would seem as solipsistic as some medieval autobiographies, in which the gap between their intense inner spirituality and the mundane events they record seems almost unbridgeable. This is certainly the case in *The Book of Margery Kempe*, the first autobiography to be written in English, which presents 'two worlds utterly at variance – an inner life of hysterical urgings and visions, an outer experience of disparate adventures' and trivial incidents rarely rising to the level of 'symbolic event'.[93] The relationship between 'inner and outer', as Stephen Medcalf has shown, is peculiarly problematic in medieval Catholicism, in which signifier and signified, symbol and referent, are so close as to be indistinguishable. In transubstantiation, for example, the bread and wine were believed to become the actual body and blood of Christ. Margery Kempe therefore travels miles to see the place where physical blood appeared on consecrated hosts in order to convince a sceptical priest of the literal truth of this doctrine. Everything for her is 'converted into the literal', 'concretised' into a world of fleshly understanding which makes no distinction between inner vision and external event.[94]

The Book of Margery Kempe mixes these two worlds indiscriminately. Her visions of Christ and of Mary are more 'real' to her than the husband she denies his conjugal rights or the fourteen children she mentions only in passing. She is forever attempting to 'relive' Christ's life, or at least to describe her own life in terms of Christ's. On her pilgrimage to Jerusalem, for example, which she enters 'riding on an ass', she falls down on the Mount of Calvary, 'spreading her arms out wide' and crying 'with a loud voice'.[95] When her fellow pilgrims understandably lose patience with her she infuriates them all the more by repeating Christ's plea, 'Father, forgive them; they know not what they do'.[96] She forever likens her own trials to those of Christ. In Leicester she seems to switch between two scenes, one in her own life and one in Christ's. The abbot comes to meet her with some of his brothers 'and at once in her soul she beheld our Lord coming with his apostles', fainting with the devotion this inspires.[97] Any 'little pain' she endures gains in dignity by association with Christ's 'great pain', which remains as 'fresh' for her, she reminds more hardened souls, 'as if he had died this same day'.[98]

The contrast between the intensity of Margery's inner world and the insignificance of the external events she describes can have comic effects. A vision of Christ taking leave of his mother, for example, causes her to fall down in a field, roaring and weeping 'as though she would have burst'.[99] She develops a habit of rushing up to women who happen to be carrying male children and treating them like the Virgin Mary. More alarming for a modern reader are the frequent symptoms of repressed sexuality most evident in her vision of the passion, which dwells on Christ's nakedness and his physical suffering (visions of men showing her their genitals, she openly admits, are a key feature of her breakdown). Yet gory details of bursting bodies and 'rivers of blood' are mixed with such endearing touches as Margery making the Virgin Mary a hot drink after the crucifixion.[100] There can be no doubt that Margery was paranoid; Jesus has frequently to reassure her that the more she is hated by her neighbours the dearer she is to him. But it is not enough to talk of 'psychosis' and 'hysteria' as if this were a scientific 'explanation' of her spirituality rather than an alternative description.[101] Hysteria and saintliness, as William James insisted, are intimately connected, particularly in medieval autobiographies such as that of the self-tormenting Henry Suso.[102] Margery Kempe has to be understood in medieval as well as modern terms for it is through medieval processes of self-understanding that she constructs her life.

Margery Kempe, of course, was illiterate but her autobiography can nevertheless be seen as a product of intertextuality, reproducing many details of other lives as well as handbooks of medieval spirituality which were read to her. The *Meditationes Vitae Christi* attributed to St Bonaventura, for example, encourages worshippers not only to conjure up visions of scenes from Christ's life but even to enter them imaginatively, taking the child Jesus in their arms, putting him on a donkey and so on. This, as we have seen, is precisely what Margery does. The mystery plays brought these scenes to life and it seems no accident therefore that it is on their return from York the day after Corpus Christi, when the cycle was performed, that Margery asks her husband to revert to a life of married chastity.[103] Her desire to emulate St Bridget of Sweden, whose *Revelations* record similar visions and a similar life of married chastity and pilgrimage, is evident not only in Margery's visit to the chamber in Rome where St Bridget lived but in Christ's comment, when Margery sees the 'stirring and moving' of the sacrament, 'My daughter Bridget never saw me in this way'.[104]

Other medieval mystics given to similar bouts of sobbing and weeping whose lives provide a model for Margery's own are Mary of Oignies, Angela of Foligno and Dorothy of Mantua. The dominant metaphors of fire and pain through which Margery attempts to portray her experience of God's love are central to St Bonaventura's *Stimulus Amoris* and Richard Rolle's *Incendium Amoris*, both of which are read to Margery by a friendly priest.[105] Dame Julian of Norwich, of course, plays an important role in the book, guiding Margery and supporting her against her detractors.[106] Dame Julian's *Revelations of Divine Love* anticipate the later *Life of St Teresa of Avila* in their recognition of the need to provide reasonable standards by which to evaluate and to interpret spiritual experience. For the excesses of Margery Kempe and other medieval mystics had made only too apparent the dangers of such an intense inward life unbalanced by external controls.

Margery's conversion, a dramatic recovery from eight months of postnatal depression, signalled by a vision of Christ visiting her bedside 'most beauteous . . . in a mantle of purple silk', occupies only the 'proem' and opening chapter of her autobiography.[107] It marks merely the beginning of her spiritual life. With a Calvinist such as Bunyan, however, whose prime concern is to count himself among the elect, everything centres on his conversion, the extended spiritual crisis at the heart of *Grace Abounding*, which was probably based upon his 'testimony' to his religious 'experience', a word that took on a special meaning for seventeenth-century puritans. Such personal witness was a requirement of entry into churches like the independent Bedford church to which Bunyan belonged.

Grace Abounding, like *The Book of Margery Kempe*, has little to say about contemporary history. The Civil War, for example, provides merely one of several examples of providential protection. Bunyan also skates over his childhood, pausing only to insist on the inevitable depravities of childhood before proceeding to the heart of the matter, that period of spiritual turmoil between the first indication of grace brought by a conviction of sin and the achievement of a settled faith marked by the assurance of final perseverance. For this was 'the most significant phase of a Calvinist's life',[108] the subject of minute scrutiny at special 'experience-meetings' and the centre of the many autobiographical pamphlets published after the advent of unrestricted printing in the 1640s.[109] Bunyan's period of crisis, oscillating between joy and despair as he feels himself elect or reprobate, took only two years of his life but occupies two-thirds of his autobiography.[110]

Bunyan's conversion is in many ways 'conventional', following the traditional Calvinist pattern of awakening through a sermon, conviction of sin, promise of repentance and then relapse. What rescues it from mere conventionality are such realistic details as the game of tip-cat during which he is convicted of sin and the setting in which he is shaken from complacency, when he overhears 'three or four women sitting at a door in the sun . . . talking about the things of God'.[111] There is a similar down-to-earth quality about the miracles he longs for as a token of election, wanting to make the puddles dry and the dry patches puddles.[112] He writes with self-deprecating irony both about his self-hatred ('I was more loathsom in mine own eyes than was a toad') and about his euphoria ('I thought I could have spoken of his love, and of his mercy to me, even to the very crows that sit upon the plow'd lands before me'). He can smile too about the evaporation of this confidence; having felt he could not forget this moment for forty years he finds himself questioning it within forty days, falling from euphoria to despair, longing 'to leap with my head downward, into some Muckhill-hole'.[113]

Bunyan captures with vivid precision the oscillating moods of his manic-depressive temperament, the neurotic anxiety which makes him abandon the idle pastime of bell-ringing through fear that not only the bells but the whole steeple will fall on him, the paranoia which leads him to imagine God making fun of him before the angels and such physical symptoms of his psychological turmoil as the 'clogging and heat at my stomach . . . as if my breast-bone would have split in sunder'.[114] There is ample evidence here of psychopathic melancholia and split personality.[115] But to describe Bunyan's progress as a development 'from severe maladjustment (accompanied by hallucinations and paranoiac symptoms) to a successful integration of the personality', as in the case of Margery Kempe, is merely to exchange twentieth for seventeenth-century terminology.[116] The vividness and individuality with which Bunyan portrays his inner world enable him to escape from the 'mould' provided by the puritan psychology of conversion.

The conventional nature of Calvinist conversion-narratives is amply illustrated by the many puritan autobiographies published in the second half of the seventeenth century. The conversion-narrative can be distinguished from the more disciplined but less dramatic lives narrated by the Jesuits, John Gerard and William Weston, the stately progress of Anglican bishops recorded in their innumerable and unexciting memoirs, the reflective narratives of educated Presbyterians such as Richard Baxter, the illustrations of inner light afforded by Quaker journals such as those of George Foxe, the Ranting adventures of a Lawrence Clarkson or Joseph Salmon, or the pseudo-biblical *Acts of the Witnesses of the Spirit* recorded by Lodowick Muggleton. The distinct form of the conversion-narrative is directly traceable to the major theologians of the Reformation, Luther, whose spiritual anguish became 'the standard emotional repertoire of seventeenth-century autobiographers', and Calvin, who 'institutionalised the believer's inner anxiety and made it into a vital component of his theological system'. The *Institutes* open with the insistence that 'true and solid wisdom' consists in 'the knowledge of God and of ourselves', encouraging the believer to cultivate an awareness of his or her inner depravity. For 'we cannot aspire to Him in earnest until we have begun to be displeased with ourselves.' Book Three analyses in further detail 'how the Christian should conduct his inner war against sin and despair', sharing his secrets with others and also helping to ease their sorrows.[117]

Behind Luther and Calvin, of course, looms St Paul, whom they can be said to have rediscovered. And it is Paul who is Bunyan's precursor-poet, the model on whose life Bunyan bases his own. The very title, *Grace Abounding to the Chief of Sinners*, combines two Pauline texts (Romans 5:20 and I Timothy 1:15) while Paul himself is paraded in the preface as a model for all conversion–narrators:

> *It was* Pauls *accustomed manner,* Acts 22. *and that when tried for his life,* Acts 22 *and* 24. *even to open before his Judges the manner of his Conversion: He would think of that day and that hour, in which he first did meet with Grace: for he found it support unto him.*[118]

The Acts of the Apostles and the Letter to the Romans, in which the doctrines of predestination and of justification are most clearly spelt out, provide the foundations on which Bunyan's autobiography is built.

For Bunyan, then, as for so many of his contemporaries, intertextuality means frequent quotation of the Bible, the only book with which they were thoroughly familiar. *Grace Abounding* accordingly veers from one biblical text to another with Paul (and Romans in particular) the primary source. It is Paul's insistence that grace is entirely beyond man's control that first sets Bunyan asking, 'How can you tell that you are Elected?' Encouraged by Christ's promise, 'And yet there is roome' (Luke 14:23), but depressed by his calling only 'to him whom he would' (Mark 3:3), Bunyan finds comfort in Paul's assurance that 'nothing can separate us from the love of God' (Romans 8:39).[119] He dwells obsessively on single biblical phrases such as 'Thou art my love' and 'He is able', fearing to have sold his birthright like Esau before coming to rest once more in the words of St Paul to the Hebrews that he has come indeed to Mount Sion.[120] Bunyan's life is quite literally built upon the Bible, constructed from the words of St Paul.

But if Bunyan writes his life in the Pauline mould many readers of Bunyan have had their piety moulded by *Grace Abounding*, which became the model for many similar conversion-narratives.[121] This is how literary forms fashion religious experience, providing the structures through which believers make sense of their lives. The Calvinist conversion-narrative made popular by Bunyan dictated the manner in which many Protestant minds have been fashioned. Consider, for example, a key moment in Bunyan's conversion, when he is wakened from melancholy introspection 'walking to and fro in a good Man's shop' by the sound of rushing wind and a voice asking, 'Didst ever refuse to be justified by the Blood of Christ?', a question to which his 'heart answered groaningly *No*', thereby silencing 'all those tumultuous thoughts that did use, like merciless hell-hounds to roar and bellow, and make a hideous noise within me'.[122] Compare with this the account given in Carlyle's pseudo-autobiographical *Sartor Resartus* of Professor Teufeldröckh's 'conversion' from fear ('The Everlasting No') to joy ('The Everlasting Yea'). Carlyle's fictive self is similarly miserable 'after much perambulation' when his spirits too are lifted by a question which he poses to himself, 'What art thou afraid of?' The worst that can befall him, he realizes, is death and hell and these he is prepared to face head on.[123] The same burning intensity (and the same biblical metaphor of fire) can be found in Carlyle as in Bunyan, the same vivid conversion from misery and doubt to joyful assurance. The Calvinist structures of feeling and thought continue to inspire Carlyle's insistence upon the eternal value of his inner life.

Carlyle, of course, was writing in the wake of Romanticism, which provided 'The Classical Age of Autobiography',[124] the period of Rousseau, Goethe and Wordsworth. Rousseau's *Confessions*, like those of Augustine, begin by addressing God rather than man, conjuring up a vision of the last judgement at which he is summoned to present his work. 'I have bared my secret soul as Thou thyself hast seen it', he claims, inviting 'the numberless legion of my fellow-men' to gather round, 'hear my confessions', 'groan at my depravities, and blush for my misdeeds'.[125] His confessions, in fact, soon become self-justification while God quickly disappears into the background. Newman's *Apologia pro Vita Sua*, the final text to be discussed, is a more genuinely religious autobiography although it too contains more than a hint of the Romantic, egotistical sublime. It too was written in self-justification, in answer to Kingsley's notorious charge that Roman clergy in general and Newman in particular did not care for truth. Such a basic challenge to his integrity could only be met, Newman felt, by telling the story of his life, dwelling on the most 'suspect' part, the period prior to his conversion to Rome.

Newman's first contact with Christianity was through Calvinism, leading him to believe that 'the inward conversion of which I was conscious' would last for eternity and

> confirming me in my mistrust of the reality of material phenomena, and making me rest in the thought of two and two only supreme and luminously self-evident beings, myself and my Creator.[126]

In one of the few glimpses that Newman gives of his childhood, he confesses to a preference for the world of the imagination, especially that of the Arabian nights, over the 'real world'. Life itself, he thought, might be a dream in which he was an angel and the experiences of his senses illusory, 'my fellow-angels by a playful device concealing themselves from me and deceiving me with the semblance of a material world'.[127] He seems never to have had a strong sense of the reality of the external world in comparison with his inner certainties.

Newman's sense of himself and of God as the strongest realities in his life is confirmed by later passages in the *Apologia*:

> I am a Catholic by virtue of my believing in a God; and if I am asked why I believe in a God, I answer that it is because I believe in myself, for I feel it impossible to believe in my own existence (and of that fact I am quite sure) without believing also in the existence of Him, who lives as a Personal, All- seeing, All-judging Being in my conscience.[128]

Newman finds it difficult, in fact, to reconcile this certainty with the condition of the world around him, which seems to 'give the lie' to his inner consciousness:

If I looked into a mirror, and did not see my face, I should have the sort of feeling which actually comes upon me, when I look into this living busy world, and see no reflexion of its Creator.

He launches into an eloquent, terrifying portrait of the world, full of conflict, alienation, evil, disappointment, pain and suffering, concluding that 'if there be a God, *since* there is a God, the human race is implicated in some terrible aboriginal calamity' for which he finds the most convincing explanation in the doctrine of original sin. A series of logical steps takes him from this to the belief in an infallible guide protecting mankind against such an awful world, and this, of course, is the Church.

It is not logic, however, which makes the *Apologia* convincing; it is the portrait of a man's emotional need for faith leading him to a place he had earlier despised. As Newman himself admits,

I had a great dislike of paper logic ... It is the concrete being that reasons; pass a number of years and I find my mind in a new place; how? the whole man moves; paper logic is but the record of it.[129]

The successive chapters of the *Apologia* necessarily include much paper-work, recording in detail the reading and writing that took him further and further away from his Calvinist roots through a liberal phase at Oriel in the 1820s and the dramatic events of the Oxford Movement towards the climax of his conversion.

This, according to the *Apologia*, was the end of the story. The final chapter begins, with total confidence:

From the time that I became a Catholic, of course, I have no further history of my religious opinions to narrate ... I have had no changes to record, and have had no anxiety of heart whatever.[130]

The publication of Ward's biography in 1912, however, showed this to have been far from the case, documenting as it does the extreme depression into which Newman had fallen in the early

1860s when a succession of failures and his support for the role
of the laity in the Church had brought him under suspicion at
Rome. 'Anxiety', he had written, was 'sucking life out of me'.
He felt like 'some wild incomprehensible beast' captured by a
triumphant Church to be shown off in public without being
used to counter the prevailing scepticism of the age.[131] His life
seemed quite literally to be coming to an end in ignominy and
neglect. Kingsley's attack, in fact, played into his hands,
enabling him to relive past glories and to re-present his life as
a triumphant victory for faith over the obstacles placed in its
path.

The *Apologia*, then, like all the autobiographies I have
considered, is very much a fiction, a literary construct, a
product of intertextuality, though like a true Romantic,
Newman quotes mainly from his own work, citing numerous
excerpts from his earlier letters and articles. Newman was a
great hoarder of documents, including an autobiographical
sketch begun in 1812 and not finished until 1884.[132] Some of
these have served not only to delay his canonization but to
deconstruct the clear consistent image of himself built up in
the *Apologia*. He can hardly have been unaware of the fictive
nature of his autobiography, writing as he did in *Historical
Sketches*,

> A Saint's writings are to me his real 'Life' . . . I mean a narrative
> which impresses the reader with the idea of a moral unity,
> identity, growth, continuity, personality.[133]

Such consistency is only possible in fiction.

One particular moment of intertextuality links the *Apologia*
with Augustine and the whole tradition of religious autobiography I have traced. A particular phrase of Augustine's
convinces Newman that catholicity is more important in a
church than antiquity or occupation of the middle ground. It is
a phrase quoted by Wiseman in an article in the *Dublin
Review*, a phrase repeated by one of Newman's friends:

> 'Securus judicat orbis terrarum'. He repeated those words again
> and again, and, when he was gone, they kept ringing in my ears
> . . . a mere sentence, the words of St Augustine, struck me with

a power which I never had felt from any words before . . . they were like the 'Tolle, lege, – Tolle, lege,' of the child, which converted St Augustine himself.[134]

Newman's conversion-narrative, at this point at least, is modelled upon Augustine's just as Augustine's was modelled on earlier narratives of a divine calling. There are many similarities between Augustine and Newman,[135] but not the least is their awareness that it is through the reconstruction of the self, meditation on the past and recognition of its meaning, that faith in God finds its most coherent and convincing expression.

REALISM IN THE NOVEL: FROM METAPHYSICS TO METAFICTION

The novel is generally regarded as the most 'realistic' of literary genres but what is actually meant by this term tends to vary. First used in the mid-nineteenth century, when the pre-Raphaelites were demanding in painting a meticulous attention to detail, realism involved for Zola the refusal to omit what others regarded as morbid or disgusting. For Auerbach it meant the serious treatment of mundane subjects, for Lukács the depiction of the world as it really was. 'Real', for the positivists, was synonymous with 'certain', 'precise', empirically verifiable, necessarily excluding any theological or metaphysical abstractions.[136] Many of the major realist novelists, most notably George Eliot, have been positivists, committed to explaining in scientific terms how it is that 'superstitious' people come to believe in the 'supernatural'.

Such realism is formal and philosophical at the same time, describing in meticulous detail the only objects believed to be accessible to definite knowledge, the 'facts' of human experience. It is also, I want to emphasize, deeply ideological, a product of a particular discourse, an extremely limited way of looking at the world, which in George Eliot's case can be linked with a number of specific sources, most notably the radical German theologians she herself translated, Strauss and Feuerbach. Classic realist texts such as hers have become a particular target of structuralist and Marxist criticism because they impose upon their readers under the guise of 'realism' a strongly prejudiced view of what the world is like. George Eliot has been accused of claiming to give a 'transparent' representation of a 'self-evident reality' which turns out on closer inspection to be a product of liberal humanist ideology.[137] Liberal humanism, of course, continues to dominate not only the novel but all forms of discourse in the twentieth century but it has met with resistance from a number of Catholic writers, notably Evelyn Waugh, Graham Greene and Flannery O'Connor, all of whom can be seen to challenge the unexamined assumptions of the 'modern' secular world, the 'rational' view that miracles never happen and that religious experience is an illusion.

Such confident assertions about the 'real' world have also been undermined by metafiction, self-conscious novels which parade in their text the awareness that both the narrative world and the 'real' world are human constructs. Reality, in other words, is at least in part a matter of faith, of what we choose to be the case. Religion, in such a world, cannot be anything other than a fiction (though it might also turn out to be true). In the extremely rough outline of the development of the novel which follows, I will focus first on the abandonment of metaphysics by the liberal humanist tradition represented by George Eliot and Iris Murdoch before considering Waugh, Greene and O'Connor as examples of Christian novelists who have offered an alternative ideology, a theology. I will end by asking to what extent a work of metafiction such as Vonnegut's *Cat's Cradle* can escape accusations of ideological bias.

The novel, according to Lukács, was born from disbelief, raised amid the ruins of theology. While epics are the literary products of integrated ages of faith, when the world seems adequate to the demands of the soul, novels are the expression in literary form of 'problematic' ages of doubt: 'The novel is the epic of a world that has been abandoned by God.' Even Cervantes, writing in an age of faith, is seen by Lukács to have undermined its authority by representing belief as a form of madness, a fanatical and illusory devotion to an invisible ideal. For Lukács, writing in the First World War, the world certainly seemed a godless place which could only acquire meaning in literature. The novelist portrays with melancholy irony the necessary but hopeless struggle of ideality against reality.[138] Like *The Decameron*, whose narrators escape from the plague to a paradisal garden, suggesting that fiction provides not 'an achieved salvation . . . but a glimpse, a mere metaphor of that salvation' in a world radically fallen,[139] *The Theory of the Novel* was to have been written in the form of a dialogue, placed in the mouths of refugees from the horrors of the Great War.[140] For them, however, there was not even the comfort of a supreme fiction, only the sad knowledge of an external world which was hostile or indifferent towards man's inner aspirations.[141]

   This melancholy view, reminiscent of the prelude to *Middlemarch* or an authorial intrusion by Hardy, soon gave place in Lukács to an alternative Marxist faith in which realism played a more positive role. No longer a matter of mere mirror-reflection, the precise description of the surface details to be found in writers such as Zola, realism became a representation of profound underlying laws of the kind observed in the narratives of Tolstoy. Detailed description could be superficially accurate but insignificant, in the way that 'a collage of photographic material may provide an incorrect, subjective and arbitrary reflection of reality'.[142] The great European realists, Lukács went on to argue, avoided both the 'objective' extreme of naturalism and the 'subjective' extreme of modernism, achieving a Hegelian synthesis in 'typical' forms which treated the individual as a representative part of the whole society. Such realism was far removed from propaganda since it had nothing to do with a writer's explicit views but resulted rather from 'the picture conveyed by the work' as a whole. Great realists such as Balzac and Tolstoy could be distinguished from 'second-raters' by their ruthlessness towards their own world-views, which they were quite prepared to abandon rather than produce 'a falsified or distorted picture of reality'.[143] The Western image of Tolstoy as a 'mystic' gazing back with nostalgia at an earlier 'holy Russia' is seen by Lukács to be a distortion derived from paying more attention to his later religious opinions than his realistic art.[144] Less convincingly, Lukács is forced by his own definition of the novel to deny that this is what Dostoevsky wrote.[145]

The distinction between implicit and explicit ideology is nevertheless important. It is not to explicit statements made by authors outside their novels or even by narrators within them that the critic should turn for an understanding of the nature of their narrative worlds, it is to the work as a whole, the formal patterns which represent the reality to which the text refers, patterns which control the readers' response at a deeper level than that of surface commentary. No amount of burrowing among the sermons of Isaac Barrow, for example, will explain the meaning of *Joseph Andrews*, prominent though that latitudinarian divine may have been in the formation of Fielding's religious opinions.[146] Different types of novel, in fact, embody beliefs in different ways. What Sheldon Sacks calls 'apologues', such as Samuel Johnson's *Rasselas*, may be organized as examples of 'the truth of a formulable statement', in this case the belief that earthly happiness is necessarily transient but that the consequence is not unbearable misery because Christians should build their hope in heaven.[147] Voltaire's *Candide* exemplifies a very different belief: the world is full of inevitable suffering which cannot have been the product of a benevolent all-powerful deity and the most we can hope to do is get on with the day-to-day business of living. Neither of these novels is 'realistic' and it would clearly be inappropriate to shed tears over characters created merely to illustrate an argument. It would be equally inappropriate to condemn both as bad novels. Similarly, according to Sacks, 'satires' such as Swift's *Gulliver's Travels* need to be read in a particular manner, identifying the targets of ridicule in the world outside the novel. Only novels of the kind Sacks calls 'actions' place human relationships at their centre, focusing attention on the development of character through action.

Nevertheless, this last kind of novel represents the mainstream of the English tradition from Defoe through Fielding and Richardson to Jane Austen and the great Victorian realists. The rise of the realist novel, as Ian Watt has shown, can be connected in philosophical and economic as well as theological terms with an increased interest in the individual. For the philosophy of association it is each individual's experience which moulds his or her identity, inscribing meaning and purpose on the *tabula rasa* of the mind. The developing capitalist economy also fostered a sense of individual responsibility, bolstering the Protestant tendency to treat wealth and prosperity as a sign of divine favour.[148] Calvinist introspection, as we have seen, contributed to a massive outpouring of autobiography in the second half of the seventeenth century, providing a clear model for the new literary form of the novel to follow. Defoe accordingly presents *Robinson Crusoe* and *Moll Flanders* as pseudo-autobiographies, the spiritual record of the sinfulness, soul-searching and conversion of their respective protagonists. The two forms, the novel and autobiography, as Patricia Spacks has shown, run in parallel tracks through the eighteenth century, the one self-consciously fictitious, the other basing its narrative on actual events, discovering and inventing the self in relation to other people and to God.[149]

And yet God does not feature strongly in the novels of this period, whose centre of interest remains human character. As Fielding explains in one of the self-conscious opening chapters of *Tom Jones*, 'Man ... is the highest subject ... which presents itself to the pen of our historian', for it is man alone whom he can hope to understand.[150] *Joseph Andrews* is a profoundly Christian book, focusing on the 'holy fool', Parson Adams, and his encounters with a variety of knaves and hypocrites. But it does not presume to intrude upon the parson's private prayer. And although Richardson dwells in greater detail on the inner consciousness of his heroines, he too remains content to hint at their piety, the root of their personal morality. Sterne, of course, claimed to have adopted the most religious level of proceeding, 'for I begin with writing the first sentence – and trusting to Almighty God for the second'.[151] But neither Mr. Shandy nor Uncle Toby shows much interest in theology. 'God only knows who is a hypocrite', opines the latter, insisting that our primary duties lie in this world.[152]

The Gothic rage for the supernatural (for ghosts and other paranormal experiences rather than a direct relationship with an orthodox deity) can be seen as a rebellion against the restraints of realism which were soon reimposed by the practical good sense of Fanny Burney, Maria Edgeworth and Jane Austen, whose heroines bare their consciences but not their devotions before the reader. The nineteenth century, of course, brought an astonishing mass of religious novels, many of them crudely didactic even by the standards of 'apologue' and 'satire'. These have been catalogued along denominational grounds, Anglican, Catholic, Nonconformist and so on.[153] Jesuits are made to die cruel deaths, converts to languish in their convents and doubters to die in dismal isolation and disgrace. As Thackeray observed in *Punch* in 1851,

> Unless he writes with a purpose, you know, a novelist in our days is good for nothing . . . this author or authoress with the most delicate skill insinuates Catholicism into you, and you find yourself all but a Papist in the third volume.[154]

The novel, in other words, was seized on as a powerful instrument of propaganda precisely because it could convey a real sense of the world as understood by a Catholic, or a dissenter, or a doubter, a world composed of feelings and experience rather than abstract formulas.

George Eliot could not resist the temptation to laugh at the crude didacticism evident in such 'oracular' novels.[155] She poked fun at *Westward Ho!*, for example, in which the 'preacher' in Kingsley so often overcomes the 'painter', the author labelling his heroes and villains with a clumsy force which was an insult to his readers' judgement.[156] It was also to the analogy of painting that she turned in that manifesto of realism, chapter 17 of *Adam Bede*. The everyday scenes of Dutch painting, she promised, would also find a place in her novels, which would give 'a faithful account of men and things as they have mirrored themselves in my mind'.[157] No view of life, however, can be an undistorted reflection of the real world and she necessarily coloured her canvas according to her view of what the world really was. She refused to write blatant propaganda, not wanting to lapse 'from the picture to the diagram'. Her narrators may not, like Kingsley's, harangue us; they are more avuncular, leading us gently to their more exalted philosophical point of view.[158] But they have a very definite point of view.

All George Eliot's novels, in fact, present Christianity through the reductive lenses of Strauss and Feuerbach, whose

Life of Jesus and *Essence of Christianity* she translated. The three clergymen depicted in *Scenes of Clerical Life* learn to place more importance on human than divine love. Adam Bede learns humility through the Feuerbachian 'baptism' of suffering while Dinah Morris, the Methodist preacher, grows to lean more on her innate intuition than on the Bible. Maggie Tulliver accepts the guidance of à Kempis, imitating Christ in self-sacrifice, but without any hope of sharing in the resurrection. Savonarola withdraws his claims to supernatural vision, so winning Romola's devotion. Felix Holt pours scorn on all unprovable metaphysical beliefs while Dorothea Brooke loses all faith in anything but a 'divine' struggle of good against evil. Even for Daniel Deronda his discovery of Judaism involves a sense of historical mission rather than a spiritual call.

All these novels, then, explain supernatural belief in purely human terms, which is also the strategy adopted by *Silas Marner*, which George Eliot herself called 'a sort of legendary tale' given 'more realistic treatment', celebrating in Wordsworthian fashion 'the remedial influences of pure, natural human relations'.[159] There is, of course, a fairy-tale element in the story of an old miserly weaver who has lost all faith in God and man being robbed of his gold but 'redeemed' by the love of a little girl. But the only mysteries allowed by the narrator are those of the human heart. The superstitious citizens of Raveloe regard everything to do with 'the world outside their experience', including the linen-weaver himself, as 'a region of vagueness and mystery'.[160] His cataleptic fits add to this aura of mystery with which he is surrounded although he no longer regards them as a sign of divine providence, having learnt from his experience in Lantern Yard, where neither man nor God speak up to acquit him of robbery. In spite of the rumours circulating in the Rainbow Inn, where they are forever talking about ghosts, there is nothing supernatural about Silas Marner.

Belief in such a supernatural providence, according to Feuerbach, is no better than trust in chance.[161] Nancy Lammeter's trust in the former, which is the reason why she refuses to adopt Eppie, is therefore akin to the Cass brothers' trust in the latter. The narrator constantly insists that they would be better to obey 'a law they believe in . . . the orderly sequence by which the seed brings forth a crop after its kind',[162] a phrase which echoes Strauss, who also insists that 'all occurrences . . . follow in a certain order of sequence' and therefore rules out all miracles.[163]

The episode of the mythical pedlar held to be responsible for the stealing of Marner's gold seems also to be related to Strauss's analysis of the growth of legendary elements in the gospel material, a product of imagination working upon memory. The only hard piece of historical evidence that can be linked with Marner's robbery is the discovery of a tinder-box in the road leading away from the village, which is then associated with a suspicious-looking pedlar. In general conversation around Raveloe, we are told,

> the balance continued to waver between the rational explanation founded on the tinder-box, and the theory of an impenetrable mystery that mocked investigation.[164]

Neither of these two extremes, of course, turns out to be true. They reflect the two extreme approaches to the gospels, the rationalistic search for 'natural' explanations (rocks beneath the surface of the water on which Jesus was seen to walk) and the entirely supernatural explanation sought by the orthodox. Strauss believed he had solved the dilemma by proposing his 'mythical point of view', which found varying degrees of historical truth at the heart of the gospel narratives, the 'real' truth of which was the character of Jesus as it came gradually to be interpreted by his disciples.[165]

The episode of the pedlar provides an example of the level of superstition prevalent in the Raveloe community. It also prepares the reader to interpret from a 'mythical point of view' the theological discussion between Dolly Winthrop and Silas Marner which takes place later in the same chapter. The carol that Dolly makes her son sing celebrates the incarnation:

For Jesus Christ our Saviour
  Was born on Christmas Day.

But it has no meaning for Silas, not only because it comes from a different liturgical tradition from the one he was brought up in but because he lacks the human experience required to give it meaning: 'the fountains of human love and faith in a divine love had not yet been unlocked' in his heart. The divine qualities of the human heart are what the narrator sees in Feuerbach's terms as the real meaning of Christian doctrines. Silas *is* redeemed by a little child, of course, not the holy child celebrated in the carol but an ordinary human baby. As he tells Eppie, his face shining 'in a sort of transfiguration', she is the 'precious child' who was 'sent to save me'.[166] The doctrine of the incarnation has been demythologized.

Angels and devils are also demythologized in *Silas Marner*, reduced to metaphors of human experience. Godfrey Cass accordingly meditates upon the virtues of his 'good angel', Nancy Lammeter, whom he woos with 'tacit patient worship'.[167] But such innate tendencies towards good must battle against such evils as 'the demon Opium' by which his wife is enslaved. Her remaining good instincts are described as 'white-winged delicate messengers' which fail to reach her poisoned heart.[168] On a metaphysical level, of course, George Eliot rejects the idea of angelic interference in the course of human affairs as strongly as Strauss:

> In the old days there were angels who came and took men by the hand and led them away from the city of destruction. We see no white-winged angels now. But yet men are led away from threatening destruction: a hand is put into theirs, which leads them forth gently towards a calm and bright land, so that they look no more backward; and the hand may be a little child's.[169]

This is the 'reality' of the world George Eliot paints, operating in accordance with strict scientific laws but nevertheless affording the possibility of human redemption from evil.

The form of realism adopted by George Eliot was welcomed in France in the 1880s as 'idealistic' in comparison with the 'morbid' and 'materialistic' naturalism espoused by Zola, whose critical opponents advocated instead the 'mystic realism' of Tolstoy and Dostoevsky, writers for whom ultimate reality remained beyond scientific explanation.[170] Tolstoy's characters catch a dying glimpse of this reality, the wounded Prince Andrey, for example, wondering to whom he should pray and feeling that 'nothing is certain except the nothingness of everything I can conceive, and the majesty of something I cannot understand'.[171] Levin's recovery of his religious faith in *Anna Karenina* is equally unclear and irrational. He vows to continue praying even though 'I shall still be unable to understand with my reason why I pray'.[172] Tolstoy's own attempts to explain his religion in non-fictional terms, however, and even his late novel, *Resurrection*, were more 'rationalistic', seeking to 'cleanse' Christianity both of dogma and of mystery.[173]

Dostoevsky presents a more sustained challenge to the rationalism implicit in the realist novel. His believers, Shatov in *The Devils*, Kirillov in *The Possessed* and Alyosha in *The Brothers Karamazov*, have no answer to the intellectual problems of evil and suffering. The rationalist arguments seem irrefutable but the need to believe remains. Ivan's evidence of innocent suffering, young children praying in vain to a 'dear, kind God' to protect them, forces Alyosha to admit that he would not consent to be the architect of such a world and to rest his belief on Christ, the ultimate in innocent victims. In Ivan's parable of 'The Grand Inquisitor', however, the returning Christ is rejected by the Church because the freedom he demands is too difficult for ordinary human beings, who will continue to require precisely what he rejected in the temptations in the wilderness: miracle, mystery and authority.[174] Ivan's rational scientific view of the world, of course, is undermined by the scheming immorality of his 'disciple', Smerdyakov, and Alyosha reasserts the truths of revealed religion at the very end of the novel. Where Dostoyevsky himself stands, as Bakhtin observed, is never entirely clear. His novels resist reduction to monologue, preserving 'a plurality of independent and unmerged voices and consciousness, a genuine polyphony of fully valid voices'.[175] Different ideologies, in other words, compete within the text.

The English novel, however, with very few exceptions, maintained its liberal humanist stance, continuing to present human relations as the highest subject of realist fiction. D. H. Lawrence, for example, may use religious language, his novels resounding with biblical phrases, but only as metaphors for human experience. True salvation, put most bluntly in the story of *The Man Who Died*, in which the risen Christ, recovering from his wounds after the crucifixion, learns not to forbid women to touch him, lies in fulfilled sexual relations.[176] Other major figures in the liberal humanist tradition, such as E.M.Forster and Virginia Woolf, find any form of supernaturalism unacceptable. The elaborate rituals and self-conscious fictions of Hinduism depicted towards the end of *A Passage to India* are found infinitely preferable to the arrogant theology of Christianity and Islam, which, to the agnostic Fielding, is merely 'a game with words'.[177] Again, the implicit claim is that the novelist can show us what 'really' is the case more effectively than the theologian.

Even a novelist as sympathetic to Christianity as Iris Murdoch seems to regard religious language in a naïve realist or positivist manner as a mistaken attempt to name metaphysical entities which do not exist rather than a symbolic expression of realities beyond human comprehension. 'Metaphysics is devilish', warns Theo, the ironically named religious atheist and pursuer of Buddhist self-denial, in *The Nice and the Good*; 'Nothing about that can be said'.[178] Stuart Cuno comes to a similar conclusion in *The Good Apprentice*, refusing to use the word 'God' because it had always seemed to him 'something hard and limited and small, identified as an idol, and certainly not the name of what he found within himself'.[179] His uncle offers him a number of modern existentialist reconceptualizations of the word, assuring him that all traditional dogmas are being redefined in this way by 'the theological rescue party'. But Stuart insists that 'God' is 'the proper name of a supernatural Person' in whom he cannot believe,[180] a position also reached by Cato Forbes, whose rebellion against his father's old-fashioned rationalism brings him temporarily into the Roman Catholic priesthood from which he resigns at the end of *Henry and Cato*.

Murdoch portrays her many Christian characters sympathetically, especially in earlier novels such as *The Sandcastle* and *The Bell*. But their beliefs are seen to be illusions, projections of their inner needs. She seems to accept, as Plato could not, that art offers merely 'magical structures to conceal the absence of God or his distance'.[181] In *Nuns and Soldiers* it is not only Guy Oppenheimer who calls Christianity too 'soft', 'sentimental and magical', offering a false comfort for the facts of suffering and death.[182] Christ himself appears to the ex-nun Anne in a vision and tells her quite brutally that her thoughts are as imaginary as his words, refusing to play the part of magician and saviour.[183] She is left to treasure her vision of Christ as a godless inspiration to human virtue, the only reality Murdoch seems prepared to affirm.

The liberal humanist tradition, however, has not had a monopoly over the modern novel. The three Catholic novelists to be considered now, Evelyn Waugh, Graham Greene and Flannery O'Connor, all insist on the 'reality' of the supernatural. Both *Brideshead Revisited* and *The End of the Affair* employ narrators who begin as rationalist, agnostic liberal humanists before coming to recognize the limitations of their vision of the world. O'Connor too portrays her prophetic figures through the eyes of 'well-adjusted' humanists who regard them as insane. In all three cases, readers are challenged to abandon the secular assumptions of their age, to admit the depth of evil in themselves and in the world, to acknowledge their need of redemption. It is a dangerous strategy, especially as all three novelists seem to delight in the irrationality of their position, building their hope in revelation upon despair of the modern world.

This is particularly true of Evelyn Waugh, who adopted characteristically defiant attitudes on the least attractive of doctrines, such as hell and original sin, welcoming the papal definition of the assumption precisely 'because it defied rationalism'.[184] As Pope Sylvester is made to say in Waugh's historical novel about Helena, mother of Constantine and discoverer of the true cross, 'Nothing "stands to reason" with God'.[185] Waugh himself stood firmly against bringing reason to bear upon revelation; for him, 'the more difficult it was to believe, the more obviously true it was'.[186] His faith was founded upon despair about the world other people called 'real', a world which he found 'unintelligible and unendurable without God'.[187] His early novels are full of the absurdity of this world, which even Prendergast in *Decline and Fall* wonders why God made. His later work, especially the *Sword of Honour* trilogy, presents the supernatural as the only real world, the only reality worthy of serious consideration.

This is certainly the project of *Brideshead Revisited*, which Waugh recognized as his first religious novel, the first 'to represent man more fully, which, to me, means only one thing, man in his relation to God'.[188] Charles Ryder, whose sacred and profane memories are the subject of the novel, portrays his younger self as a typical rationalist, the product of unquestioned secular assumptions that Christianity was historically without foundation and psychologically disastrous, the source of innumerable 'complexes' and 'inhibitions'. The sadder, wiser narrator recalls:

> no one had ever suggested to me that these quaint observances expressed a coherent philosophic system and intransigent historical claims; nor, had they done so, would I have been much interested.

Only later, the narrator adds (and then only in the revised edition of the novel), did he come to examine those claims more closely and 'to accept the supernatural as the real'.[189]

The rational Ryder continues to argue that it is only his religion which prevents Sebastian from being 'a happy and healthy man'.[190] He is given a perfect example of the complexes engendered by Nanny Hawkins and the catechism when Bridey's reference to their 'living in sin' leads to Julia's passionate outpouring of guilt and misery, focused upon the cross. That outburst, however, turns later to prayer; at least, Ryder assumes that her murmurs are a relic of 'pious rhyme' handed down through 'centuries of bedtime whispering'.[191] Julia's faith eventually forces her to leave Ryder, a clear example of what Waugh clearly sees as an inevitable conflict between human and divine, relative and absolute values.

Ryder, of course, comes in the face of death to accept his own need for such an eternal flame as burns in the tabernacle at Brideshead. But it is in spite of the Marchmains that he does so. Nothing in the history of his alcoholic friend, his impulsive mistress, their insistently pious mother, their primly moralistic brother, or their rakish father (finally penitent though he is) could account for Ryder's conversion, which is the product of a divine 'Twitch upon the Thread'. This inelegant phrase of Father Brown's supplies the title of the second part of the novel whose theme, as Waugh emphasized in his 1959 preface, is 'the operation of divine grace'.[192] It may be assisted by human folly, in particular the worldly blinkers which prevent the rational Rex Mottram from recognizing that what the priest tells him might in fact be 'real'. The secular Hooper, symbolic of the drabness of the modern world, 'the suffocating ordinariness of common reality',[193] revolts Ryder even more, forcing him to seek refuge in an alternative 'reality' made 'real' in the novel by hints and symbols rather than explicit commentary.

'The hidden presence of God in an atheistic world'[194] has also been identified as the main subject of Graham Greene's work. His 'Catholic novels', from *Brighton Rock* of 1938 to *The End of the Affair* of 1951, abandon 'normal' human experience for the extremes of sinfulness and saintliness, the realization of grace operating even in the gangster world of Pinkie's Brighton and through the whiskey priest in *The Power and the Glory*. Charles Péguy's assertion that the sinner is at the heart of Christianity, that no one is as 'competent' in that faith as the sinner, except perhaps the saint, provides the epigraph to *The Heart of the Matter*, in which the hero chooses to commit suicide rather than injure any of the three persons he loves (his wife, his mistress and God), who are equally real to him.

It is in *The End of the Affair*, however, that Greene offers his most powerful challenge to rational liberal humanism and its exclusion of God both from the real world and from the 'realistic' world of fiction. The narrator, like Ryder, begins as an agnostic but comes, grudgingly, to accept the existence of a God whom he continues to hate and to whom he pleads, at the end of the novel, to be left alone. He has learnt in the meantime that grace is irresistible, that God's mysterious plot, like those of his own novels, is moving inexorably to a predestined end. The early part of the novel is full of dark references to 'that other', 'that third, whom I hated without yet knowing him'.[195] A first reader of the novel, lulled into accepting the liberal humanist assumptions of the narrator, can have little inkling that this third person, the lover for whom Sarah abandons both her husband and Bendrix himself, is God. So convinced is the narrator that she is having another adulterous affair that he has her followed by a private detective who discovers apparently convincing evidence of her new love, a scrap of paper which appears to be a draft of a passionate love letter. This, as the reader later learns, is in fact part of a diary charting the progress of her love for God from the time of its inception (a rash vow conditional on Bendrix surviving the direct hit of a German bomb upon his house) through a period of resistance to a final joyful capitulation.

All this remains incredible to the rational narrator: 'We had agreed so happily to eliminate God from our world'.[196] Sarah herself goes to absurd lengths to convince herself that God does not exist and that her vow need not therefore be honoured, paying regular visits to the grotesquely old-fashioned atheist Smythe who attempts to 'explain away' not only divine but human love, succeeding only in confirming her conviction of their reality. Her husband's dismissal of the 'superstitious' belief in a material God maintained even by such profound thinkers as Pascal and Newman as the result of 'glandular deficiency' has a similar effect, driving her into a Catholic church to dwell on 'that material body on that material cross'. In a 'flaming rage, and in defiance of Henry and all the reasonable and the detached', she dips her finger in the holy water and makes the sign of the cross.[197]

The assault on rationalism is taken even further by the introduction of miracles into the novel, which Greene himself came to regard as 'an appalling mistake'.[198] The detective's son claims to have been cured of appendicitis by the 'sainted' Sarah visiting his bedside and touching his stomach. The fanatic rationalist is cured of his unsightly spots by a lock of her hair:

> at the time of publication it was difficult to say who were the most scandalised – non-Catholic readers at the introduction of miracles into realist fiction, or Catholics at the attribution of miracles to a woman like Sarah.[199]

It remains open to readers to find 'rational' explanations for these miracles, as their narrator does. They will be very reluctant, however, to accept his brand of rationalism.

Greene's later work is increasingly less committed to supernaturalism. The most sympathetic figure in *A Burnt-Out Case*, for example, which announces itself as merely 'an attempt to give dramatic expression to various types of belief, half-belief and non-belief',[200] is the agnostic doctor who attempts to synthesize evolutionary theory with Christian moral values along the lines of Teilhard de Chardin rather than the more orthodox Catholics who attempt to make a Schweitzer-style saint of the enigmatic and exhausted Querry. Greeneland continues to be a bizarre place which cannot be fitted into a watertight doctrinal system. The only sense the atheistic Dr Fischer can make of the world is to present God in his own image as greedy for our humiliation, playing practical jokes upon his guests, giving them presents to keep them going rather than commit suicide but inflicting shame and suffering on all in the end. The benign *Monsignor Quixote* insists on doubt as a necessary part of faith, his nightmare being that Christ is saved from the cross by a legion of angels, allowing no room for his followers to doubt. The only tangible result of his death is that the communist mayor begins to be similarly doubtful about his own creed. Greene may now be less convinced of the reality of the supernatural than he was but his novels continue to pour doubt upon other ideologies which claim to be more real.

Flannery O'Connor launches an even more aggressive assault upon rational notions of reality. 'All novelists', she recognizes, 'are fundamentally seekers and describers of the real'; what differs is their view of reality, which for her centred upon a transcendent God revealed in the incarnation, a mystery which defies complete encapsulation in language. Mystery, however, is a great embarrassment to the modern mind, which likes to give a scientific explanation for everything.[201] In order to counteract this tendency a Christian writer, she confessed, is often driven to the grotesque, the perverse and the unacceptable, shocking modern readers into recognizing that what they take to be natural is, in fact, distorted.[202] Her two volumes of short stories, *A Good Man Is Hard To Find* and *Everything That Rises Must Converge*, present a collection of overconfident rationalists violently disabused of their shallow assumptions about human nature. They include young Joy Hopewell, who finds an itinerant Bible-seller not quite as innocent as she had assumed (not only does he rape her but he walks off with her wooden leg), the confident Mrs Cope, who finds that she cannot in fact cope with

a group of local thugs, the grandmother whose happy
humanism is completely shattered by 'The Misfit', a violent
criminal for whom a world without Christ is not worth
preserving, and the socially conscious liberal widower whose
attempts to 'save' the lame negro Johnson founder upon a
failure to recognize either the strength of evil within him or
the depths of his desire to be saved by no one but Jesus.[203]

This is the whole point of *Wise Blood*, to which O'Connor was
forced to add an 'Author's Note' correcting what she saw as a
widespread misreading of the novel:

> That belief in Christ is to some a matter of life and death has
> been a stumbling block for readers who would prefer to think it
> a matter of no great consequence. For them Hazel Motes'
> integrity lies in his trying with such vigour to get rid of the
> ragged figure who moves from tree to tree in the back of his
> mind. For the author Hazel's integrity lies in his not being able
> to.[204]

This figure, of course, is Jesus, whom Hazel has spent his
whole life trying to escape. 'Nothing matters but that Jesus
don't exist', he insists, setting himself up as the first prophet of
'the Church Without Christ . . . where the blind don't see and
the lame don't walk and what's dead stays that way'.[205] But
behind this obsession with Christ, we are led to see, is a deep
craving for faith, a fundamental rejection of the secular
assumptions of much of modern America.

The same ideological attack upon secularism pervades *The
Violent Bear It Away*, in which the rational schoolteacher
Rayber tries to rehabilitate the young Francis Tarwater,
'infected' as he has been by the prophetic ravings of his
grandfather. Rayber too has to struggle against 'irrational and
abnormal' tendencies within himself, such as the love he bears
for his mentally retarded son Bishop. He rages about Francis
'being led away from reality',[206] undertaking a programme of
'rational' activities, visits to museums and so on. He sets a
glass of water in front of Francis, whose ardent desire is to
baptise young Bishop, and then proceeds to drink it. But
Francis refuses to be reclaimed for rationalism, ending the
novel with a clear acceptance of his prophetic vocation.

Readers are left, as in Waugh and Greene, to question their own version of reality.

This question of the relation between fiction and reality, which realism asks its readers to forget, is brought into the open by metafiction. For what people call the 'real' world is seen to be itself a fiction, a construct of liberal humanist ideology. Novelists such as Kurt Vonnegut and Thomas Pynchon subvert common-sense notions about the everyday world, which they portray as more absurd than any fantasy dreamt up by science fiction.[207] The only religion consistent with such a world is that propounded by the prophet Bokonon in *Cat's Cradle*, who argues that all religion consists of lies. This is why religion, as opposed to science, is 'the one real instrument of hope'.[208] His complex cosmogony, he realizes, is a pack of lies. But there is no alternative, no escape from 'the cruel paradox of Bokononist thought, the heartbreaking necessity of lying about reality, and the heartbreaking impossibility of lying about it'.[209] We are condemned to fictions which we know to fall short of the truth.

Bokonon presents God as an unconscious agent of fate whose motives remain inscrutable. 'Anyone who thinks he sees what God is Doing', *The Books of Bokonon* insist, is a fool.[210] 'What is the *purpose* of all this?' asks man in the first book:

> 'Everything must have a purpose?' asked God.
> 'Certainly,' said man.
> 'Then I leave you to think of one for all this,' said God. And He went away.[211]

Undermined in this passage are both conventional notions of God *and* the insatiable demands of rational man. The novel ends by quoting Bokonon's final lines, written before he is frozen alive in ice-nine, which regret not having written 'a history of human stupidity' and express a final wish to be preserved for eternity 'lying on my back, grinning horribly, and thumbing my nose at You Know Who'.[212] Both Bokonon and Vonnegut refuse to offer comforting illusions about 'reality'; the most they can rise to is fiction.

However doubtful metafiction may be about its ability to capture the 'truth' of the 'real' world, it cannot in the end avoid being read as some kind of reflection, however distorted, of that world. In the case of Vonnegut, clearly, the world seems chaotic and pointless. The Catholic novelists considered earlier, while equally gloomy about the prevalence of evil and suffering, perceive the world as redeemed by revelation. The incarnation, in which the Creator Himself suffers and overcomes the worst evil that the world can offer, is for them the most important reality. The liberal humanist tradition offers a very different description of the 'real' world. All these portraits of reality, however, are both ideological and theological, deeply imbued with value-judgements about the nature, purpose and origin of a world either sustained or abandoned by God.

CHAPTER 4

Metaphorical Theology: The Poetry of Faith

THE DYNAMICS OF METAPHOR: METAPHYSICAL WIT

A sensitivity to literature, I have suggested, acts as a safeguard against literalism, the tendency to talk of God 'in straightforward language' as if we had privileged access to His diaries.[1] Religious language is not a matter of giving names to clearly discernible objects; it is a complex web of metaphors and symbols pointing towards an imperfectly understood reality. Metaphors, I want now to show, provide perhaps the most important means by which language is stretched beyond the literal in order to talk of God. They play an important role in the Bible and in traditional doctrinal discourse. But they are absolutely central to poetry, which has been defined as 'organized violence committed on ordinary speech'.[2] They abound in Gerard Manley Hopkins, who stretches language to breaking point, and in the metaphysical poets, who violate expectations by linking sacred and profane in a series of striking metaphors.

'Far the most important thing to master', wrote Aristotle of poetic language, 'is the use of metaphor . . . for the ability to use metaphor well implies a perception of resemblances', of the similarities between different objects which allows one to be described in terms of another. It is the use of linguistic 'riddles', 'unfamiliar usages', according to Aristotle, which confers 'dignity' upon poetic diction, raising it above 'the level of the commonplace'.[3] The same point has been made at greater length by Russian formalists and structuralists, who see 'defamiliarization' and the foregrounding of figures of speech as the essence of literary or poetic language. There are, according to Roman Jakobson, two main axes of language:

selection, which is based upon the perception of similarity and generates metaphor, and combination, which is based upon spatial and temporal contiguity and gives rise to metonymy. Poets project one axis of language upon the other, producing an unlikely combination such as 'ships plough the sea' or 'my car beetles along'. It is this which gives poetry its potential to generate new meaning.[4]

Recent studies of religious language, as we have seen, stress the cognitive element in metaphor, which is not merely a matter of ornament, 'a decorative way of saying what could be said literally'. The 'substitution theories' of metaphor elaborated by classical rhetoric, which regard metaphors as replaceable by literal translations, and the 'emotive theories' propounded by logical positivism and linguistic analysis, which see metaphor as literally 'meaningless', semantically deviant and philosophically dishonest, are equally objectionable from this point of view. For the former, poetry becomes merely entertainment, for the latter meaningless expletives or downright lies. Vaughan, they argue, cannot possibly have seen eternity or Blake have dined with the prophets Isaiah and Ezekiel. In the face of this philosophical attempt to impose rigorous logical and scientific limits upon language, it is necessary to spell out the dynamic potential of poetry to generate new meanings, to celebrate in metaphor 'a unique cognitive vehicle enabling us to say things that can be said in no other way'.[5]

The 1960s saw a number of competing accounts of the dynamics of metaphor, including Max Black's 'interaction theory', discussed above, in which the two terms of a metaphor such as 'man is a wolf' are seen to interact upon each other, the latter providing a lens through which the former is seen in a new light, both terms needing to be held in a tension irreducible to a single statement.[6] Other critics also stressed the need for 'stereo-scopic' or 'bi-focal' vision, holding both halves of a metaphor together in a complex tension which recognizes both similarities and differences:

> Metaphors are literally absurd. Men are self-evidently not mice; life is not a play, nor is it a dream, and we only retain the power of the metaphor to make us look at men and mice, life and plays,

in a new way, as having anything in common, while we retain a firm grasp of their difference. Without that tension they would be dead metaphors and would relapse into cliché, or into a new literalness.[7]

The 'tensive' quality of metaphorical language, according to Philip Wheelwright, stretches understanding beyond the limits of the literal.[8] More recently, Paul Ricoeur has written of the 'split-reference' or 'tensional' quality of a metaphor, which simultaneously affirms and denies that something is the case. There is, he argues, an implicit 'and is not' in any positive metaphorical statement. As with all literary devices, the literal sense is suspended so that a second level of reference can come into effect.[9]

Theology has always been irredeemably riddled with metaphor. The gospels, as we have seen, make Jesus repeatedly risk and often suffer the misunderstanding of the literal-minded. In Mark the disciples mutter stupidly, 'We have no bread', when Jesus warns them against the leaven of the pharisees (16:8). In John Nicodemus asks how a man can enter his mother's womb a second time in order to be 'born again' (3:4). 'The kingdom of God is within you', says Jesus in Luke (17:21) while the Gospel of Thomas makes him sound as if he had read Ricoeur: 'the Kingdom is within you, and it is outside of you' (Logion 3). It is quite clear, as Frye comments, that whatever he *did* mean,

> He did not mean that the kingdom of God is 'within' in the sense that our hearts and lungs are inside us, or in the sense, say, that a swallowed safety pin is within a baby. All serious discussion of the passage begins by rejecting the demotic [literal] or descriptive meaning, and then discusses what kind of metaphor is signified by the word *entos*.[10]

Christian doctrine, too, inevitably resorts to metaphor. Even Aquinas, it has been argued, in saying that metaphors are used 'improperly' of God, should rather be seen as recognizing the inadequacy of all language than enjoining silence or more straightforward discourse. Since we cannot understand God as He is, Aquinas claims, we are forced to talk of Him indirectly, in terms of analogy or comparison with more directly observable phenomena.[11] Believers who might be tempted to think that 'God' is quite literally the name of a person are instructed that He is, in fact, three persons, each represented by a metaphor. For He is (and is not) a Father, He is (and is not) a Son and He is (and is not) a Spirit, wind, or breath. Even the pronoun in these statements is metaphorical, for He is quite clearly not of the masculine gender.

Literal understanding of any of these terms, as Sallie McFague insists, is idolatrous, worshipping a construct of human language as if it were a real object:

> When a model [a sustained or extended metaphor] becomes an idol, the hypothetical character of the model is forgotten and what ought to be seen as *one* way to understand our relationship with God has become identified as *the* way ... the distance between image and reality collapses: 'father' becomes God's 'name' and patriarchy becomes the proper description of governing relationships at many levels.[12]

The point is not to replace one metaphor with another, addressing God continually as Mother instead of Father, She rather than He, or to invent a Goddess of our own creation, but to recognize the metaphorical status of all these terms.

The Old Testament, in fact, is full of feminine metaphors of God carrying Israel and giving birth in pain, suckling her at the breast, comforting her and covering her nakedness. Gnostic texts too make Jesus speak of the Holy Spirit as 'the true Mother', medieval mystics such as St Anselm and Dame Julian of Norwich stress the nourishing, nurturing aspects of God's love and St Teresa of Avila, who resorts constantly to metaphor in an attempt to portray the mysteries of mystical experience, describes the prayer of quiet in terms of a mother feeding her baby, 'without its moving its lips ... for the soul loves without using the understanding'.[13] In all these examples, the maternal images, because they are unfamiliar, advertise their metaphorical status.

It is, however, only too easy for metaphors to become over-familiar, to grow

> old and moribund, losing the vital tension of opposing meanings, dramatic antithesis, paradox, which was theirs at

their inception. They become fossilized and enter into everyday life . . . no longer living metaphors, but merely ex-metaphoric corpses.[14]

A dead metaphor loses the tension between its two senses, settling on a single meaning. The metaphor which gave rise to the eucharist, for example, Christ's outrageous assertion over the breaking of bread that 'This is my body', can easily lose its literal sense. The bread becomes a special kind of wafer so different from our staple diet that its miraculous transformation ceases to suprise. People get used to eating their God. But if the sacrament is to continue to point to a mysterious reality it must preserve both literal and figurative meanings:

> liturgy can only act as a disclosure of God to those who surrender their claim to know beforehand what it means and who will allow its literal meaning to serve each time afresh as the starting-point for the discovery of further meaning.[15]

Christ's sacrifice can be 'realized' anew each time that the sacrament is celebrated only if the congregation refuse to be dulled by familiarity and habit to its extraordinary claims.

Literature, as we have seen, sets out to defamiliarize, foregrounding its violation of the literal and advertising its difference from ordinary language. No one could read these stanzas from 'The Wreck of the Deutschland', for example, without noticing that something extraordinary is being done with language:

> Not out of his bliss
>   Springs the stress felt
> Nor first from heaven (and few know this)
>   Swings the stroke dealt –
> Stroke and a stress that stars and storms deliver,
> That guilt is hushed by, hearts are flushed by and melt –
>   But it rides time like riding a river
> (And here the faithful waver, the faithless fable and miss).
>
>   It dates from day
>   Of his going in Galilee;
> Warm-laid grave of a womb-life grey;
>   Manger, maiden's knee;

The dense and the driven Passion, and frightful sweat:
Thence the discharge of it, there its swelling to be,
Though felt before, though in high flood yet –
What none would have known of it, only the heart, being hard
at bay,

Is out with it! Oh,
We lash with the best or worst
Word last! How a lush-kept plush-capped sloe
Will, mouthed to flesh-burst,
Gush! – flush the man, the being with it, sour or sweet,
Brim, in a flash, full! Hither, then, last or first,
To hero of Calvary, Christ's feet –
Never ask if meaning it, wanting it, warned of it – men go.[16]

The temptation here, for the literal-minded at least, is to dismiss these lines as affected and pretentious nonsense. Hopkins, it is true, often stretches the patience of his most passionate admirers as well as the elasticity of the English language. But the point is that these stanzas do 'mean' something; they are, in fact, about the central elements of the Christian faith: the incarnation and crucifixion of Christ and the suffering and commitment of the believer. They cannot, of course, be paraphrased but I will attempt to explain *how* they achieve their meaning.

The poem as a whole celebrates what at first seems shocking, the death in a shipwreck of five German nuns who are seen to be joined with Christ in their suffering. These stanzas (numbers six to eight in the poem) prepare the ground for the dramatic description of their death, calling upon Christ. It is Christ's suffering not His joy, the first verse insists, which brings people to faith, making them feel the 'stress' which 'springs' from His crucifixion. 'Stress' has special connotations for Hopkins, 'instress' referring to the dynamic force which shapes beauty in the world and which affects beholders of that beauty. It is the 'stress of selving in God', Hopkins wrote in a sermon, which 'forced out drops of sweat or blood, which drops were the world'.[17] 'Stress' here, in the poem, is a form of grace but the literal sense of 'strain' is also very much present. It is 'felt' first by Christ but also by believers in their 'strokes' or moments of extremity, when they are 'delivered' into the hands of the elements.

The grace of suffering is said to 'spring', to leap that is from Christ's delivery into life (his birth) and sin (the cross), but it also wells up like a spring from the heart. For guilt is 'hushed', hearts 'flushed' and 'melted', by his suffering. The internal rhymes play upon accidental similarities of sound (which Hopkins did not believe to be entirely accidental) to reinforce the similarities of sense between the overwhelming and silencing of guilt, the melting of ice and the flooding of the heart with compassion for Christ. 'Flushing' can mean to spurt or rush out, to cleanse, to throw out fresh shoots, to blush and to grow hot. Here it has all these senses, all of which are involved in the melting of the believer's heart. Christ's stress, in the last two lines, is said to 'ride' time 'like riding a river', another water metaphor for the travelling of the gospel through time, the historicity of the accounts of Christ's birth and suffering. Those who treat it as a fable 'miss' the whole point that, however difficult it may be to get at the actual events, faith must kneel before Christ on the cross.

The metaphorical density of Hopkins's language, then, is complex rather than confused, the multiple meanings needing to be held together in tension. The second stanza focuses on the physical details of Christ's birth and death, his coming and his 'going' being intimately connected. He is entombed in Mary's womb, his 'warm-laid grave', since he is born to suffer on the cross. The horrifying nature of crucifixion brings nails 'driven' into His body, sweat which is 'frightful' in two senses (being both born of and inspiring fear), the 'swelling' of wounds and their 'discharge'. 'Charge', too, has a double meaning, referring also to the energy or instress of God's creation (as in 'God's Grandeur', with which 'the world is charged'). The discharge of Christ's wounds comes 'thence' (from the cross) but its 'swelling to be' is in the heart, giving birth to faith. It may have been 'felt before' (it certainly was by Christ) but it only comes 'out', only issues in faith, when the heart is 'hard at bay', hard-pressed as the hart when hunted (a metaphor to be pursued further by Francis Thompson). The linguistic density, the mixing of metaphors here, is quite astonishing. Yet it all 'makes sense'.

Finally, in the third stanza quoted here, men are seen to fall at Christ's feet, to submit wholly to Him, to achieve their goal in God, only at the 'last', in the face of death. The metaphor of flagellation conveys the violence required, the suffering which alone brings submission. Faith is seen as instructive and immediate, the taste of an individual in the mouth of God, bursting like a ripe and luscious berry, which itself, in an almost absurd metaphor, has a plush 'cap'. It is the climax of identity when a man 'fills' his 'being' with faith, obeying an instinct beyond conscious intention ('meaning it'), desire ('wanting it'), or external pressure ('warned of it'). The metaphorical journey to Calvary is completed through a flood of figurative language, all of which enriches the cognitive 'meaning' of the poem. It may be mannered writing but it is not mere ornament. As von Balthasar says of Hopkins's sacramental celebration of 'God's revelation in Christ throughout the universe',

> what has to be interpreted is not concepts (of 'universal' abstract truths) but images (of the unique, personal, divine-human truth) and here poetry is the absolutely appropriate theological language.[18]

The poetic quest for novelty, as Samuel Johnson complained, can be taken to extremes. Accepting that wit is not merely a matter of ornament, that Pope's phrase, 'What oft was thought, but ne'er so well expressed',[19] ignores poetry's cognitive content, 'depresses it below its natural dignity, and reduces it from strength of thought to happiness of language', Johnson goes on to criticize the 'unnatural' way in which in the metaphysical poets 'the most heterogeneous ideas are yoked by violence together'. He also objects to their elaboration of metaphors into complex conceits:

> the force of metaphors is lost when the mind by the mention of particulars is turned more upon the original than the secondary sense, more upon that from which the illustration is drawn than that to which it is applied.[20]

Yet the tension between the literal and the metaphorical senses is precisely what allows poetry to say something new. Donne, by describing sexual attraction in theological terms and religious experience in sexual images, canonizing his lovers and demanding to be ravished by God, may antagonize the eighteenth-century lexicographer who wants to impose discipline and control upon language, but opens up in the process the area of overlap between the two kinds of ecstatic experience.

The ecstasy of the mystic and the lover are even more shockingly juxtaposed in Crashaw's 'Hymn to Saint Teresa', whose chaste love and self-sacrifice are celebrated in overtly sexual metaphors:

> She never undertook to know
> What death with love should have to doe;
> Nor hath she e're yet understood
> Why to shew love, she should shed blood,
> Yet though she can not tell you why,
> She can *love*, and she can *dye*.[21]

There is the standard playing here with the sexual connotations of 'dying' but also a profound recognition of the similarities *and the differences* between spiritual and carnal love. Both kinds of love defy reason, involving pain and self-sacrifice. Yet the loss of blood involved in the one is hardly martyrdom, just as sexual climax is hardly death. The tension in these metaphors derives from the perceived difference between the two kinds of love.

The metaphysical wit of Donne, Crashaw, Herbert and others belongs to a long tradition of Christian meditation going back from the *Spiritual Exercises* of St Ignatius Loyola through medieval and patristic piety to the New Testament itself.[22] For meditation necessarily proceeds by metaphor, drawing the mind from the tangible 'realities' of the senses to the 'realities' of the spiritual world. Herbert, for example, surprises his readers by redescribing the familiar message of redemption in the commonplace images of pulleys and porches, pearls and leases, banquets and feasts (the last four of these coming straight from the parables). One of his best-known poems consists of a whole series of images thrown out at the mystery of prayer:

PRAYER the Churches banquet, Angels age,
  Gods breath in man returning to his birth,
  The soul in paraphrase, heart in pilgrimage,
The Christian plummet sounding heav'n and earth;
Engine against th'Almightie, sinners towre,
  Reversed thunder, Christ-side-piercing spear,
  The six-daies world transposing in an houre,
A kinde of tune, which all things heare and fear;
Softnesse, and peace, and joy, and love, and blisse,
  Exalted Manna, gladnesse of the best,
  Heaven in ordinarie, man well drest,
The milkie way, the bird of Paradise,
  Church-bels beyond the starres heard, the souls bloud,
  The land of spices; something understood.[23]

Two of the early metaphors here are biblical, Christ often presenting the kingdom in terms of a banquet and Genesis describing the creation in terms of God breathing life into man. Prayer, Herbert suggests, is man breathing back to God. 'Angels age' is more complex, even contradictory, since spiritual beings are beyond time's grasp. In prayer, however, time and eternity meet (as we shall see in T. S. Eliot's 'Little Gidding'). The idea of the soul being paraphrased is even worse than the same fate befalling a poem, while the heart can hardly go on a literal pilgrimage. Both metaphors point to the miraculous element in prayer. The next few metaphors are more down to earth: the seemingly unbridgeable chasm between heaven and earth can in fact be 'measured'; contact can be made as by a plummet, though the struggle involved in the enterprise makes it a form of spiritual warfare by which sinners strive to 'bring down' the Almighty. Rather than God hurling thunder at men, men attempt to reach God by this means (R.S. Thomas, as we shall see, presents them hurling gravel at His window).

Returning to biblical images, Herbert presents prayer as a piercing once more of Christ's side, an excessive device for drawing his attention (but the excess, of course, comes rather in His submitting to such treatment and thereby opening a channel of prayer). Prayer 'transposes' the 'six-daies world' both by transforming the mundane and by entering a different dimension of time symbolized by the sabbath, when all secular work should cease. Prayer is seen as a kind of music which does not require great skill to follow. It is likened to the highest emotions of which men are capable and also the highest food. It is God 'dressing down' to mix with man, while he in turn must wear his Sunday best if the two are going to meet. The poem ends by turning from the mundane to the most exotic images. The milky way, of course, is not only the distant group of stars but the pilgrim route to Santiago. The bird of Paradise is not only an exotic creature but a means of regaining Eden. Most astonishingly of all, the church bells are actually heard beyond the stars, the soul is kept alive by prayer and its stammered phrases are finally understood by God.

Prayer is only understood, of course, by God, to whom it is addressed.[24] If any of these metaphors were adequate to describe it, the others would be unnecessary, since the concept would have been exhausted. Individually partial, together they build up a picture of what prayer is like, in terms that men can begin to understand. In Herbert, then, as in the Christian tradition as a whole, it is the sheer variety and plurality of metaphors which provide such a rich source of poetic understanding, enabling believers to transcend the limits of ordinary language, to glimpse and to encounter a reality which they cannot fully understand.

SYMBOL AND SACRAMENT: THE ROMANTIC IMAGINATION

If metaphors operate at the level of language, as a 'free invention of discourse', making connections which would not otherwise have been made, symbols are more firmly 'bound to the cosmos', taking root in physical objects.[25] They need also to take root in the psyche, whether as Jungian archetypes, a psychic residue of the experience of the race, or as more personal images of a reality beneath the level of discourse. 'The Cross is a symbol', to be explored more fully in a moment, 'because it stands for a truth which words cannot completely express'.[26] A traffic light, on the contrary, is an artificial sign whose meaning is entirely arbitrary. 'Real symbols', according to Karl Rahner, differ from conventional signs in being the self-expression or self-realization of an essential truth, Christ himself being the *Realsymbol* of the Logos.[27] There is always an element of mystery surrounding a symbol, an opacity, a surplus of meaning, an enigma which no interpretation should attempt to eradicate. The deeper meaning to which the symbol points remains inexhaustible and ultimately inexpressible. In theology as in literature symbolism involves a rejection of the positivist belief that reality can be dis-covered, laid bare by language. No-one, for example, not even Melville himself, can say precisely what Moby Dick 'stands for'.[28]

Religious symbols, as Tillich insisted, 'participate in the reality of that to which they point', opening up a reality 'beyond' or 'within' the physical objects themselves and unlocking elements within ourselves that correspond to that reality at the deepest level. They cannot be 'invented' ; they grow organically in the soil of the unconscious and they die when they can no longer find sustenance there.[29] In the sacraments, Tillich recognized,

> Nature participates in the process of salvation. Bread and wine, water and light, and all the great elements of Nature become the bearers of spiritual meaning and saving power.[30]

He could only deplore the widespread loss of sacramental thinking and feeling evident in the Protestant churches of the United States, which he saw as part of a wider alienation from nature on the part of modern man.[31]

Mircea Eliade has also deplored what he called 'desacralization', the disappearance of a sense of the sacred. Man cannot live without symbolic significance, however, and modern culture continues to swarm with 'half-forgotten myths, decaying hierophanies and secularised symbols', a 'mythological litter' which continually assumes new forms.[32] The question remains whether the traditional symbols of Christianity can continue to command a response or whether, as many poets have suggested since the Romantics, we need continually to create new symbols. I will consider to begin with how traditional symbols operate, first that of the cross, resounding as it does through the poetry and devotion of two thousand years, and secondly the sacraments, particularly that of baptism. I want then to explore the less conventional symbolism of Romantic and Symbolist poets from Wordsworth, Blake and Coleridge to Yeats and Eliot.

The cross itself is perhaps the most important of Christian symbols. No arbitrary choice, it was the historic instrument of Christ's death, transformed through his resurrection from a symbol of degradation to one of triumph. The empty cross, in particular, points beyond crucifixion to victory over suffering and death.[33] At least some of the resonance of this Christian symbol, however, derives from the universal symbolism of the Cosmic Tree, the immortal and life-giving pillar of the universe, to be found in ancient Indian, Chinese and Germanic myths as well as Genesis:

> The Byzantine liturgy sings even now, on the day of the exaltation of the Holy Cross, of 'the tree of life, planted on Calvary, the tree on which the king of ages wrought our salvation', the tree which 'springing from the depths of the earth, has risen to the centre of the earth' and 'sanctifies the Universe unto its limits'.[34]

Christian veneration of the 'sacred tree', in other words, makes the literal means of Christ's death a universal symbol of salvation, liberating the imagination to explore its multiple meanings.

As early as the apocryphal gospels the cross is presented as participating symbolically in the process of redemption. In the Gospel of Peter, for example, the soldiers guarding the tomb see three men emerging from the sepulchre followed by a cross, which pronounces a solemn 'Yea' to the voice from heaven which cries, 'Thou hast preached to them that sleep' (Peter 10:39–42). In the Gospel of Barnabas the cross even rises with Christ (12:1). One of the earliest poems to draw upon the inexhaustible reservoir of symbolic meaning to be found in the cross is the anonymous Old English 'Dream of the Rood', in which a gloriously bejewelled cross appears in a vision, shining before men and angels, a symbol of terrible beauty and triumphant suffering. Like the Word in the opening chapter of St John's gospel, this cross shines in the dark. It also wears armour, symbolic of Christ's combat against evil and death, and gold, symbolic of his kingship.

This poetic cross is fully personified, endowed with a number of human qualities, alternating between pride and humility in relating how it was hewn down by soldiers and driven through with 'dark nails'. It admits to shaking with fear when 'mankind's brave king' marched up, climbed upon it and embraced it. But it 'durst not bow to the ground . . . dared not lean from the true' or abandon its dreadful duty. Literally, of course, all this is absurd. How could a tree feel and say all these things? Symbolically, however, the poem explores the profound mystery of the cross, balancing Christ's human suffering, the 'deep wounds' and 'wide-mouthed hate dents' inflicted here upon the tree, against His transcendent triumph, the majesty with which he defeats his enemies.[35]

The rich symbolism of the cross could be traced throughout literature, from medieval lyrics lamenting the miseries of Mary's son[36] to Renaissance celebrations of his triumphant majesty. Chapman's 'Hymn to Our Saviour on the Cross', for example, sees the crucifixion as a victory in battle, the outstretched arms symbolic of world-encompassing triumph, the crown of thorns becoming a garland of laurels.[37] Donne, in 'The Cross', plays with the multiple meanings of that word, while in 'Good Friday, 1613. Riding Westward' he meditates on its paradoxes. Should he turn towards Calvary, he realizes,

> There I should see a sun, by rising set,
> And by that setting endless day beget;
> But that Christ on this Cross, did rise and fall,
> Sin had eternally benighted all.[38]

The puns here are far from trivial for they point towards the mystery at the heart of faith, that the dying and rising of the Son is the light and salvation of the world.

The English Hymnal for 'Passiontide', as might be expected, dwells on the symbolic significance of the cross. Isaac Watts's famous hymn, 'When I survey the wondrous Cross', paints a richly unrealistic (some would say over-rich, even rococo) picture of the crucifixion, in which Christ's 'dying crimson' is seen to 'spread' over his body 'like a robe', symbolizing at the same time the humanity which suffers and the godhead which is garbed in majesty, a paradox also expressed by the richness of the 'crown of thorns'. Significantly, the stanza in which this richly symbolic language occurs is marked with an asterisk in *The English Hymnal,* indicating that it can be 'conveniently omitted ... without doing violence to the context', while *Hymns Ancient and Modern* omits it altogether.[39] Is it the violence such poetry does to language which makes an over-protective committee discard it? Or perhaps they fail to find cognitive 'content' here, merely rich ornamentation. Other symbolic celebrations of the cross, however, have emerged unscathed, including J.M.Neale's 'one and only noble tree', which exceeds all others not only 'in foliage' and 'in blossom' but in the 'sweetest weight' it bears.[40]

In an altogether grimmer and more realistic context, the poets of two world wars continued to turn to the cross as a symbol of human suffering. Siegfried Sassoon insists that it is Christ who stands before him in the form of an English soldier shouldering planks, 'stiff in the glare' of rockets and flares while others invoke His name only to curse.[41] Wilfred Owen sees training troops as 'teaching Christ to lift his cross by numbers'[42] while Edith Sitwell begins her account of the 1940 night raids,

> Still falls the Rain –
> Dark as the world of man, black as our loss –
> Blind as the nineteen hundred and forty nails
> Upon the cross.[43]

Man, in other words, continues to cause Christ additional suffering and the cross continues to serve as a symbolic focus for meditation on suffering of all kinds. Its use can never be restricted to 'believers' only; its meanings evade strict control since they lie beyond the realm of words.

Sacraments, on the other hand, can be reserved for the initiated, using the *symbolon* or fragment of a divided tablet as a token or badge of belonging. The Latin term *sacramentum,* signifying a pledge of good faith or oath of allegiance, replaced the Greek term *mysterion* in the early church, representing a religious rite whose 'meaning' was spelt out by neo-platonic theologians as a visible sign of an outward and invisible reality. 'A word comes to an element', said Augustine, 'and a sacrament is there.' That word, in scholastic theology, became the all-important form, transforming the original material into a new substance.[44] It became only too easy for a 'literal' understanding to concentrate upon the product and to ignore the symbolic process:

> Seminary manuals and popular catechisms explained the meaning of the sacramental rites with minimal reference to their liturgical celebration. Baptism would be discussed in terms of the pouring of water to the accompaniment of a brief ritual formula, and the whole solemn ritual of prayers, singing, exorcism, renunciation of Satan, profession of faith, giving of salt, use of two different kinds of oil, lighted candles, baptismal robes and the rest were totally ignored.

These 'ceremonies', according to the Catechism of the Council of Trent, were not an 'essential' part of the sacrament and did not affect its 'validity'.[45]

Neglect of symbolism, however, is even more common among disbelievers in the sacraments, such as the Protestant Scripture Reader quoted by Newman whose account of the Benediction of the Blessed Sacrament saw no symbolic significance, only a priest entering 'with a long wand in his hand', lighting candles, taking 'a gold star' from 'a small cupboard on the altar', screwing it on a candlestick and placing it under a 'beehive' before bowing down before it. Newman concludes:

> I am not blaming this person for not knowing a Catholic rite, which he had no means of knowing, but for thinking that he knows it, when he does not know it, for coming into the chapel, with this coxcombical idea . . . in his head, that Popery is a piece of mummery, which any intelligent Protestant can see through.[46]

Reverence for the sacraments involves a reluctance to spell out precisely what they mean, a recognition of their mysterious nature.

A sacrament such as baptism combines archetypal symbolic resonance with particular historical reference. It employs water, 'the commonest archetypal image of the unconscious', which is both a threat of death through drowning and a promise of rebirth, regeneration, renewal, cleansing and refreshment. 'This wholesome water', writes Cyril of Jerusalem, 'has become for you both a tomb and a mother.' The Sarum rite of baptism refers to 'the spotless womb of the divine font'.[47] To these universal symbolic associations of death and rebirth, deluge and recovery, descent into abysmal depths and defeat of the sea-monster, Christianity brings its own specific biblical allusions. 'It was water', says Tertullian, 'that was first commanded to produce living creatures'; it was Noah who survived the flood to enjoy a new covenant with God; it was Moses who brought the Israelites safely through the Red Sea in which Pharaoh's armies were drowned; and it was Christ who broke the power of the dragon Behemoth through his baptism in the river Jordan, as He later harrowed hell.[48] Baptism, in other words, draws upon universal symbols but gives them fresh meanings.

Many of these symbolic meanings may be lost to a literalistic age though they are preserved in the liturgy of the Easter Vigil, when candles are lit from a large fire outside the church to celebrate the risen Christ as 'the light of the world', to 'inflame' believers with new hope of 'eternal light' and to purify their minds. The Easter proclamation celebrates the victory of life over death not only in the risen Christ but in the renewal of nature:

> Rejoice, O earth, in shining splendour,
> radiant in the brightness of your King!
> Christ has conquered! Glory fills you!
> Darkness vanishes for ever!

Christ's blood becomes not only the symbol of His atoning sacrifice, the ransom for men's sin, but the consecration of their homes in the new passover night. The liturgy of the word taps the rich vein of water-symbolism in the Old Testament, from the waters of Genesis and the liberation from the Red Sea in Exodus to Isaiah drawing water from the wells of salvation (12:2–6) and the psalms thirsting after God (41) and longing to be cleansed (50). The liturgy of baptism itself, of course, involves the congregation being sprinkled with blessed water as they renew their vows.[49] To enter into all this symbolism, to accept its power to redescribe the world, is indeed a form of rebirth.

Poetry, as we have seen, revels in such violation of the literal, the Romantic and Symbolist movements especially involving a rebellion against rationalism and positivism respectively. To see the natural world through the eyes of the imagination as symbolic of a deeper reality than that described by Newtonian physics is the essence of Romanticism:

> To see the world in a grain of sand:
> And a heaven in a wild flower,
> Hold infinity in the palm of your hand
> And eternity in an hour.[50]

For Blake there is no division between the natural object and the spiritual reality which it symbolizes. The two cannot be separated. He opposes wholeheartedly the dualism which attempts to divide body from soul and to impose reason and morality upon nature. He even makes Isaiah admit that the God of Israel is a product of 'Poetic Genius': 'I saw no God, nor heard any, in a finite organical perception; but my senses discovered the infinite in everything'.[51] The imagination, in other words, perceives God *in the world*.

For Wordsworth, too, God is divined by the poetic and prophetic imagination *in* the natural world. 'Tintern Abbey' celebrates the feelings evoked by a landscape which has been treasured in the memory, issuing not only in acts of kindness but in a 'sublime' mysticism,

> that blessed mood,
> In which the burthen of the mystery,
> In which the heavy and the weary weight
> Of all this unintelligible world
> Is lighten'd.

In such moments, he claims, we 'become a living soul' and 'see into the life of things'.[52] Wordsworth's vocabulary is 'naturally' religious, as Keble insisted in his *Lectures on Poetry*, because he saw nature as a sacrament, a symbolic revelation of God.[53]

The Prelude can certainly be read as a profoundly religious poem, tracing the effect of such epiphanic 'spots of time' upon Wordsworth's imagination, imbued as it was with a sense of the sacred, of the symbolic significance of the natural world in which all that 'he beheld respired with inward meaning'.[54] The cliff which rears up and appears to threaten the boat-stealing boy, for example, symbolizes the divine power of nature, which is also recognized at later moments,

> when the light of sense
> Goes out in flashes that have shown to us
> The invisible world,

forcing us to see that 'our home is with infinitude'. The torrents, rocks and crags of the Alpine landscape

> were all like workings of one mind, the features
> Of the same face, blossoms upon one tree;
> Characters of the great Apocalypse
> The types and symbols of Eternity,
> Of first, and last, and midst, and without end.[55]

Nature, in other words, is an organic part of God, a physical expression of his 'personality'.

When, in the final book of *The Prelude*, Wordsworth stands on the summit of Snowdon and hears the roar of waters ascending through a gap in the clouds to the moonlit 'starry heavens' above, he finds there another symbol of the sacred imagination,

> The perfect image of a mighty mind
> Of one that feeds upon infinity;
> That is exalted by an underpresence,
> The sense of God, or whatsoe'er is dim
> Or vast in its own being.

In the 1850 version this becomes the fully orthodox 'recognition of transcendent power'.[56] As Harold Bloom has said, 'what Wordsworth is giving us here is his vision of God', symbolized by and participating in the forms of the natural world.[57]

The Prelude claims that 'Poets, even as Prophets' are 'connected in a mighty scheme of truth' and 'enabled to perceive / Something unseen before'.[58] The Romantic conception of poets as prophets, as Stephen Prickett shows, can be traced back at least as far as Robert Lowth's *Lectures on the Sacred Poetry of the Hebrews* and translations of Isaiah,[59] works which had a profound influence not only on Coleridge but also on Hopkins, who looked back on Wordsworth as one of those rare spirits who had 'seen something' beyond the grasp of ordinary men. Wordsworth's 'Intimations of Immortality', according to Hopkins, gave human nature one of 'those shocks' the 'tremble' from which was still spreading.[60] His own view of nature was equally sacramental, not only giving glory to God for all the 'dappled things' he 'fathers forth' but seeing Him *in* his creatures:

> for Christ plays in ten thousand places
> Lovely in limbs and lovely in eyes not his
> To the Father through the features of men's faces.[61]

The Romantics, in other words, treat the natural world as a revelation, celebrating 'the translucence of the Eternal through and in the Temporal', which is how Coleridge defined a symbol, insisting that 'it always partakes of the Reality which it renders intelligible'.[62]

Thomas Carlyle, drawing upon the same German Romantic tradition as Coleridge, insists, through the ecstatic ravings of Professor Teufelsdröckh, that symbols are an 'embodiment and revelation of the Infinite'. The universe, in his eyes, becomes 'one vast Symbol of God'. Whereas 'extrinsic symbols', such as flags, are arbitrary and accidental, 'intrinsic symbols' contain within themselves the truth they reveal. Christ, accordingly, can be seen as 'our divinest Symbol ... a Symbol of quite perennial, infinite character'. Eventually, of course, like clothes, most symbols grow old and need to be replaced, the function of poets and prophets being to 'shape new Symbols, and bring New Fire from heaven'.[63] But Carlyle refuses to separate signifying symbol from signified concept, insisting on the paradox of 'Natural Supernaturalism', the sacredness of 'this fair universe' through every part of which 'the glory of a present God still beams'.[64] Here, as in Wordsworth, the Romantic concept of the symbol should not be dismissed as a form of secularization but recognized as a poetic form of natural theology.

If Romanticism can be seen as a reassertion of religious values in reaction to eighteenth-century rationalism, Symbolism could be called a rebellion against the limitations of nineteenth-century positivism and its denial of the realm of mystery. Just as the Romantics were concerned with 'Intimations of Immortality', feelings that often lay too deep for words, the Symbolists were preoccupied 'with half-uttered or half-glimpsed meaning' which words could only evoke or suggest.[65] Arthur Symons began his account of *The Symbolist Movement in Literature* with a quotation from Carlyle, going on to claim that art was returning in the Symbolists 'to the one pathway' which led 'through beautiful things to the eternal beauty'. Mystery was no longer to be feared as it had been by a materialistic age but celebrated in symbols 'by which the soul of things can be made visible'. He presented the Symbolist movement as 'a kind of religion, with all the duties and responsibilities of the sacred ritual'.[66] Many of the French poets whom Symons discussed did eventually return to the Catholic Church, where they found the architectural and ritual beauty, the mystery and the mysticism for which they were seeking. It is not, however, to them but to a major English religious poet who came under their spell, T.S. Eliot, that I want to turn in order to explore the poetic resonance of traditional Christian symbols.

Another major modern symbolist, W.B. Yeats, found it necessary to replace Christianity with his own esoteric set of symbols, 'expressing his obsessive uncertainties' and 'suggesting what discourse cannot handle'.[67] Yeats acknowledged that he was 'very religious' but, having been deprived of his childhood Christianity by the onslaught of positivist science, turned to poetry for 'a new religion, almost an infallible Church of poetic tradition'.[68] For Yeats, seeking to initiate an age of imagination and emotion to replace the cold age of criticism and science, the question was,

How can the arts overcome the slow dying of men's hearts that we call the progress of the world, and lay their hands upon men's heart-strings again without becoming the garment of religion as in the old times?[69]

His answer lay in a rich and sumptuous symbolism which was never allowed to settle into fixed 'reference' to 'eternal truths'.

For Eliot the question was different: how to restore and to regenerate the ancient symbols of the Christian tradition. Eliot's discovery of Symons and Symbolism in 1908, he was later to admit, changed the course of his poetic development.[70] He was to remain obsessed with words and their imprecision, the Word and its ineffability, and the Symbolist task (as Mallarmé had seen it) 'to purify the dialect of the tribe'. An early 'pre-Christian' poem such as 'Gerontion' explores the need for salvation, the search for significance and meaning in life, even in a dry, lifeless, loveless old man:

> Signs are taken for wonders. 'We would see a sign!'
> The word within a word, unable to speak a word,
> Swaddled with darkness. In the juvescence of the year
> Came Christ the tiger.[71]

The infant or wordless Christ, on whose mystery Lancelot Andrewes had dwelt, becomes in the poem a symbol whose full potential remains unrealized.[72] The old man, Gerontion, cannot take the necessary leap of faith towards the terrifying truth of the incarnation, symbolized here by a paradoxical combination of 'swaddled' infant and fierce Blakean tiger.

The Waste Land too remains uncommitted to the shattered and seemingly lifeless symbols of the Judaeo-Christian tradition:

> What are the roots that clutch, what branches grow
> Out of this stony rubbish? Son of Man,
> You cannot say, or guess, for you know only
> A heap of broken images, where the sun beats,
> And the dead tree gives no shelter, the cricket no relief,
> And the dry stone no sound of water.

The biblical allusions (Isaiah 32, Ecclesiastes 12 and Luke 23) find no resonance in a sterile land desperately in need of rejuvenation. The waters of the Thames are no longer refreshing and symbolic of procreation (as they are in Spenser's 'Prothalamion') but filthy and sterile. The sexuality of the modern world (the typist and the young man carbuncular) is similarly sterile, heading either for a Wagnerian apocalypse or an Augustinian purging by fire. The universal symbols of regeneration, of death by water bringing the resurrection of nature, seem too feeble to effect any change in a land barren of faith. For to the anthropologists on whom Eliot drew, 'good positivists' such as Sir James Fraser and his disciple Jessie Weston, 'the magico-religious life of archaic humanity' was only 'a mass of childish superstitions'.[73] The final section of the poem refuses therefore to allow the disciples to experience Christ's resurrection, providing no water for the waste land, only the thunderous commands of the Upanishads and a few fragments of literature. Language literally breaks down, shattering into small pieces with only a hint of possible redemption.[74]

Eliot's later poetry, however, rediscovers the meaning and vitality of traditional Christian symbols. The 'Four Quartets' still struggle with the problem of language:

> Words strain,
> Crack and sometimes break, under the burden,
> Under the tension, slip, slide, perish,
> Decay with imprecision, will not stay in place,
> Will not stay still.[75]

But the poem operates at the level of symbols and sound rather than semantics. Each quartet, for example, focuses on one of the four elements (air, earth, water and fire), exploring their symbolic significance in Christian terms. 'Little Gidding' in particular points to the possibility of redemption from the fire of sexual desire by the purging fire of the Holy Spirit, the war-time air-raids bringing an additional layer of meaning to this symbol:

> The dove descending breaks the air
> With flame of incandescent terror
> Of which the tongues declare
> The one discharge from sin and error.

The only hope, or else despair
Lies in the choice of pyre or pyre –
To be redeemed from fire by fire.[76]

The symbolic tongues of Pentecost celebrate the Word which transcends the limitations of ordinary language. It is only through symbols that Eliot is able to express his commitment to Christianity, the ruins of Little Gidding themselves becoming symbolic of the possibility of active communal faith, representing a place 'where prayer has been valid'. The words of Dame Julian combine with those of Dante and other Christian mystics to proclaim a shared historical reality in which these symbols have given meaning to life.

The primary symbols of the Christian faith, as will become clear in the final section of this chapter, continue to fascinate contemporary poets, however they may struggle to interpret them. It is the freedom such symbols provide to explore their plurality of meaning which makes them so much more rewarding for poetry than dogma. They should not, of course, be seen as an alternative to doctrine but as a richer, more emotive mode of exploring the mysteries at the heart of the Christian faith, a complementary mode of theological reflection.

PARADOX AND AMBIGUITY: THE MODERN DILEMMA

Paradox and ambiguity, like metaphor, symbolism and other poetic devices, are an admission of the limits of logic, an expression of the contradictory nature of experience. In literal 'steno-semantic' terms, Philip Wheelwright complains, 'there can be but two possible replies to the primary question of religious ontology [Is there a God?]: the reply of positivism and that of supernaturalism'.[77] Many modern Christians, however, feel the need to say with Simone Weil that there both is and is not a God. Their positive spiritual experience of love and acceptance makes them feel that there is an object corresponding to their experiences (what Newman called an 'Object correlative' to their inner needs and feelings), while their negative experiences of rejection, disappointment and despair compel them to doubt this assurance, to recognize that the concepts and categories which shape their mode of perception may have been distorted.[78]

Poetry, for Cleanth Brooks, was 'the language of paradox' with 'The Canonisation' providing the canonical example. For Donne's poem 'is a parody of Christian sainthood . . . of a sort that modern man, habituated as he is to an easy yes or no, can hardly understand'. Regarding rhetoric as a 'cheap trick' or 'mechanical exercise' Brooks's literal reader insists that this poem is about *either* love *or* sainthood, not *both*.[79] Even something as basic as a table is paradoxical, appearing solid and stable in spite of being composed of a mass of rapidly rotating particles, so that both descriptions are necessary to do justice to its seemingly contradictory properties.[80] Poetry, as Empson showed, positively celebrates such ambiguities, the multiple nuances of language being held together in the unity of a work of art.[81] Theology too, according to Ruth Page, should open itself to ambiguity, to 'change, diversity and polyvalence . . . the way in which anything may be interpreted in a variety of ways according to one's perspective'.[82]

Christian doctrines, however, are already full of paradox, of logically contradictory statements. Christ, for example, in the Chalcedonian definition, is *both* fully man and fully God, a paradox which imposes limits upon orthodoxy and also stretches the limits of language. The fathers rejoiced in such paradoxes, none more than Augustine, balancing providential grace against human free will and expressing the paradox of the fortunate fall. Athanasius speaks of the incarnation in language riddled with metaphor, symbol and paradox.[83] So too does Tertullian, countering Marcion's heretical insistence on the impossibility of God becoming fully man with a celebration of its absurdity: just because it is absurd it is to be believed . . . it is certain because it is impossible'.[84] These paradoxes are not empty signs of the inexpressible (it would be less impressive, for example, to say that 'Ultimate Reality is both a tomato and a banana'). Nor are they merely ornamental, giving pith and force to a paraphrasable claim. Christians believe that they are 'forced by the "facts" to say that God is Three in One'.[85]

Faced with these apparent contradictions medieval scholastic theology, in the eyes of an urbane literary humanist such as Erasmus, made itself ridiculous by attempting to clarify the mystery of the incarnation, asking totally inappropriate questions:

> Could God have taken on the form of a woman, a devil, a donkey, a gourd or a flintstone? If so, how could a gourd have preached sermons, performed miracles, and been nailed to the cross?

Erasmus, in contrast, celebrates the folly of the cross, the paradox that Christ, 'the wisdom of the Father, was made something of a fool ... to help the folly of mankind', being 'made sin so that he could redeem sinners'.[86] Erasmus paradoxically praises folly, beginning with the literal sense of the term and proceeding to unpack its ambiguities, to explore ways in which what appears foolish to the worldly-wise is, in fact, true wisdom.

Paradox assumes a more urgent tone in less equable temperaments than Erasmus. Luther, for example, conscious of the depth of human sin, pushes the paradox of the incarnation to extremes, making Christ 'the greatest transgressor, murderer, adulterer, thief, rebel, blasphemer &c that ever was or could be in all the world'.[87] Pascal, Newman and Kierkegaard, I want to argue, are profoundly paradoxical theologians because they recognize the deeply contradictory nature of a faith which roots its triumph and its glory in suffering and sin. Such a faith, the only 'explanation' to be found for an ambiguous and otherwise incomprehensible world, is wrestled with by poets of all periods, from Dante through Milton and Cowper to the present day. It is a particular preoccupation of contemporary poets such as Geoffrey Hill and R. S. Thomas, with whom this chapter will end.

It was to Pascal that T. S. Eliot turned for an example of paradoxical religious thought, the attempt as in a poem to hold apparent contradictions in profound tension and unity:

> I can think of no Christian writer, not Newman even, more to be commended than Pascal to those who doubt, but who have the mind to conceive, and the sensibility to feel, the disorder, the futility, the meaninglessness, the mystery of life and

suffering, and who can only find peace through a satisfaction of the whole being.[88]

The *Pensées* themselves may not be noted for their unity, composed as they are of fragments which Pascal was in the process of classifying when he died. They were, apparently, to have been marshalled into systematic arguments against scepticism in his intended *Apology for the Christian Religion*. They are certainly paradoxical, presenting Christianity as the 'answer' to man's mixed condition, his combination of misery and greatness. For the world itself struck Pascal as ambiguous:

> Nature offers me nothing that does not beget doubt and anxiety. If I saw there nothing to indicate a Divinity, I would draw a negative conclusion; if I saw everywhere the marks of a Creator, I would repose undisturbed in faith. But seeing too much to deny and too little to assure me, I am in a pitiful state.[89]

The world proclaims only 'the presence of a God who hides himself', Isaiah's *Deus absconditus*.[90]

Man himself, according to Pascal, is also ridden with contradictions:

> He wants to be great, but sees that he is small; he wants to be happy, but sees that he is miserable; he wants to be perfect, but sees that he is full of imperfections; he wants to be the object of love and esteem among men, but sees that his faults deserve only their hatred and contempt.[91]

A whole section of the *Pensées* is devoted to enumerating man's 'Misery' while another extols his 'Greatness'. It transpires, however, in the section called 'Contrareities', that his greatness lies mainly in his recognition that he is wretched.[92] Christianity alone, according to Pascal, offers a satisfactory 'explanation' of these contradictions in terms of the fall and the redemption, enabling man to know what a paradox he is.[93]

Newman, in his *Apologia*, follows a similar path, finding that the external world fails to confirm his inner certainty of God. He draws a dismal picture of the world, full of 'alienation', 'aimless courses' and 'random achievements'. His horror reaches a crescendo when he considers the paradox of humanity,

> the greatness and littleness of man, his far-reaching aims, his short duration, the curtain hung over his futurity, the disappointments of life, the defeat of good, the success of evil, physical pain, mental anguish, the prevalence and intensity of sin, the pervading idolatries, the corruptions, the dreary hopeless irreligion . . . all this is a vision to dizzy and appal; and inflicts upon the mind a sense of a profound mystery, which is absolutely beyond human solution.[94]

What is beyond man, however, is not beyond God, and so Newman turns to revelation, with its doctrine of original sin, and an infallible Church as the guardian of that revelation. His most famous poem encapsulates his paradoxical view of providential grace working within a fallen world as a 'kindly light amid the encircling gloom'.[95]

But the most ardent preacher of the paradoxes of Christianity, with an even more tortured temperament and a fully developed Protestant sense of sin, was Søren Kierkegaard, who has been called 'the poet of religion'.[96] Resisting all attempts to rationalize Christianity, Kierkegaard revels in its absurdity. His 'dialectical theology' stresses the distance between a transcendent God and His finite creatures, the gap between eternity and time, holiness and love, religion and morality, divine grace and human responsibility. It is a gap only bridged by the supreme paradox of the incarnation, captured in Luther's stark contradiction, 'This Man is God.' Kierkegaard hammers home the scandal of the cross to believers dulled by familiarity to its outrageous paradoxes. He presents Abraham's preparedness to sacrifice *his* son as a paradigm of faith responding in *Fear and Trembling* to a God who demands what is absurd and irrational. Christianity, for Kierkegaard, is not a coherent philosophy of life; it hangs upon a paradox which the finite mind cannot hope to comprehend.

It is not merely in the modern period, of course, not only as a result of existential anguish or structuralist exegesis, that poets have fed upon the paradoxes and ambiguities of the Christian faith. Dante's famous letter to Can Grande, for example, spells out the 'polysemous' quality of the *Divina Commedia*, which required interpretation at each of the four levels common to biblical exegesis of the time: literal, allegorical, moral and anagogical. 'Polysemous' he glosses as 'of more senses than one' for 'it is one sense which we get through the letter, and another which we get through the thing the letter signifies'.[97] The end of the *Purgatorio*, as Stephen Prickett has shown, dramatizes the difference between divine revelation and the highest truth to which reason can attain. The poet leaves Virgil in triumph, crowned and mitred, invested, that is, with the symbols of worldly and ecclesiastical power, having reached the highest step of human understanding.[98] Confronted, however, by his beloved Beatrice in the Masque of Revelation, he trembles with fear, turning to his mentor as a child to its mother only to discover that Virgil has disappeared. Beatrice rebukes him for his unrestrained tears: does he not realize that in Paradise man is supposed to be happy?[99] She shames and shocks him into a recognition of the difference between man and God, the distance between the finite and the infinite. The glimpse that Dante catches of the mystery of the incarnation is oblique, indirect and ambiguous: the symbolic griffin, whose twofold nature is reflected in Beatrice's eyes, in which 'even like the sun in the mirror the two-fold beast shone ... now with the one, now with the other nature'.[100]

The paradoxical and ambiguous nature of Christianity overcomes all efforts to iron it out. Milton, for example, insists that 'No passage of Scripture is to be interpreted in more than one sense'.[101] But *Paradise Lost*, precisely because it attempts to spell out divine motivation, teeters on the brink of a thousand heresies. His image of deity, it has been claimed, is

no less marvellous than that of the Divina Commedia. Milton's God is surprising enough to be a universal father figure, enigmatic enough to be the subject of interminable scholastic debates, sublime enough to be awe-inspiring; remote enough from our wishes to be partly true. And certainly there is no divine image in English literature half so interesting.[102]

But not only does Milton separate the Father from the Son; he seems at some points even to sympathize with Satan's rebellion against divine authority, leaving it open for Blake to claim that he 'wrote in fetters when he wrote of angels and God, and at liberty when of devils and Hell . . . because he was a true poet, and of the Devil's party without knowing it'.[103] Far from ironing out ambiguity Milton opens up the tensions and difficulties of the Christian faith.[104]

Many of the most famous English hymns hinge upon paradox. It is not simply, as Robert Lowell suggests, that their seemingly cheerful surface sometimes conceals a morbid and gloomy view of life:

> stiff quatrains shovelled out four-square
> they sing of peace, and preach despair.[105]

Faith, in Marvell's words, is itself a paradox 'begotten by Despair / upon impossibility'.[106] For a tortured soul such as William Cowper, Christ is the only light in darkness, the only remedy for sin, bringing a joy which only 'sometimes . . . surprises / The Christian while he sings'. Cowper longs

> for a closer walk with God
> A calm and heavenly frame.

But he does *not* possess it. The 'blessedness' he knew when he first 'saw the Lord', the 'peaceful hours' he 'once enjoyed', have vanished, leaving 'an aching void / The world can never fill'. He pleads therefore for the dove to return, hating the sins that first drove it away. Only *then* shall he recapture the calm faith that *was* his.[107] The suicidal poet of Olney, encouraged by constant Calvinist introspection, represents an extreme example of the paradox of faith, which finds joy and salvation in the agony and degradation of the cross.

This paradox is perhaps most perfectly captured in Hopkins' celebration of 'The Windhover', which is at its most beautiful when it submits to the wind, hanging on 'the rein of a wimpling wing / In his ecstasy', symbolizing the glory Christ achieves in abandoning divine power to embrace the suffering of the cross:

Brute beauty and valour and act, oh air, pride, plume, here
Buckle; AND the fire that breaks from thee then, a billion
Times told lovelier, more dangerous, oh my chevalier.[108]

'Buckle' here, as Empson explained, has two senses: the
confident arming of Christ the redeeming knight and also the
physical denting of the crucified body.[109] The ambiguity of the
word expresses the paradox of the cross, a symbol *both* of
terrible suffering *and* of triumph. Other natural processes
described in the poem symbolize the same paradox: the soil is
made to 'shine' when it is ploughed and embers 'gash
gold-vermilion' when they fall and 'gall themselves'. Christ's
gashes, the wounds he willingly endures, are his greatest
glory.

Contemporary poets struggle to accept this paradox. That
the world is fallen and full of suffering they see but that
Christ's suffering can set this right, can reconcile man and
God, bringing redemption and atonement, is more difficult to
believe. Ted Hughes, for example, finds a less beautiful bird
than does Hopkins to symbolize the struggle for survival in a
harsh modern world. *Crow* retells the biblical myths of
creation, fall and redemption:

> Man's and woman's bodies lay without souls,
> Dully gaping, foolishly staring, inert
> On the flowers of Eden.
> God pondered.
>
> The problem was so great, it dragged him asleep.
>
> Crow laughed.
> He bit the Worm, God's only son,
> Into two writhing halves.
> He stuffed into man the tail half
> With the wounded end hanging out.

The head half he stuffs into woman, from where it continues to
peer out through her eyes, calling to be reunited with its other
half in sexual union. God goes on sleeping; Crow goes on
laughing. God then tries to teach Crow to say the word 'Love',
but Crow is so disgusted at what he sees in the world,

especially human sexuality, that he retches and flies off, leaving man and woman fighting on the grass with God struggling in vain to part them.[110] When God, in disgust with man, turns to heaven, and man, in disgust with God, turns to Eve for consolation, Crow tries to reconcile them:

> Crow nailed them together
> Nailing Heaven and earth together –
>
> So man cried, but with God's voice.
> And God bled, but with man's blood.
>
> Then heaven and earth creaked at the joint
> Which became gangrenous and stank –
> A horror beyond redemption.[111]

The attempt to 'join' man and God in the incarnation fails, in Hughes's eyes, to 'redeem' the horrors of the world.

Even 'Christian' poets such as Geoffrey Hill find it difficult to understand or to accept the concept of the atonement. He is 'staggered' by the 'burden' of the cross, like Thomas in 'Canticle for Good Friday', watching the wood spit 'each drop / Of deliberate blood'.[112] In 'Lachrimae' it is easier to be 'at one' with 'eternal loss' than with eternal salvation, to sympathize with a suffering rather than a triumphant Christ:

> Crucified Lord, you swim upon your cross
> and never move. Sometimes in dreams of hell
> the body moves but moves to no avail
> and is at one with that eternal loss.
>
> You are the castaway of drowned remorse,
> You are the world's atonement on the hill.[113]

Hill himself admits that his poetry struggles with 'the sense of *not* being able to grasp true religious experience'.[114] He describes the act of writing itself, 'the technical perfecting of a poem', as 'an act of atonement, in the radical etymological sense – an act of at-one-ment, a setting at one, a bringing into concord, a reconciling, a uniting in harmony'.[115] But the hyphens, as Christopher Ricks has argued, reveal the difference between the theological and the secular sense of the word, representing Hill's 'dis-ease' with the concept.[116] Hill is clearly not at ease or at one with the theological terms which he nevertheless chooses to employ.

R. S. Thomas also struggles to relate theological concepts, even the word 'God', to human experience. He cannot, for example, disentangle Kierkegaard's theology from his personal agonies, the cursing of God which his father could never forget. Young Søren had to live

> with the deed's terrible lightning
> About him, as though a bone
> Had broken in the adored body
> Of his God.

Then came his rejection of his fiancée and the attacks of the press:

> Wounded, he crawled
> To the monastery of his chaste thought
> To offer up his crumpled amen.[117]

When Thomas himself kneels in prayer, as 'In A Country Church', he receives 'no word' but the sound of the wind and 'the dry whisper of unseen wings / Bats not angels, in the high roof'. He is vouchsafed only a symbolic vision of a 'blazing' crown of thorns and a tree 'Golden with fruit of man's body'.[118] Sometimes, as 'In Church', there is only silence:

> There is no other sound
> In the darkness but the sound of a man
> Breathing, testing his faith
> On emptiness, nailing his questions
> One by one to an untenanted cross.[119]

The attempt to fix meaning upon the cross, in terms of answers rather than questions, concepts rather than symbols, is something Thomas distrusts.

For God is necessarily mysterious, only to be described indirectly. The sections of *The Penguin Book of Religious*

Verse, which Thomas edited, begin with the orthodox term 'God' but go on to explore other modes of representing ultimate reality: 'Self', 'Nothing', 'It' and 'All'.[120] His own preference seems to be for the 'Via Negativa', which defines God as 'that great absence', the 'silence within'. He explores 'The Gap' between language and ultimate reality, 'the blank still by his name' in the dictionary, a sign composed of 'the darkness that is a god's blood'.[121] He refuses to accept the conventional metaphors for relationship with God: 'Face to face', 'side by side', or 'near you'. He will continue to use the 'name' but 'seldomer' and more modestly than others,

> leaning far out
> over an immense depth, letting
> your name go and waiting
> somewhere between faith and doubt
> for the echo of its arrival.[122]

The word, in other words, points to a 'real' object but only indirectly and at a great distance.

Thomas's most recent volume, *Experimenting with an Amen*, seems even less confident that God can be 'contacted' as by telephone, however much we 'experiment / with the code'.[123] He flings prayer 'like gravel' at the sky's window, hoping to attract His attention. He even claims once to have detected the movement of a curtain at the window.[124] But the self-portrait that he gives in 'A Life' portrays in unflattering terms his continuing doubts about a God he is 'too pusillanimous to deny' and whom he can only affirm in poetry.[125] The paradoxes and ambiguities of Christianity are too complex to be sustained by straightforward, literal language. It requires a poetic Joshua, blowing his trumpet against the walls of literalism, to resist 'the aggression of fact'.[126]

CHAPTER 5

Theology and Drama: Acts of Faith and Doubt

LITURGICAL DRAMA: FROM THE MASS TO THE MYSTERY PLAYS

One of the most obvious ways in which faith is enacted or produced, in the theatrical sense, is liturgy. For it is in performing acts of worship that believers give tangible expression to their faith. It is in liturgy, therefore, that denominational differences are most clearly observable. And yet liturgy, in the Western churches at least, has always been a neglected area of theology, hardly a matter of theology at all but of ecclesiastical history, focusing on practical questions about the conduct of worship. Liturgical theology as such, 'the elucidation of the meaning of worship', the attempt to spell out 'the deep and ultimate logic of the Church's *lex orandi*', is a relatively recent development, gaining much of its impetus from the Eastern Orthodox churches.[1]

Liturgical forms, then, like literary forms, are theologically significant. It matters, for example, whether the priest saying mass adopts the 'eastward position', facing away from the people, because it signifies a totally different understanding of God:

> It symbolises the whole way of thinking in which God is seen as a projection 'out there' to whom we turn from the world. By contrast, the 'westward position' in which the president surrounded by his assistants faces the people across the table, focuses attention upon a point in the middle, as the Christ stands among his own as the breaker of bread.[2]

It also makes a significant difference, of course, to call the altar a table, and to place it more centrally in the church. 'The new stagecraft' of recent liturgical reform involves radical theological changes not only in the understanding of God but in a shift of emphasis from the personal to the communal and a lessening of the division between sacred and secular.[3]

There are, of course, many other modes of liturgical theology. In the regulation of worship for the day and for the year, a whole theology of time is encoded. The day is divided into liturgical 'hours' and the year into theological 'feasts'. Again, the division is not so much between 'sacred' and 'profane' but old and new: the whole of time, the whole world, is 'renewed' in 'the eschatological consciousness of the Church'.[4] It is a vision of life to which Lawrence showed himself surprisingly sympathetic, describing how it gave structure to the lives of the Brangwens:

> So the children lived the year of Christianity, the epic of the soul of mankind. Year by year the inner, unknown drama went on in them, framework hearts were born and came to fullness, suffered on the cross, gave up the ghost, and rose again to unnumbered days, untired, having at least this rhythm of eternity in a ragged, inconsequential life.[5]

Tolstoy too presents liturgy as transforming life, his Jerusalem pilgrim in *The Two Old Men* seeing a labourer in the fields lit up by the sun in the new light of the easter candles.[6]

Liturgy, then, is rooted in daily life, enacting the revelation that is perceived in Christ, the human 'icon' of the divine (Col. 3:10). The Christian community, in Pauline theology, is 'modelled' anew 'on the heavenly man', becoming God's new temple (I Cor. 15:49; 3:16–17). The sacraments can be seen in the light of this theology to celebrate and to enact in symbolic and dramatic forms our participation in the body of Christ:

> Baptism, with confirmation, expresses our participation in Christ's setting out upon his mission at the descent of the Spirit in the Jordan baptism; penance and the anointing of the sick express our participation in Christ's ministry of forgiveness and healing; order and the eucharist our participation in the meals Christ has with his disciples; marriage our participation in Christ's resurrection union with his people.[7]

It is important that these sacraments are fully enacted for they require the participation of the whole person. Liturgy cannot and should not, Moltmann warns, be reduced to 'doctrinal and moral instruction'. These 'liberating feasts' represent (and re-present) our Christian freedom through symbolic drama.[8]

Drama and ceremony are not therefore 'optional extras' in a liturgy dominated by language; they are 'an integral part of Christian ritual'.[9] Even the new eucharistic rite of *The Alternative Service Book*, according to its authors, can 'sustain liturgical drama of a high order'.[10] The documents of the Second Vatican Council, which made the historic switch from Latin to the vernacular, also stress the importance of music and sacred art in the celebration of the new rites, which 'should be distinguished by noble simplicity ... within the people's powers of comprehension', aiming at 'noble beauty rather than sumptuous display'.[11] The dramatic reforms of the liturgy which recent years have seen are not, therefore, intended to reduce their dramatic quality, whatever their actual effect.

The development of liturgy into elaborate ceremonial, the transformation of the simple meals of the early church into the solemn mass of the High Middle Ages, is often presented as a victory of form over content. Since the Latin liturgy of the word was not understood by the laity, it has been argued,

> The rite which had originally been a service of Bible reading and preaching was now transformed into a magnificent, if somewhat meaningless, pageant. Played out on the splendid stage of the larger Gothic church, lighted from jewelled windows of stained glass, clothed in the sumptuous late-medieval vestments, with the flames of the candles flickering and the sweet-scented smoke of the incense ascending, it presented a complex of light and colour and movement, which engaged the heart, if not the head, of the medieval Christian.[12]

It is by no means certain, however, that the medieval Christian was so dismembered or his pageants so meaningless. The dramatic moments of the liturgy, such as the elevation of the host at the moment of consecration, which became the climax of the mass in the thirteenth century, highlighted by the ringing of bells and lighting of torches, can be related directly to theological developments, in this case the Western acceptance of the doctrine of transubstantiation, defined at the Fourth Lateran Council in 1215.[13]

All drama, it has been argued along anthropological lines, is a development from ritual, ancient Greek sacrificial and fertility rites being the source of tragedy and comedy respectively.[14] While this remains a matter of speculation, however, the recognition of dramatic elements in the liturgy of the Middle Ages and the development of integral plays from those elements can be fully documented. It is difficult sometimes to draw the line between liturgy and drama, and it would probably be wrong (and certainly unfashionable) to insist on a Darwinian process of organic evolution from one to the other. But it is clear that participants in the liturgy of the Middle Ages recognized the symbolic significance of their actions and that much of the drama of the period drew deeply from the liturgy. In examining both these phenomena more closely I want to draw attention yet again to the theological significance of liturgical drama.

Evidence of theological meaning being 'read into' the drama of the liturgy survives in many allegorical interpretations of the mass. A Syriac homily from as early as the fifth century dwells on the dramatic symbolism of the offertory procession, in which Jesus 'is being led to death on our account', the deacons who set the paten and cup on the altar and cover them being seen to 'typify His burial'. They do not, the homilist hastens to add, represent the Jews but the watching angels, while the celebrant 'bears in himself the image of our Lord' and the other priests in the sanctuary the apostles at the sepulchre.[15] None of these commonplace allegorical readings of the mass, it should be realized, goes so far as to suggest that the priest impersonates Christ:

> the officiant does not pretend to be Christ. He does not act the part of Christ but *ex parte Christi*, on behalf of Christ, who is conceived as supernaturally present without surrendering divine identity to his minister. The priest, following the text, commemorates Christ, recalls his words in indirect discourse, and, in doing so, is asked by the rubrics to simulate the posture narrated in the words – to raise his eyes towards heaven as he

breaks the bread and lifts the cup. For a priest suddenly to presume that he was Christ, to impersonate Christ, would be imposture.[16]

The difference between liturgy and 'realistic' drama is clear on this point at least, since the latter demands the identification of actor and role. Not all drama, however, is 'realistic', the musical *Godspell* positively discouraging such identification, calling the leading figure 'Stephen-Christ' and distributing the other roles at random among the disciple-clowns. So even this distinction is not as clear as it might seem.

The most sustained surviving interpretation of the dramatic symbolism of the mass comes from the ninth-century Bishop of Metz, Amalarius, and his followers, whose work seems 'closer to literary criticism than to theology' in the scholastic sense.[17] Like some modern literary critics Amalarius was accused of misleading the laity. He was also denounced as a heretic and blamed for the rise in 'theatrical mannerisms' and 'histrionic gestures' among the clergy.[18] His analysis of the mass manages to squeeze every ounce of potential significance from the tiniest rubric but also brings out very clearly the dramatic elements in the liturgy: role-play, plot-structure, shifts in mood, staging and even choreography.

Amalarius recognizes that the roles of the participants in the mass are fluid:

At times the celebrant is the High Priest of the Temple sacrificing the holocaust on the Day of Atonement, at other times he is Christ, and at one point he is Nicodemus assisting Joseph of Arimathea at the entombment. The congregation can be the Hebrews listening to the prophecies of the Messiah, the crowd witnessing the Crucifixion, the Gentiles to whom the Word was given after it had been rejected by the Hebrews, and the elect mystically incorporated into the body of Christ.

On Palm Sunday they carry palms and become the crowds welcoming Jesus into Jerusalem while at Christmas they become the shepherds of Bethlehem (a role they regularly assume during the Gloria). Following the communion they become the disciples receiving the blessing of Christ before the

ascension.[19] Sometimes they are even allowed to be themselves. None of these roles, of course, is fixed; they are merely
potential meanings which an imaginative mind can (and did)
find in the mass.

Amalarius also analyses the 'plot' of the mass from the
framing introit ceremonies, which are eschatological in
emphasis, through the liturgy of the word, the offertory, the
canon and the consecration (which is not for him the climax) to
the communion, in which the risen Christ is shared by His
people. He observes shifts of mood, for instance from the
expectant hope of the introit to penitential sorrow in the Kyrie
and back again to exultant triumph in the Gloria. He is alert to
the significance of the dual stage on which the dramatic action
proceeds, the presbyterium being 'the plane of eternity, from
which the ascended Christ looks down on suffering humanity'
and the altar being the 'stage of history upon which, amid the
mobs of Jerusalem and the sorrowing disciples, the incarnate
Christ is crucified and dies'. The two planes 'intersect at the
moment of the sacrifice'.[20] He is even aware of the 'choreography' of the mass, the deployment of deacons and celebrants
around the altar. When the subdeacons, for example, wait to
receive Christ's body at the altar they are seen as the three
Marys visiting the sepulchre, to be told by the angel that he is
risen.[21] This, of course, was the first element of the liturgy to
be developed into a fully-fledged play.

The claim that 'religious ritual *was* the drama of the early
Middle Ages',[22] that the Church provided a stage, performers,
an audience and the rudiments of mimetic action (if not
complete impersonation), does not depend upon the imagination of Amalarius, influential though he was in the
medieval perception of dramatic symbolism in the liturgy. An
eleventh-century disciple, Honorius of Autun, for instance,
called the priest 'our tragedian' who 'represents . . . the
struggle of Christ' in 'the theatre of the church'. Even his
silence is eloquent, since it

> signifies Christ as a lamb without voice being led to the
> sacrifice. By the extension of his hands he delineates the
> stretching out of Christ on the cross. By the singing of the
> preface he expresses the cry of Christ hanging on the cross.[23]

Amalarius and his disciples are important because they spell out what is implicit in the dramatic development of medieval liturgy, articulating the theological competence underlying contemporary liturgical performance.

Apart from the mass itself, it was the Easter liturgy which seems to have lent itself to the most dramatic developments. The Eastern ceremonies of the adoration, deposition and elevation of the cross, along with the visit to the sepulchre, 'highly infused' as they are 'with devotional and dramatic feeling', were adopted by Rome in the seventh century and soon became widespread.[24] The *Regularis Concordia*, for example, a tenth-century code compiled at Winchester for English Benedictine monasteries, gives a clear indication of their dramatic power. The 'Adoration of the Cross' it describes begins with two deacons holding the cross upright between them and singing Christ's reproach, 'Popule meus, quid feci tibi?' ('My people, what have I done to you?'). The cross is then laid on a small cushion before being unveiled and adored, the abbot prostrating himself before it and reciting the penitential psalms 'cum magno cordis suspirio' ('with deep heartfelt sighs').[25] It is perhaps stretching the term to call these 'stage directions' since they are also a plea for sincerity, but the rudiments of drama are certainly here.

'The Interment of the Cross in the Sepulchre' has even more explicit directions about scenery and props. A part of the altar should contain 'a likeness of the sepulchre' ('quaedam assimilatio sepulchri') with a curtain stretched around it behind which the cross is laid, having been 'enfolded in a linen cloth'. It is then guarded throughout the night of the vigil before being visited by the three Marys and raised in triumph on Easter morning.[26] Some versions of these rites adore, bury, visit and raise the host rather than the cross. The whole ritual, in fact, seems to have developed from the Good Friday reservation of the sacrament in a special vessel understood to symbolize Christ's tomb.[27]

Dramatic variations on this Easter theme include an enactment of the Harrowing of Hell, to precede the elevation of the host, recorded in a fourteenth-century Benedictine ordinal from Barking. The abbess with her whole convent gathered in a side-chapel with the doors closed, representing ('figurantes') the souls of the patriarchs waiting in Limbo for Christ's liberation. A priest then approached, the vicar of Christ ('repraesentabit personam Christi'), and sang the antiphon 'Tollite portas' (Lift up your gates) three times, knocking each time upon the door with his Resurrection Cross. The door then opened to allow the whole convent to stream out of the chapel carrying palms and lighted candles, proceeding to the sepulchre from which the host was raised, to be displayed in a monstrance while the congregation would sing 'Christe resurgens' (O rising Christ). The procession then made its way to the altar 'in the manner in which Christ preceded the disciples after the Resurrection into Galilee'.[28]

It seems to have been a splendid ceremony, full of theologically significant dramatic symbolism, in spite of the fact that no one appears to have been bold enough to play the part of the devil and ask, 'Who is this king of glory?' A similar ceremony for the consecration of churches, from ninth-century Metz, in which the bishop circled the building three times, knocking each time on the portal and issuing Christ's command, went even further in requiring an answer from 'one within' who then had to exit 'as if taking flight' on the bishop's triumphal entrance.[29] They may have been bolder in Metz than in Barking but both examples illustrate how closely liturgical symbolism could approach dramatic impersonation.

Liturgical drama as such is normally considered to have begun with the evolution of an integral play about the visit to the sepulchre, called the 'Quem quaeritis' after the opening question addressed by the angel at the tomb to the three Marys, 'Whom do you seek in the sepulchre?' These embryonic plays or tropes are supposed to have begun with musical embellishments of the Easter services. But antiphonal chanting soon developed into dramatic dialogue and ceremonial procession into more complicated role-play. These tropes, in the tenth century at least, remained very much a part of the liturgy, with the church as 'stage', clerical performers and ecclesiastical costumes and props (a thurible, for instance, to suggest the spices carried by the Marys).[30] But the *Regularis Concordia* is very clear about the mimetic, representational function of its 'Visit to the Sepulchre', in which one of the brethren sits quietly at 'the place of the sepulchre . . . holding a palm in his hand' while three others, 'vested in copes' and 'bearing in their hands thuribles with incense', move towards the sepulchre 'haltingly, in the manner of seeking for something'. The rubric continues: 'These things are done in imitation [ad imitationem] of the angel seated on the tomb and the women coming with spices to anoint the body of Jesus.' Having asked his question and delivered his message, the angel lifts the veil of the sepulchre to reveal nothing but 'the shroud in which the cross had been wrapped', which they take up and spread out before the clergy 'as if demonstrating that the Lord has risen'.[31] This short scene is genuinely dramatic because the devices of mimetic action, impersonation, gesture, dialogue and music combine to produce an overall meaning which is more than the sum of its separate parts.

The Easter plays seem to have changed much less than the other dramatic forms of the Middle Ages, presumably because of their centrality to the Christian message. What accretions there were brought material mainly from the gospels. An Italian version of the visitation, for example, introduced Peter and John racing to the sepulchre while a sepulchre-play from Fleury of the late twelfth century included an impressively dramatic encounter between 'one in the likeness of a gardener' who refuses to let Mary Magdalen touch him. The rubric reads, 'let him draw himself back . . . as if avoiding her touch.' The same actor reappears at the climax of the play in splendidly symbolic ecclesiastical attire, including a white dalmatic and infula, a 'costly phylacterium' on his head, a cross in his right hand and a gold garment in his left, representing the risen Christ in all his unquestioned glory.[32] The same play, in other words, moves swiftly from psychological realism to bold symbolism.

There is a 'narrative inconsistency' in the portrayal of Mary Magdalen in many of these plays, illustrating the fact that their interest centres on liturgical worship of Christ rather than characterization for its own sake. She is presented mourning in the garden *after* the angel has told her and the other Marys of the resurrection. It is an inconsistency brought about by the conflation of different gospel accounts, an inconsistency which persists in some of the later mystery cycles, showing the 'determining power of their liturgical model'.[33] Some vernacular plays, however, reveal a genuine interest in her conversion. The early-thirteenth-century Bene-diktbeuern Passion Play, for example, develops her part to embrace scenes from her early life, including a famous episode in which she buys cosmetics from a merchant 'to entice young men', whom she addresses like a medieval Marlene Dietrich, offering an alternative 'vision of divine glory':

> Seht mich an,
> jungen mann
> Lat mich eu gevallen.
>
> (Hey, look at me
> You young men.
> Let me give you pleasure).

When she falls asleep an angel appears, singing of Jesus and the new life he brings. Her song about the pleasures of the world is interspersed with the angelic song of redemption until she repents, replaces her 'worldly attire' with a 'black mantle' and pours her cosmetics over Christ's feet.[34] The passage from Luke (7:38), traditionally associated with Mary Magdalen, has been expanded into a powerful dramatization of the conflicting values of predatory desire and self-giving love.

The late medieval mystery cycles, of course, are full of such psychological 'realism'. Many of the most famous examples are comic. The Wakefield Master, for example, introduces a sub-plot about sheep-stealing into his well-known 'Second Shepherd's Play', makes Cain invite Abel to kiss his arse before telling God that he is 'out of hys wit' and portrays Noah's wife as a nagging shrew.[35] Joseph has a tough time in all the cycles, particularly in 'The Trial of Joseph and Mary' in the *Ludus Coventriae*, a play denounced by one modern critic for mixing deep reverence with biting satire and presenting Mary's plight 'in the tone of a tragical farce of the servant-girl who has slipped up'.[36] In fact, the audience are carefully manipulated by the dramatist, who makes them sympathize more and more with the wronged maiden as even her supporters in the play threaten to desert her. Where they do laugh at the sexual innuendoes they are made to feel as guilty as the characters who are forced eventually to beg her forgiveness.[37]

This embracing of both farcical and potentially tragic elements within a plot structure which is fundamentally comic, resolving all the difficulties in a triumphant ending, is not, of course, limited to medieval drama. Auden too, in his account of 'The Temptation of St Joseph' in his Christmas Oratorio, *For the Time Being*, has his chorus make fun of the suspicious husband:

> Joseph, have you heard
> What Mary says occurred;
> Yes, it may be so.
> Is it likely? No.[38]

Auden, like the medieval dramatists he translated, was only too aware how unlikely the Virgin Birth was (and is). It requires faith to be able to see the bizarre and even shameful elements of life within an overall comic vision.

It certainly required a faith as strong as that of the Middle Ages to shatter, as in the gospels, the classical demands of literary decorum, to mix genres and styles so recklessly. Yet, in Auerbach's terms, the mystery plays achieved a breakthrough in the Western representation of reality:

> this great drama contains everything that occurs in world history . . . all the heights and depths of human conduct and all the heights and depths of stylistic expression . . . there is no basis for a separation of the sublime from the low and everyday, for they are indissolubly connected in Christ's very life and suffering. Nor is there any basis for the concern for the unities of time, place, or action, for there is but one place – the world; and one action – man's fall and redemption.[39]

The mystery plays can afford to indulge in comic realism because the reality they represent is fundamentally comic, subsuming tragedy and suffering in resurrection and eternal joy.

Even Auerbach, however, found it hard to stomach the interpretation of farcical scenes in the passion plays of the mystery cycles. The Wakefield 'Buffeting of Christ', for example, begins with the torturers driving Christ on like a donkey. But they have to dehumanize their victim, who threatens to undermine the whole structure of their society, in order to torture him as they do. Caiaphas and Annas in the same play are portrayed with similar psychological realism (and anachronism) as a bellicose bishop and a smooth canon-lawyer respectively.[40]

'The Crucifixion' in the York cycle is equally horrific, with the soldiers responsible for nailing Christ to the cross callously competing over who can do the more professional job, complaining when their measurements prove to be false and cursing when they hoist up the cross. Yet when they finally complete their gruesome business Christ, who has been silent all the while, can still bring himself to plead for their forgiveness. The soldiers mock even his most moving speech, which they liken to the jangling of a jay and the patter of a pie.[41] The contrast is dramatically powerful and theologically significant. For if Christ can forgive even these soldiers there is hope for everyone.

In spite of such powerful dramatic effects the mystery cycles remained overtly didactic. Characters such as the Expositor in the Chester cycle intervene regularly to underline the doctrinal teaching which was the avowed purpose of the whole enterprise. Far from inviting the 'suspension of disbelief' the plays demand wholehearted faith in the reality of the truths represented. At the end of the Wakefield 'Crucifixion', for example, Nicodemus turns directly to preach to the audience and in the final stanza of the Chester cycle the actor playing Christ does the same, completely abandoning his stage role.[42] Occasionally, as in the *Ludus Coventriae*, when Peter and John preach to the people of Jerusalem (represented by the audience), 'doctrinal instruction . . . occurs naturally, within the flow of the action'.[43] But it normally involves complete abandonment of dramatic illusion as currently understood.

It should nevertheless be recognized that the mystery cycles achieve their most effective theological teaching through their 'staging' of the history of the world, presenting a 'moving picture', an animated stained-glass window, of the medieval theology of time, God's artefact, which is not mere linear progress but full of vertical meaning, figural significance: 'The events chosen for dramatisation are those in which God intervenes in human history' to express His will.[44] The fixed locations of their staging underline these figural connections, Isaac and Christ being prepared for sacrifice upon the same stage mountain. The need for selection of the most important Old Testament prefigurings of Christ clarifies what contemporary exegesis often over-complicated:

> Where theology had sought out these figural patterns with an ingeniousness and exhaustiveness that finally came near to defeating itself, the drama took from theology only the central, unequivocal figures, and played them one after another, creating thereby a dramatic structure of considerable economy and narrative tightness.[45]

The English mystery cycles, then, were not liturgical drama as such, being performed mainly by lay people outside church buildings. But they were performed on Corpus Christi, a liturgical feast instituted in the thirteenth century to celebrate the gift of the eucharist. The mass itself, which involves a memorial representation of Christ's sacrifice, can only be perceived as a subject of celebration in the overall context of God's action in history, redeeming man from the effects of sin and providing new hope of eternal life. To play this whole story on the stage, as Kolvé has shown, 'is in the deepest sense to *celebrate* the Corpus Christi sacrament, to explain its necessity and power, and to show how that power will be made manifest at the end of the world'.[46] This helps to explain the plot of the cycles, beginning with the fall of the angels and ending with the final judgement. The feast of Corpus Christi cannot, of course, be held entirely responsible for the form of the surviving cycles.[47] But it provided a suitable occasion for combining devotion and drama.

RENAISSANCE TRAGEDY AND REFORMATION THEOLOGY

Medieval drama, for all its occasional solemnity, was basically comic in structure, incorporating suffering within a joyful celebration of God's providential plan of redemption. Suffering, to invert the famous ending of *The Mayor of Casterbridge*, brought merely moments of pain in a general drama of happiness. Renaissance theatre, however, is normally seen as narrowing the scale of events from the divine to the human perspective. Time became no longer the massive arena of redemption in history but the smaller 'theatre' of an individual's life, 'where despite his mortality man could reveal his authentic dignity and gain a personal immortality'.[48] Renaissance drama, according to Curtius, was 'anthropocentric', abandoning religion for ethics and focusing on 'the play of man's psychological powers'.[49] Théodore de Bèze, for example, writing in 1550, turned the story of *Abraham Sacrifiant* into a tragedy, which is what it is called on the title-page of Arthur Golding's English translation, by stressing the conflict between divine and human values and making God's command 'a simple, irrational test of obedience, crushing in its effect on an anguished human being'.[50]

Bèze, of course, was a Protestant, his view of the world and of its creator shaped by the major Reformation theologians Luther and Calvin who presented faith in precisely these terms of unquestioning obedience. The world of the *Institutes* was not created for pleasure; it is full of potential disasters, of which Calvin gives some appallingly graphic examples:

> Various diseases repeatedly trouble us: now plague rages; now we are cruelly beset by the calamities of war; now ice and hail, consuming the year's expectation, leads to barrenness, which reduces us to poverty; wife, parents, children, neighbours, are snatched away by death; our house is burned by fire. It is on account of these occurrences that men curse their life, loathe the day of their birth, abominate heaven and the light of day, rail against God, and, as they are eloquent in blasphemy, accuse him of injustice and cruelty.[51]

God's 'secret plan', according to Calvin, may be 'incomprehensible' (in St Paul's words, He has 'mercy on whom he will have mercy, and whom he will he hardeneth', Romans 9:18), but remains 'irreprehensible',[52] not to be judged by 'the mind of man', which is 'so completely estranged from God's righteousness that it conceives, desires, and undertakes, only that which is impious, perverted, foul, impure, and infamous'.[53]

It is important to recognize the harsh view of man, God and the universe presented by the dominant theological discourse of Elizabethan England (dominant certainly in the Thirty-Nine Articles) since Renaissance tragedy can be seen, at least in part, as an 'anxious' and 'confused' reaction to this 'provocative theology', both a reflection and a subversive interrogation of this dominant ideology.[54] The term ideology, of course, should not be understood in Marx's sense as a matter of 'false consciousness', 'a defective perception of clearly perceptible facts'. It is rather the complex and unavoidable construction of a sense of the world and the self through a variety of material, social and cultural practices. It includes both theology and, as I argued in the first chapter, liturgy, which inscribes both subject and object of worship in a particular discourse.

Although it is possible to talk of a *dominant* ideology, such as Calvinism in Elizabethan England, a number of competing ideologies can be found at any given historical moment, including residual elements from a previously dominant discourse (such as the recently abandoned Catholicism) and emergent elements of ideologies yet to become fully articulate (such as Baconian science, already beginning to 'push God upstairs' and concentrate on the observable laws of the physical world). These codes constitute the language available to theologians and dramatists, who can only interrogate them from within, 'staging' their inherent difficulties by displaying them in practice, in particular dramatic situations. Literature can serve sometimes to bolster ideology, when readers or audience are encouraged merely to identify with the characters and regard everything that occurs as 'natural'. But a dramatist can, as Brecht saw, drawing on the example of Renaissance models, struggle to prevent such simple identification by alienating the audience and making them aware of the constructed ideological nature of their sense of the world, of themselves and of God.[55]

This dramatic interrogation of ideology need not be a deliberate or conscious process. Tragedy rarely involves 'an outright denial of religious faith', more often 'a sceptical probing of those hard facts of life with which faith has to reckon'. It tends to arise particularly during historical periods when 'faith and scepticism are in a state of unresolved tension'.[56] Tragedy involves, in Nietzschean terms, a shattering of boundaries, 'severing the certainties' and 'exploding the solidity of explanations', asking questions to which there can be no satisfactory answers.[57] Other theories of tragedy have seen it as an attempt to make the universe intelligible, whether optimistic about reconciliation of discordant elements in an eternal justice, like Hegel, or despairing of an irredeemably hostile universe, like Schopenhauer or Unamuno.[58] My focus for the moment will be on the way tragedy asks theological questions about the existence of evil in a world created by an omnipotent and benevolent God. It is this apparent contradiction, 'explained' by Christianity in terms of the fall, which Renaissance tragedy probes to the limit.

The Tragical History of the Life and Death of Doctor Faustus dramatizes precisely the tensions and difficulties of this particular problem in the theological language of its time. The fact that critics are almost equally divided between supporters of Marlowe's orthodoxy and of his atheism indicates how delicately balanced the question is.[59] There are, of course, residual 'medieval' elements in the text, most notably its morality-play structure, which emerges both in the psychomachia between the Good and Bad Angels for Faustus' soul and in the scenes of diabolic clowning, turned though they are into anti-popish plots. Emergent scientific aspirations are also treated sympathetically not only in the opening scene but in the genuine excitement Faustus experiences in probing 'the secrets of astronomy' (vii 2).[60] Protestant theology, however, provides the dominant discourse of the play, contributing to its almost Manichean division between the spiritual powers of good and evil.[61] Faustus seems quite literally to be torn between rival pictures of the world.

These contradictory elements are apparent in the variant descriptions of hell in the play. The 'perpetual torture-house' into which the damned Faustus is made to gape as its jaws open to receive him is described by the Bad Angel in terms as graphic as any medieval baptistery:

> There are the furies, tossing damned souls
> On burning forks, their bodies boil in lead:
> There are live quarters broiling on the coals,
> That ne'er can die. (xix 118–21)

Earlier, however, Mephostophilis has twice given a much more 'modern' account of hell as eternal separation from God and from 'the eternal joys of heaven' (iii 80):

> Hell hath no limits, nor is circumscrib'd
> In one self place, but where we are is hell. (v 122–3)

In terms of dramatic presentation it is the mental torture of Faustus, separated from Christ in the final scene, which most powerfully affects a modern audience.

At one level, the play dramatizes the orthodox Christian answer to the problem of evil. It is the result of the fall, first of the angels and then of man, both exemplifying the sin of pride, particularly intellectual pride, a curiosity to know more than God has allowed. Faustus, straining in the opening scenes against the accepted limits of human knowledge, turns to magic:

> a world of profit and delight,
> Of power, of honour, or omnipotence . . .
> A sound magician is a demi-god. (i 52–61)

Like Adam, losing his soul in order to eat of the tree of the knowledge of good and evil, Faustus enters into a pact with the devil to gratify his thirst for knowledge. His blood at first congeals, preventing him from signing his contract, as if 'unwilling I should write this bill'. 'Why streams it not', he asks, 'that I may write afresh?' Mephostophilis, however, provides fire to help the blood flow, enabling Faustus to announce, in bold blasphemy of Christ, 'Consummatum est' (v 65–74). Even towards the end of the play he remains proud of his blasphemous rebellion, countering the scholars' 'God forbid!' with a piece of desperate bravado: 'God forbade, indeed; but Faustus hath done it' (xix 64). This is Faustus (and behind him, Marlowe?) at his most subversive.

In his final hour, however, Faustus experiences the full horror of his separation from God and from the Saviour whose redeeming blood he had earlier scorned:

> O, I'll leap up to my God! Who pulls me down?
> See, see where Christ's blood streams in the firmament!
> One drop would save my soul, half a drop. Ah, my Christ! –
> Rend not my heart for naming of my Christ;
> Yet will I call on him. (xix 145–9)

The pronouns here (*my* Christ, *my* God) emphasize the closeness Faustus feels towards them even at this stage. But after he calls on Lucifer his vision of the Son fades, to be replaced by the appalling sight of the Father:

> see where God
> Stretcheth out his arms and bends his ireful brows.
> Mountains and hills, come, come, and fall on me,
> And hide me from the heavy wrath of God! (150–4)

When the devils enter to take him away it is the judgement of God, again, which frightens Faustus more than anything: 'My God, my God! Look not so fierce on me!' (187).

The fierceness of Faustus' God has alarmed many critics, especially in the context of the Calvinist view that, since He is ultimately responsible for everything, He must have willed Faustus' choice of evil, predestining him to the wickedness which He then punishes. It is an objection Erasmus made to Luther:

> Who will be able to bring himself to love God with all his heart when He created hell seething with eternal torments in order to punish His own misdeeds in His victims as though He took delight in human torments?[62]

Donne issued similar warnings against the Calvinist tendency to limit God's mercy, to make God less than human.[63] So did the 'objector' in Lawne's abridgement of the *Institutes*, only to be told that 'it is a point of bold wickedness even so much as to enquire the causes of God's will'.[64] Even Calvin acknowledges the difficulty: 'To some it seems too hard, and alien to the mercy of God that any who flee for refuge in calling upon the Lord's mercy are wholly deprived of forgiveness.' But he disposes of the problem by saying with 'the author of the Hebrews' that it is not God who refuses to forgive but the reprobate who are 'stricken by God's just judgment with eternal blindness on account of their ungratefulness'. Those who are denied 'softness of heart', however, can only credit themselves with the deficiency.[65] God, it seems, makes all the decisions but men take all the blame.

This paradox or contradiction (depending on your point of view) is explored by *Dr Faustus* in dramatic terms. The question the play poses, as a tragedy, engaging the sympathies of its audience for its hero, is whether Faustus 'deserves' to be damned. The play is open, it is argued, to a Calvinist reading (that Faustus is wicked because he is damned) as well as an Arminian one (that he is damned because he is wicked). Marlowe 'stages' the contemporary theological debate, which polarized the two views, exposing through controversy 'the contradiction in the hypothesis that God is good and omnipotent', given the degree of evil in the world.[66]

To what extent, then, is Faustus presented as responsible for his choice? In the opening scene he concocts from a combination of biblical texts a brilliant Calvinist double-bind:

Stipendium peccati mors est Ha! *Stipendium etc.* The reward of sin is death: that's hard. *Si pecasse negamus, fallimur, et nulla est in nobis veritas.* If we say that we have no sin, we deceive ourselves, and there's no truth in us. Why, then, belike we must sin, and so consequently die. (i 39–44)

There seems no escape from this vicious circle (for the reprobate, at least). Is Faustus one of those whom God, in Calvin's words, 'allows . . . to be blinded by Satan'?[67] Faustus likes to think that he is free but Mephostophilis claims (in the B text, admittedly) that it was he who directed his eyes to the dangerous passages of scripture which first misled him (B 1988–93).[68]

The dramatic suspense of the play, of course, depends upon the audience feeling that Faustus is free to repent at any time (even at the very end). He makes a number of moves towards

repentance, especially in scene six, when the two angels
deliver contradictory messages:

> *Good Angel*   Faustus, repent; yet God will pity thee.
> *Bad Angel*   Thou art a spirit; God cannot pity thee.

Faustus insists that there are no limits to God's forgiveness:

> Be I a devil, yet God may pity me;
> Yea, God will pity me if I repent.

To this the Bad Angel replies, 'Ay, but Faustus never shall
repent', a prediction (or is it a recognition of predestination?)
which Faustus confirms, echoing St Paul and Calvin:

> My heart is harden'd, I cannot repent.
> Scarce can I name salvation, faith, or heaven,
> But fearful echoes thunder in my ears,
> 'Faustus, thou art damn'd!' (vi 12–21)

It is the Calvinist nightmare, already seen in Bunyan's
autobiography and Cowper's hymns, of being irredeemable.

Faustus returns a little later to the same question, whether
it is too late for him to be saved. Again the two angels disagree:

> *Bad Angel*   Too late.
> *Good Angel*   Never too late, if Faustus will repent.

He calls upon Christ, only for Lucifer to appear, together with
Beelzebub and Mephostophilis, insisting that 'Christ cannot
save thy soul, for he is just' (vi 80–7). Lucifer admits, however,
that he has a vested 'interest' in Faustus' damnation. The Old
Man who makes a final attempt to persuade Faustus to repent
claims, on the contrary, that he need not 'persever' in evil or
despair; grace is still available to him (xviii 42, 61–3). Only
after the demonic Helen has 'sucked forth' his soul will the Old
Man admit that Faustus has successfully 'excluded' the 'grace
of heaven'. The chorus, too, by pointing the moral that Faustus
was enticed 'To practise more than heavenly power permits'
(Epilogue, 8), implies that he had a choice in the matter.

The chorus, however, cannot be allowed to have the final word. There is no final answer to the problem of evil, which this play explores in terms clearly derived from contemporary debates. Whether in fact Christian teaching on the subject amounts to profound paradox or contradiction is also a matter for dispute. What is important to recognize is the extent to which dramatic form explores and displays potential contradiction, providing a vehicle for the probing of faith. It also dramatizes what is often lost in the abstractions of systematic theology, the human implications of particular doctrines. To see Faustus' final moments on stage is to be brought face to face with the awfulness of damnation, to realize in human terms what the doctrine really 'means'.

Some of Shakespeare's tragedies can be found to interrogate in similarly ambiguous ways the Reformation doctrines of evil and damnation, stretching theological language beyond its technical boundaries and exploring its human significance.[69] One learned study of 'Shakespeare's dramatic employment of theology' insists that the theology remains subordinate to characterisation and plot, designed solely to 'illumine the state of mind or course of action of a dramatic character'.[70] The very frequency of the words, 'God, hell, devil and heaven' is seen by another as an indication of their metaphorical status, a reduction of their theological significance. Newly coined metaphors, such as 'mine eternal jewel', are also taken to throw 'a more general and a more indefinite atmosphere' around the Christian doctrines of the soul and the devil.[71] But I want to claim a more serious theological role for the plays, insisting on their potential to explore and to supplement Reformation discussion of the nature of evil.

Macbeth is perhaps the most obvious example of a play which explores the nature of evil, demonstrating the inadequacy of the optimistic view, represented by Richard Hooker, that 'evil as evil cannot be desired'.[72] The play 'displays' the development of what King James himself called a 'cauterized conscience', which becomes so inured to evil that it is incapable of repentance, 'senseless of sinne'.[73] It is not enough, as Helen Gardner insists, to say that Macbeth is 'driven by ambition':

> The mystery of the perverted will, the attraction of the dreadful, and the imagination of all that is meant by damnation are far more

powerfully presented in *Macbeth* than in the explicitly metaphysical and theological tragedy of *Dr Faustus* . . . Shakespeare
has presented the thing itself, the hardening or incapacity for
penitence on which so many preachers dwelt, and for which
Calvin provided so ghastly an explanation.[74]

King James, of course, insisted on human freedom and
responsibility, that the devil can only deceive 'such as first
wilfully deceive themselves, by running into him'.[75]

Macbeth runs into the witches quite literally on the heath
and immediately echoes their language. He is fascinated by
their predictions (which turn out to be foreknowledge) but is
aware from the moment that they begin to be fulfilled that
'this supernatural soliciting . . . cannot be good', or he would
not

> yield to that suggestion
> Whose horrid image doth unfix my hair,
> And make my seated heart knock at my ribs
> Against the use of nature. (I iii 133–6)

Malcolm's appointment as Prince of Cumberland provokes
what Macbeth himself immediately recognizes as evil, in the
pervasive light/dark, day/night oppositions of the play:

> Stars, hide your fires;
> Let not light see my black and deep desires. (I iv 50–1)

In the famous soliloquy at the end of the first act in which he
spells out the moral duties which should prevent him mur-
dering Duncan Macbeth claims that he is prepared to risk
hell, to 'jump the life to come' (I vii 7), as confidently as his wife
asserts, 'A little water clears us of this deed' (II ii 67). But they
are both shown to be mistaken. Lady Macbeth is driven mad by
guilt while Macbeth himself, as soon as he has murdered
Duncan, dwells on his inability to pronounce 'Amen' to the
innocent 'God bless' of the grooms:

> Had I but died an hour before this deed
> I had lived a blessed time; for from this instant
> There's nothing serious in mortality –

> All is but toys, renown and grace is dead,
> The wine of life is drawn, and the mere lees
> Is left this vault to brag of. (II iii 88–93)

The technical theological language of blessedness, mortality and grace, mixed with this bold metaphor of the soul as the wine of the body, takes on additional meaning. There is also more than a hint here, as in the 'poison'd chalice' of evil (I vii 11), of eucharistic symbolism (inverted, of course, in the witches' 'black mass' over their cauldron).

Macbeth charts in terrifying fashion the successive stages of its hero's descent into evil, the hardening of his heart to embrace the murder of his friend, the taunting of his servants and the callous reception of his wife's death. Life is by now evacuated of all significance, 'a walking shadow',

> a tale
> Told by an idiot, full of sound and fury,
> Signifying nothing. (V v 24–8)

This, in human terms, is what damnation means, the deliberate rejection of the gift of grace. *Macbeth*, unlike *Dr Faustus*, does not raise questions about the nature of God. The fact that the witches know what will happen to him does not mean that he is 'predestined' in the Calvinist sense (not, at least, if we accept Augustine's argument that supernatural foreknowledge fails to reduce human free will). Macbeth is shown quite clearly to choose evil. But the play certainly explores the nature of that evil and also of that 'hardening' of heart so central to Reformation theology.

If *Macbeth* deals with the evil that men choose, *King Lear* focuses upon the suffering that they cannot avoid. However foolish he may have been, Lear finds himself facing afflictions that bear no relation to his offences. He is 'a man / More sinned against than sinning' (III ii 59). He has been likened to Job, described by Calvin as complaining similarly against the 'hideous windes' that beset him but learning from his affliction 'what our estate is'. Lear in some ways obeys what Calvin calls the Christian duty in the face of affliction, to 'bethynke us of our byrthe' and 'consider our selves, both what we bee, and whence we come'.[76] Lear, stripped of all the paraphernalia of authority, can be said to learn what 'unaccommodated man is', 'a poor, bare, forked animal' (III iv 105–8). He penetrates to the depth of human depravity, the 'sulphurous pit' of sexual appetite and hypocrisy (IV vi 110). He also learns to have more care for 'poor naked wretches', 'houseless' and 'unfed', of whom he had previously 'ta'en / Too little care' (III iv 28–35).

Having learnt all this, however, and having been reconciled to Cordelia in the tender prison-scene, Lear is made to suffer yet more affliction: the loss of his daughter, closely followed by his own death, the ultimate test of any theology. What explicit theology there is in the play itself, necessarily natural theology given Shakespeare's changing of the Christian setting of his source to a pagan one, is certainly shown to be inadequate. The superstitious Gloucester sees the gods as 'wanton boys' who 'kill us for their sport' (IV i 36), Edgar views them as just but uncaring punishers of 'our pleasant vices' (V iii 170–1) and Albany finds them ineffectual when called upon for help. 'The gods defend her!', he cries, on hearing of Cordelia's plight, only for Lear to enter immediately carrying her dead body (V iii 255).

None of these natural theologies, then, can account for the harshness of human experience represented in the play. It is important, however, to see that they are all pagan views, corresponding closely to the attitudes generally attributed to heathens in the Elizabethan period, which are given clear expression, for example, in Sidney's *Arcadia*. There are the superstitious, like Gloucester, the atheistic, like Edmund, Regan and Goneril, and the virtuous heathen who anticipate Christian attitudes, of whom Cordelia is the most obvious example, Christian before her time.[77] She is constantly portrayed as a saintly figure; even her tears are seen as 'holy water' in her 'heavenly eyes' (IV iii 30). She calls upon both the 'blest secrets' of medicine (IV iv 15) and the 'kind gods' to cure her father's madness and to bring 'restoration' (IV vii 13–16, 58). She asks too for his 'benediction' (58).

Perhaps the most important thing about Cordelia, however, is that she says very little, choosing rather to act out her theology in self-sacrificing love. Her motto from the beginning has been simple, that actions speak louder than words, making it possible to give a Wittgensteinian interpretation to her famous reply to her father, 'Love, and be silent' (I i 61). Certainly, if Lear is 'redeemed' in Bradley's famous phrase,[78] it is through her. The saintly language which surrounds her provides the barest possibility of a Christian reading of the play, a tentative and totally implicit answer to the problem of suffering the tragedy poses.[79] As with Marlowe, it is not by his answers that Shakespeare contributes to theology but by his questions.

The Theatre of the Absurd: Godotology

The theatre of the absurd, the term given to a group of plays which combine an existential anxiety about the apparent meaninglessness of life with a total disrespect for the conventions of realism, finds its focus in the spiritual crisis of 'modern man', who remains desperate to believe but incapable of faith. Arthur Adamov's *Confession* voices the dilemma, expressing both a continuing need to pray and a terrible disbelief that there is anyone to pray to. The old language no longer carries weight, for it has been used too readily for too long:

> The name of God should no longer come from the mouth of man. This word that has so long been degraded by usage no longer means anything . . . To use the word God is more than sloth, it is a refusal to think, a kind of short cut, a hideous shorthand.[80]

Deprived of a proper object for their faith, the deuteragonists of Adamov's absurd play *Ping Pong* devote their lives to the mysteries of the pin-ball machine, burying their despair in the comfort of routine. It is a classic example of 'bad faith', Sartre's term for inauthentic existence, the failure to face up to the truth of the human condition.

That truth, according to Camus, is that man is an exile, a stranger in a meaningless and hostile universe, newly awakened to the falsity of traditional myths which had previously provided him with a purpose. He continues to seek unity and harmony in the world but is doomed to disappointment. The absurdity of life consists in the imbalance between these spiritual cravings and the unaccommodating world. Even Kafka is seen by Camus to have fallen into the trap of hope, reaching for transcendental answers to the problems of existence. The authentic existentialist refuses all such consolation.[81]

There is, however, as Esslin observes, a contradiction between these existentialists' recognition of the irrationality of the human condition and the extreme rationality of their arguments, a clash between their unconventional theories, about existence preceding essence, for example, and their highly conventional characterization, which fails to break away from the coherent, consistent people of realist drama. The theatre of the absurd makes that break, totally abandoning the rational and realistic. It does not

> argue *about* the absurdity of the human condition; it merely *presents* it in being – that is in terms of concrete stage images . . . what *happens* on the stage transcends, and often contradicts, the *words* spoken by the characters.[82]

Absurd plays, as I hope to show, mainly through some of Beckett's work, do not argue *about* the death of God and the meaninglessness of life. They present traditional theological language as absurd and inappropriate, failing to address the reality of the human condition. They can be seen themselves, however, to be returning to 'the original, religious function of the theatre', to make people aware of their 'precarious and mysterious position in the universe'. Theatre, in this sense, continues to be a form of ritual, making people experience as 'a living reality' what they may otherwise have known only 'in the conceptual sphere'.[83]

The theatre of the absurd, of course, hits humanist beliefs as hard, if not harder, than theological faith. Ionesco, for example, who exposes the pointlessness and lovelessness of suburban marriage in *The Bald Prima Donna*, was labelled a 'messiah' of 'anti-realism', ushering in a 'bleak new world from which the humanist heresies of faith in logic and belief in man will forever be banished'. He defended himself by announcing his dislike of messiahs and his opposition to all ideologies, which he saw as fossilized forms of language to be challenged and overthrown by the living language of the stage.[84] The whole point of *The Chairs* is that there can be no absolute, infallible message for mankind. The Old Man and his wife pin all their hopes on the Orator, who is to announce to the world the condensed wisdom they have accumulated over a lifetime, only for there to be no real audience (only empty chairs) and no message (the Orator turns out to be deaf and dumb). The 'meaning' of the play, Ionesco explained, lies in the chairs themselves, symbolically undermining the 'essences' in which people continue to believe, proclaiming both 'the absence of people' and 'the absence of God'.[85]

One way of exposing the hollowness of traditional religious myths and their failure to speak to men cut off from their 'religious, metaphysical, and transcendental roots' (in Ionesco's words)[86] is to retell them with significant differences. This is the strategy of Arrabal's *Automobile Graveyard*, in which the hero, Emanou, born in a stable to a carpenter father, leaves home at thirty to play the trumpet and to seek for meaning in a squalid and hypocritical world (the graveyard, for example, being run like a luxury hotel). He is betrayed by a kiss, beaten and finally led to death with his arms tied to the handle-bars of a bicycle, having made no difference at all to his society. Grass's *The Wicked Cooks* involves a similar parody of the last supper and passion, with the Count, possessor of a mysterious recipe for cabbage soup, trading his knowledge for the hand of his lover only to forget his secret and be driven to suicide, unable to fulfil his part of the bargain. In both of these plays the claims of Christianity to be a revelation of the secret of the universe are presented as absurd.

This too is the theological significance of Beckett's plays, which are pervaded by irreverent, even blasphemous, references to biblical myths, in particular that of the crucifixion and resurrection of Christ. The very setting of *Waiting for Godot*, a country road with a tree next to a 'low mound', has been seen to symbolize a negation of the Christian message: an empty cross and a closed tomb.[87] The audience, certainly, are not left long in doubt about the tree, for Vladimir is soon speculating about the two thieves crucified along with Christ, one of whom was saved and the other damned. 'It's a reasonable percentage', he opines. Estragon, however, can make no sense at all of his friend's theological terms:

> Vladimir   Suppose we repented.
> Estragon   Repented what?
> Vladimir   Oh . . . (*He reflects.*) We wouldn't have to go into the details.
> Estragon   Our being born? (p.11)[88]

The idea of confession, distasteful even to the more idealistic Vladimir, is totally foreign to Estragon, whose only regret is that he was ever given life. Asked if he remembers the gospels, he can only recall the attractive colour of the Dead Sea on the maps of the Holy Land. Vladimir begins, uninvited, in fact positively discouraged, to refresh his friend's memory of the crucifixion, only to be interrupted throughout. When he refers to 'Our Saviour' Estragon interjects, 'Our what?', before pressing the matter further: 'Saved from what?' The theological terms find no resonance in his own experience.

Vladimir, however, warms to the task of biblical scholarship in spite of his friend's total lack of interest:

> Vladimir   . . . how is it that of the four Evangelists only one speaks of a thief being saved. The four of them were there – or thereabouts – and only one speaks of a thief being saved . . . Of the other three two don't mention any thieves at all and the third says that both of them abused him.
> Estragon   Who?
> Vladimir   What?
> Estragon   What's all this about? Abused who?
> Vladimir   The Saviour.
> Estragon   Why?
> Vladimir   Because he wouldn't save them.

The conversation proceeds with Vladimir wondering why everybody believes the more optimistic version and Estragon supplying a simple answer: 'People are bloody ignorant apes' (pp. 12–13). He seems, at this stage of the play at least, to have no interest whatsoever in Christ or in salvation. His most positive suggestion is that they should both hang themselves (p.17).

The subject of crucifixion, however, continues to dominate the play. Vladimir, for instance, rebukes Lucky for daring to 'crucify . . . Such a good master' (p.34) while Estragon justifies going about barefoot by the example of Christ. 'But where he lived', Vladimir objects, 'it was warm, it was dry.' 'Yes', replies Estragon, 'And they crucified quick' (p.52). The implication, presumably, is that the suffering of the tramps in the cold is even worse than that of Christ. Nor do they experience any joy in the resurrection with which Act Two begins. The tree miraculously sprouts 'four or five leaves' overnight and Estragon's first words to Vladimir, who has just sung a song about a dog stealing bread, being beaten to death and then buried, are, like those of Christ to Mary Magdalen, 'Don't touch me' (pp. 57–8). Even Vladimir's mysterious bladder infection seems to have been cured (a sign of returning fertility?). But Estragon continues to hanker after death:

Estragon   The best thing would be to kill me, like the other.
Vladimir   What other? (*Pause.*) What other?
Estragon   Like billions of others.
Vladimir   (*sententious*). To every man his little cross. (*He sighs.*) Till he dies. (*Afterthought.*) And is forgotten. (p.62)

Suffering and death, in other words, are universal. What is different in the claim made by Christians is that the man who suffered and died in this particularly gruesome manner was God. The two tramps find this difficult to believe. They wait by the tree for the arrival of Godot, as if for confirmation of this claim.

But is Godot God? Not exactly, of course, since he is also, among other things, a French racing cyclist.[89] Nevertheless, Godot shares a number of attributes with the traditional concept of deity, including, if we are to believe the young boy (Middle English, evangel) who is his messenger, a white beard and a propensity to do nothing (pp. 91–2). His grace is certainly arbitrary, even fortuitous. When the tramps address

'A kind of prayer ... A vague supplication' towards him, his reported reply is

Vladimir	That he'd see.
Estragon	That he couldn't promise anything.
Vladimir	That he'd have to think it over. (p.18)

They have some difficulty in explaining to Pozzo precisely who Godot is:

Vladimir	Oh, he's a ... he's a kind of acquaintance.
Estragon	Nothing of the kind, we hardly know him.
Vladimir	True ... we don't know him very well ... but all the same ...
Estragon	Personally I wouldn't know him if I saw him. (p.23)

All these statements, of course, would apply equally well if they were talking about God.

Godot also has affinities with the conception of God advanced by Lucky:

> a personal God quaquaquaqua with white beard quaquaquaqua outside time without extension who from the heights of divine apathia divine athambia divine aphasia loves us dearly with some exceptions for reasons unknown ... (pp. 42–3)

He may not show much emotion (either suffering or surprise), or even speak, but He does, in His inscrutable wisdom, divide the elect from the damned, separating the sheep from the goats. Godot is similarly arbitrary, treating the goat-minding boy with kindness but beating his shepherd brother (p.51). The reaction of the tramps to what they believe to be his arrival in Act Two fits exactly into the pattern of Calvinist election and reprobation. Estragon shrieks, 'I'm accursed!' and 'I'm in hell' while Vladimir shouts, 'We're saved' (pp. 73–4). He continues to believe that Estragon, who thought he saw him, 'must have had a vision' (p.75) but it becomes apparent to everyone when Godot fails once more to keep his appointment that he will never come. The tramps attempt suicide, failing farcically for lack of rope and resolve to repeat their attempt the following day:

Vladimir	We'll hang ourselves tomorrow. (*Pause.*) Unless Godot comes.
Estragon	And if he comes?
Vladimir	We'll be saved.

There seems, however, to be little prospect of that and the second act ends, like the first, in spiritual paralysis:

Vladimir	Well? Shall we go?
Estragon	Yes, let's go.
	They do not move. (p.94)

Waiting for Godot, then, is a play about the desperate but unfulfilled desire to be saved. The name 'Godot', by analogy with the character Molloy names 'Mag' in order to represent 'the need to have a Ma' with 'the "g" spitting on it', recognizes the desperate need to believe in God but spits on it.[90] The same principle seems to apply in *All That Fall* to Christy, the peddler of fertilizer, also claiming to bring new life, which nobody wants to buy. Beckett provides in Godot 'a Proustian version of salvation . . . because it is concerned finally with . . . a *desired* rather than a *hoped* for salvation'. Proust, in Beckett's analysis, held sexual desire to be unfulfillable, leading necessarily to disappointment and despair, since even possession of the object fails to satisfy the needs of the subject.[91] In faith too, Beckett suggests, there can only be hopeless desire, for there is no object capable of meeting human aspirations.

Early in *Waiting for Godot* Vladimir significantly mis-remembers the Book of Proverbs: 'Hope deferred maketh the something sick' (p.10). The quotation should run, 'Hope deferred maketh the heart sick, but when the desire cometh it is a tree of life' (Proverbs 13:12). When Godot first fails to appear and Estragon wonders whether they've come to the right place, Vladimir insists, 'He said by the tree. (*They look at the tree.*) Do you see any others?' (p.14). Even this tree, however, affords no protection to the damned Estragon trying to hide from Godot. 'Decidedly', Vladimir admits, 'this tree will not have been of the slightest use to us' (p.74). They try imitating it for a while, staggering about on one leg (presumably a parody of à Kempis' ideal), hoping to ingratiate themselves:

Estragon	Do you think God sees me?
Vladimir	You must close your eyes?
	Estragon closes his eyes, staggers worse.
Estragon	(*stopping, brandishing his fists at the top of his voice*). God have pity on me!
Vladimir	(*vexed*). And me?
Estragon	On me! On me! Pity! On me! (pp. 76–7)

The tramps are clearly desperate in their need for redemption but it is a desire which Beckett presents as utterly without foundation outside themselves and therefore utterly hopeless.

Beckett's second play, *Endgame*, presents an even more hopeless picture, a godless apocalypse, with the universe stumbling to an ignominious conclusion. The characters at one point try to pray but abandon the enterprise in disgust. 'The bastard!', shouts Hamm, 'He doesn't exist' (38). The play has been seen to have killed off the idea of God, crucified by Hamm[er] and Clov (*clou* being French for nail) on 'the place of a skull' (the set has often been compared with a skull, having two small windows for eyes).[92] Clov's first words are an echo of Christ on the cross ('Finished, it's finished') while Hamm's, once he's removed the 'large blood-stained handkerchief' from his face, are reminiscent of Lamentations and Herbert's 'The Sacrifice': 'Can there be misery – (*he yawns*) – loftier than mine' (p.12). He too echoes Christ on the cross, crying out 'Father! . . . Father!', though the father to whom he calls lives in a dustbin (p.43).

Hamm himself, like the Christian God, assumes the role of both Father and Son, Master and King, eventually being placed in check and left to die on the board (chess being a dominant metaphor of the play). He is as vindictive as the God in Matthew's parable, refusing to give Mother Pegg oil for her lamp and telling her 'to get out to hell' (p.48). He may not, like the Christ of St John's Revelation, hold the keys of hell and of death, but he does at least have the combination of the food-cupboard.[93] His preaching too seems modelled on Christ's: 'Get out of here and love one another! Lick your neighbour as yourself!' (p.44). The small boy Clov sees through the window at the end of the play raises the possibility of resurrection, in the original French version of the play at least, in which Hamm asks whether the object against which he is sitting is the 'lifted stone' and if he is 'looking at the house with the eyes of Moses dying', within sight, that is, of the promised land. To all of this conjecture, however, Clov replies, quite simply, 'No'.[94] In the English version, Hamm says of this boy, 'If he exists he'll die there or he'll come here' (p.50). Since, like Godot, he never arrives, we are left to assume either that he never existed or that he is dead.

Endgame is also a comment on the awfulness of the world, seen in Nagg's old joke to be worse than a pair of botched trousers. Just as Job was told to 'stand still, and consider the wondrous works of God' (Job 37:14), Clov is instructed to raise his head 'and look at all that beauty' (pp.50–1).[95] 'Do you want me to look at this muckheap', he asks (p.47). The play totally debunks the Genesis myth of creation. Whereas God divided the dry land from the waters, calling the former earth and the latter seas and seeing 'that it was good' (Genesis 1:9–10), Clov sees the earth through one window and the seas through another, calling them both 'filth': 'I say to myself that the earth is extinguished, though I never saw it lit' (p.51).[96] The play takes place, of course, after some terrible calamity analogous to the Flood. Hamm, who in the biblical account saw his father naked, is blind in the play and keeps his parents in dustbins. He is also petrified that the evolutionary process may begin again from one of Clov's fleas or a crablouse. 'Catch him,' he cries, 'for the love of God' (p.27). The little boy too presents a threat, as 'a potential procreator' (p.50), but there is nothing in the play to suggest that the world is not going to come to an end, and with it all pain and suffering.

The same grim undermining of Christian belief can be found in many of Beckett's shorter plays. *Happy Days*, for example, portrays the ageing Winnie, increasingly incapacitated (buried in Act One to her waist, in Act Two to her neck) but facing her predicament with absurd optimism and routine 'normality'.

She begins her day with prayer, exclaiming, 'Another Heavenly Day', and refusing to complain, since she has 'so much to be thankful for'. She suffers no pain, or at least 'hardly any', and receives 'great mercies'. Her prayers, she claims, are 'perhaps not for naught' (pp.9–12).[97] The second act opens with similar optimism: 'Hail, holy light . . . Someone is looking at me still. (*Pause.*) Caring for me still. (*Pause*). That is what I find so wonderful' (p.37). She remains positive to the end, when her husband crawls painfully towards her, lacking even the energy to give her a kiss. 'Oh this *is* a happy day', she cries (p.47). But again, there is absolutely nothing in the play to justify such optimistic faith.

All That Fall, a radio play, presents another ironic reading of a biblical text, on this occasion Psalm 145, from which Mr Hardy, himself saved by totally human means when climbing, takes the text for his sermon: 'The Lord upholdeth all that fall and raiseth up all those that be bowed down' (p.39). It is a text which provokes 'wild laughter' from the Rooneys.[98] There are ironic echoes of this psalm all through the play: the 'tender mercies' which the Rooneys receive are never acknowledged while the only way 'one generation shall laud thy works to another', it seems, is by bequeathing their diseases.[99] The play abounds with symbols of infertility, whether impotence, as in the case of the aptly named Slocum, the killing of children, or the removal of their sexual organs. It has been called 'an anti-fertility ritual' after the manner of Schopenhauer, who also believed in bringing the world to a grinding halt (to take the railway sounds of the play symbolically).

Perhaps the most grotesque of Beckett's dramatic attacks upon faith is his television play, *Eh Joe*, in which the hero is tormented by a woman's voice which reminds him of his fiancée's death and taunts him for his faith:

> How's your Lord these days? . . . Still worth having? . . . Still lapping it up? . . . The Passion of our Joe . . . Wait till he starts talking to you . . . When you've done with yourself. (p.18) [100]

The passion here, of course, is ambiguous, representing both his lust and his suffering, though this is as nothing in comparison with hers. The voice describes in gruesome detail the various means by which the girl attempted to take her life before she was eventually successful, drowning after an overdose, her hands, breast and face pressing against the stones of the river-bed. The play ends:

> *There's love for you* . . . Isn't it Joe? . . . Wasn't it Joe? . . . Eh Joe? . . . Wouldn't you say? . . . Compared to us . . . Compared to Him . . . Eh Joe? (p.21)

The suffering of Christ is portrayed once again as failing to atone for the suffering of ordinary men and women on this earth.

Beckett's obsession with the crucifixion can be compared in some respects with that of Flannery O'Connor's fanatical disbelievers, for whom the most important thing is that Christ was not God and did not therefore save us. There is little doubt that Beckett's characters long for redemption. They call out to be saved, to be heard and comforted by an omnipotent and benevolent Father. Convinced, however, that no such being exists, Beckett leaves them to stew in their hopeless desire, looking as absurd as Henry, in *Embers*, who sits on the beach (after the sea of faith has ebbed) attempting to hold a conversation with his dead father, 'As if he hadn't died' (p.21).[101] His daughter asks, 'why does Daddy keep on talking all the time?', especially in the lavatory, to be told that he is praying, 'Roaring prayers at God and his saints' (p.32). Neither father replies, of course, earthly or heavenly, and Henry is left appealing alternately to 'Father' and 'Christ', who answer, in the final words of the play, 'All day all night nothing (*Pause.*) Not a sound' (p.39).

Not all of Beckett's successors, on the British stage at least, see things as bleakly, though the crucifixion dominates a number of recent plays. Peter Nichols's *Passion Play* makes the same pun as *Eh Joe*, interspersing James Croxley's adultery with excerpts from Mozart's Requiem and the St Matthew Passion. Croxley, a deeply anti-Christian restorer of paintings at work on a Victorian crucifix, attacks 'that insipid eunuch' whose initials he shares, complaining that 'we still live in the shadow of His death'.[102] He advocates free love but destroys the lives of those around him, his adultery providing a 'metaphor for the essential emptiness of a godless world'.[103]

Peter Shaffer's *Equus* explores a similar contrast between a sterile normality and a perverse spirituality. A particularly morbid painting of the crucifixion, with a spear being forced between Christ's ribs, is seen to have suggested to the young Alan Strang the blinding of the object of his worship on whom he projects his guilt, that magnificent example of God's handiwork given in the Book of Job, a horse. Alan creates his own religion, based, of course, upon the Bible, in which Equus becomes God's 'only-begotten son' (p.243).[104] His psychiatrist probes to the heart of his faith and the motive for his terrible act, reciting, 'The Lord thy God is a jealous God. He sees you forever and ever' (p.297), implying that the blinding of the horse was equivalent to killing this vindictive God. Shaffer probably comes too close to both realism and rationalism to be classified as absurd but he too dramatizes both the need to believe and its difficulties and dangers.

Tom Stoppard's *Jumpers* takes a different direction, focusing on the question of theological and philosophical language about God. Like other absurd plays, *Jumpers* encapsulates its ideas in its central image of mental gymnastics. The gymnasts, in this case, are modern philosophers, predominantly logical positivists, playing games with words, denying any absolute validity to the notions of 'good' or 'God'. The play's ridiculous hero, George Moore, not *the* George Moore but another moral philosopher of the same name, attacks their limited view of the discipline, focusing attention on what he still considers to be the most important question, 'Is God?' The God he invents, however, is 'a philosopher's God, logically inferred from self-evident premises' (pp.39–40).[105] 'I'm not at all sure', he admits, 'that the God of religious observance is the object of my faith' (p.68). His wife points out that people continue to worship what they consider to be a real person:

> One can't help wondering at the persistence of the reflex, the universal constant unthinking appeal to the non-existent God who is presumed dead. Perhaps he's only missing in action . . . and getting himself together to go BOO! (p.35)

Even the agnostic Archbishop of Canterbury, in the dream-like Coda with which the play ends, finds himself having to resort to tear-gas in order to quell rioting believers demanding 'the blood of the lamb' and 'the bread of the body of Christ' (p.84). In a final affectionate tribute to Beckett, Stoppard suggests that there is no need to despair since 'many are happy much of the time' and 'one of the thieves was saved' (p.87).

The question here, as in my opening chapter, is one of language, which, in the words of Stoppard's absurd hero, is only 'an approximation of meaning and not a logical symbolism for it' (p.24). Stoppard has been seen to have accepted a late-Wittgensteinian view of language not as names for objects but as a series of very serious language-games giving expression to particular and historical forms of life.[106] The language of theology which Beckett divorces from the context of a believing community, placing it instead into the mouths of his isolated and alienated sceptics, may not therefore be as dead as he supposes. In order to be comprehensible, however, it needs to be seen within its total context as part of a complex and pluriform set of linguistic and literary codes.

NOTES

Square brackets indicate the date of the first edition of the work cited.

1 TOWARDS A POETICS OF FAITH

Theology and literature: a creative tension

1   Walter J. Ong, *Interfaces of the Word: Studies in the Evolution of Consciousness and Culture*, Cornell, 1977, p. 334.
2   Ezra Pound, *Literary Essays*, London and New York, 1954, pp. 20–1.
3   *The Nature of Christian Belief*, A Statement and Exposition by the House of Bishops of the General Synod of the Church of England, London, 1986, pp. 14–15.
4   Sallie McFague, *Speaking in Parables: A Study in Metaphor and Theology*, Philadelphia, 1975.
5   Peter Hodgson and Robert King, eds, *Christian Theology: An Introduction to Its Traditions and Tasks*, London, 1983, p. 1.
6   Hans Urs von Balthasar, *The Glory of the Lord: A Theological Aesthetics*, 7 vols, Edinburgh, 1982, vol. I, *Seeing the Form*, pp. 9–11 and 111.
7   Terry Eagleton, *Literary Theory: An Introduction*, Oxford, 1983, p. 8.
8   R. M. Frye, *Perspective on Man: Literature and the Christian Tradition*, Philadelphia, 1961, p. 43.
9   Ong, *Interfaces*, pp. 258 and 263.
10 Roland Barthes, *Image – Music – Text*, Essays Selected and Translated by Stephen Heath, London, 1977, p. 147.
11 Julia Kristeva, *Desire in Language: A Semiotic Approach to Literature and Art*, translated by Thomas Gova and others, New York, 1980, pp. 125 and 140.

12 David Lodge, *Small World*, London, 1984, pp. 26–7.

13 Francis Mulhern, *The Moment of Scrutiny*, London, 1979, p. 26.

14 Isaiah Berlin, *The Hedgehog and the Fox: An Essay on Tolstoy's View of History*, London, [1953] 1967, pp. 39–40.

15 John Coulson, 'Religion and Imagination', in David Jasper, ed., *Images of Belief in Literature*, London, 1984, p. 8

16 See J. Hillis Miller, *The Disappearance of God*, Cambridge, Mass., 1963.

17 Julian Huxley, *Religion without Revelation*, London, [1927] 1957, p. 58.

18 Peter Walker, '*Horae Canonicae*: Auden's Vision of a Rood – A Study in Coherence', in Jasper, ed., *Images*, p. 63.

19 John Henry Newman, *The Idea of a University*, ed. Martin J. Svaglic, San Francisco, [1852] 1960, p. 237.

20 Michael Edwards, *Towards a Christian Poetics*, London, 1984, pp. 7, 12 and 142.

21 William F. Lynch, *Images of Faith: An Exploration of the Ironic Imagination*, Notre Dame and London, 1973, p. 5.

22 John Coulson, *Religion and Imagination*, Oxford, 1981, pp. v and 82.

23 Gordon Kaufman, *The Theological Imagination: Constructing the Concept of God*, Philadelphia, 1981, p. 11.

24 See for instance Paul Ricoeur, *Essays on Biblical Interpretation*, London, 1981, p. 182.

25 Nathan Scott, *The Poetics of Belief*, Chapel Hill and London, 1985, pp. 1 and 12.

26 Samuel Taylor Coleridge, *Biographia Literaria*, London, [1817], 1956, p. 167.

27 Ibid., p. 48.

28 *The Spiritual Exercises of St. Ignatius*, ed. Henry Keane, London, 1952, p. 25.

29 Ibid., pp. 29–30 and 43.

30 See David Hesla, 'Religion and Literature: The Second Stage', *Journal of the American Academy of Religion*, 46, no. 2 (1978), pp. 181–92, and Giles Gunn, *The Interpretation of Otherness: Literature, Religion and the American Imagination*, New York, 1979.

31 See F. W. Dillistone, 'Introduction', in Jasper, ed., *Images*, pp. 1–2.

32 Samuel Johnson, *Lives of the English Poets*, 2 vols, London, [1779, 1781] 1952, I 204.

33 T. S. Eliot, *Selected Essays*, London [1932], 1934, pp. 389–90.

34 Helen Gardner, *The Business of Criticism*, Oxford, 1959, p. 102; *In Defence of the Imagination*, Cambridge, Mass., 1982.

35   Helen Gardner, *Religion and Literature*, London, [1971] 1983, p. 131.
36   Ibid., p. 126.
37   Ibid., p. 136.
38   Austin Farrer, *Interpretation and Belief*, ed. Charles Conti, London, 1976, p. 9.
39   See David Tracy, *The Analogical Imagination: Christian Theology and the Culture of Pluralism*, London, 1981, p. 102.
40   Basil Mitchell, 'Common Consent', in *PN Review 13*, vol. 6, no. 5 (1979), p. 6.
41   Northrop Frye, *The Great Code*, London, [1982] 1983, p. 47.

Literalism: the common enemy

42   Max Black, *Models and Metaphors: Studies in Language and Philosophy*, Ithaca, NY, 1962, pp. 41, 46, 236–7.
43   Frye, *The Great Code*, p. 60.
44   Ibid., pp. 43–5.
45   Thomas Aquinas, *Summa Theologica*, 1a. 1, 10, quoted in Janet Soskice, *Metaphor and Religious Language*, Oxford, 1985, p. 86.
46   Tony Bennett, *Formalism and Marxism*, London, 1977, p. 116.
47   Ibid., p. 113.
48   Simone Weil, *Waiting for God*, New York, 1973, p. 32.
49   Ian Ramsey, *Christian Discourse: Some Logical Explorations*, London, 1965, p. 80.
50   Ian Ramsey, *Religious Language: An Empirical Placing of Theological Phrases*, London, 1957, pp. 26, 171.
51   Ludwig Wittgenstein, *Lectures and Conversations on Aesthetics, Psychology and Religious Belief*, ed. Cyril Barrett, Oxford, 1966, p. 71.
52   A. J. Ayer, *Language, Truth and Logic*, London, [1936] 1946, p. 9.
53   A. J. Ayer, *The Central Questions of Philosophy*, Harmondsworth, 1976, pp. 74–5.
54   Soskice, *Metaphor*, p. ix.
55   See for instance Sallie McFague, *Metaphorical Theology: Models of God in Religious Language*, London, [1982] 1983, p. 9.
56   Ramsey, *Christian Discourse*, pp. 43, 52.
57   Ramsey, *Religious Language*, pp. 138–43.
58   Frye, *The Great Code*, p. 54.
59   Francis Newman, *Phases of Faith*, Leicester, [1850] 1970, pp. 153, 161–2.
60   Coulson, *Religion and Imagination*, p. 38.
61   John Macquarrie, *God-Talk: An Examination of the Language and Logic of Theology*, London, 1967, p. 213.

62 J. L. Austin, *How To Do Things With Words*, Oxford, 1962, pp. 152–9.

63 See 'Crisis for Cranmer and King James', *PN Review 13*, vol. 6, no. 5 (1979), pp. 1, 8, 17.

64 Ian Robinson, *The Survival of English*, London, 1973, p. 56.

Theology: a matter of language

65 Macquarrie, *God-Talk*, p. 215.

66 Iris Murdoch, *Sartre*, New Haven, 1953, p. 27.

67 *The Poems of George Herbert*, introd. Helen Gardner, Oxford, 1961, p. 175.

68 Paul Ricoeur, *The Rule of Metaphor*, Toronto, 1977, p. 6.

69 W. Donald Hudson, *Wittgenstein and Religious Belief*, London and Basingstoke, 1975, p. 89.

70 Leszek Kolakowski, *Positivist Philosophy: From Hume to the Vienna Circle*, Harmondsworth, [1966] 1972, pp. 9–59.

71 Thomas Hobbes, *Leviathan*, London, [1651], 1914, pp. 20–1.

72 Scott, *Poetics*, pp. 2–3.

73 John Locke, *Essay Concerning Human Understanding*, 2 vols, Oxford, [1690] 1894, II 146–7.

74 Karl Popper, *The Logic of Scientific Discovery*, London, 1959, p. 280.

75 Soskice, *Metaphor*, pp. 99–141. The nominalist position is perhaps best exemplified by Thomas Kuhn, *The Structure of Scientific Revolutions*, Chicago, 1962. For the critical realist position see Mary Hesse, *Science and the Human Imagination*, London, 1954, *Models and Analogies in Science*, Notre Dame, 1966, and (with Michael A. Arbib) *The Construction of Reality*, Cambridge, 1987.

76 Antony Flew and Alasdair MacIntyre, eds, *New Essays in Philosophical Theology*, London, 1955, pp. 96–9.

77 Peter Donovan, *Religious Language*, London, 1976, pp. 25–6.

78 Ian Ramsey, *Religious Language*, p. 28.

79 David Crystal, *Linguistics, Language and Religion*, pp. 157–89.

80 Hudson, *Wittgenstein*, p. 62.

81 Ludwig Wittgenstein, *Tractatus Logico-Philosophicus*, trans. D. F. Pears and B. F. McGuinness, London, 1963, 3:203, 4:01.

82 Ludwig Wittgenstein, *Philosophical Investigations*, trans. G. E. M. Anscombe, Oxford, 1958, p. 18; see John Casey, *The Language of Criticism*, London, 1966, pp. 1–31.

83 Paul Engelmann, *Letters from Ludwig Wittgenstein with a Memoir*, Oxford, 1967, p. 143.

84 Hudson, *Wittgenstein*, pp. 80–6.
85 Wittgenstein, *Philosophical Investigations*, p. 373.
86 Ibid., p. 563.
87 Wittgenstein, *Lectures and Conversations on Aesthetics, Psychology and Religious Belief*, ed. Cyril Barrett, Oxford, 1966, pp. 57–9.
88 D. Z. Phillips, *Faith and Philosophical Inquiry*, London, 1970, p. 132.
89 Wittgenstein, *Philosophical Investigations*, p. 124.
90 D. Z. Phillips, *Prayer*, London, 1969, p. 50.
91 Patrick Sherry, *Religion, Truth and Language-Games*, London, 1977, p. 36.
92 D. Z. Phillips, *Death and Immortality*, London, 1970, pp. 74–5.
93 Karl Barth, *Church Dogmatics*, trans. G. W. Bromiley, 4 vols, Edinburgh [1936] 1975, vol I, 'The Doctrine of the Word of God', Part One, p. 132.
94 Macquarrie, *God-Talk*, pp. 41–9.
95 Rudolf Bultmann, *The Theology of the New Testament*, trans. Kendrick Grobel, 2 vols, New York, 1951 and 1955, II 240.
96 Robert Funk, *Language, Hermeneutic and Word of God: The Problem of Language in the New Testament and Contemporary Theology*, New York and London, 1966, p. 74.
97 Paul Tillich, *The Dynamics of Faith*, London, 1957, pp. 42–3.
98 Macquarrie, *God-Talk*, pp. 154, 166.
99 Martin Heidegger, *Existence and Being*, trans. Douglas Scott, Chicago, 1947, pp. 279–81, 360.
100 Heidegger, *Poetry, Language, Thought*, trans. Albert Hofstadter, New York, [1971] 1975, pp. 184, 208.
101. Funk, *Language, Hermeneutic and Word of God*, pp. 50–8, 67–77.
102 Ibid., pp. 110–20.
103 George A. Lindbeck, *The Nature of Doctrine: Religion and Theology in a Postliberal Age*, London, 1984, p. 18.
104 Ibid., pp. 113–14.
105 B. L. Whorf, *Language, Thought and Reality*, ed. J. B. Carroll, Cambridge, Mass., 1956, pp. 207–19.
106 See George Steiner, *After Babel: Aspects of Language and Translation*, London, 1975.
107 John Dominic Crossan, *The Dark Interval: Towards a Theology of Story*, Niles, Ill., 1975, p. 11.
108 Ibid., pp. 40–1.
109 John B. Cobb, Jr, 'A Theology of Story: Crossan and Beardslee', in Richard Spencer, ed., *Orientation by Disorientation*, Pittsburgh, 1980, pp. 151–64 (q. p. 153).

110 Lynn M. Poland, *Literary Criticism and Biblical Hermeneutics: A Critique of Formalist Approaches*, Chico, Calif., 1985, p. 119.
111 Jonathan Culler, *On Deconstruction: Theory and Criticism after Structuralism*, London, 1983.
112 Mark C. Taylor, *Erring: A Post-Modern A/theology*, Chicago, 1984.
113 Ibid., pp. 103–5.
114 Christopher Norris, *Deconstruction: Theory and Practice*, London, 1982, p. 88.

Literature: the point of reference

115 Matthew Arnold, *Literature and Dogma*, Michigan, [1873] 1968, pp. 189 and 196.
116 I. A. Richards, *Principles of Literary Criticism*, London, [1924] 1967, pp. 211, 216.
117 Ibid., pp. 220–3.
118 Ibid., p. 193.
119 Ibid., pp. 182, 191 and 222–3.
120 F. R. Leavis, *Education and the University: A Sketch for an English School*, London, 1943, p. 35.
121 Ibid., p. 119.
122 F. R. Leavis, *Two Cultures? The Significance of C. P. Snow*, London, 1962, p. 23.
123 F. R. Leavis, *English Literature in Our Time and the University*, London, 1969; *The Living Principle: English as a Discipline of Thought*, London, 1975.
124 W. K. Wimsatt, *The Verbal Icon: Studies in the Meaning of Poetry*, Lexington, 1954.
125 Cleanth Brooks, *The Well-Wrought Urn: Studies in the Structure of Poetry*, New York, 1947, p. 184.
126 Fredric Jameson, *The Prison-House of Language: A Critical Account of Structuralism and Russian Formalism*, Princeton, 1972, pp. 82–3.
127 Viktor Shklovsky, 'Art as Technique', in Lee T. Lemon and Marion J. Rees, eds, *Russian Formalist Criticism: Four Essays*, Lincoln, Neb., 1965, pp. 12, 57.
128 Terence Hawkes, *Structuralism and Semiotics*, London, 1977, p. 73.
129 Shklovsky, 'Art as Technique', pp. 12–13.
130 Coleridge, *Biographia Literaria*, p. 169.
131 Roman Jakobson, 'Closing Statement: Linguistics and Poetics', in Thomas A. Sebeok, ed., *Style in Language*, Cambridge, Mass., 1960, pp. 353–7.

132   Umberto Eco, *A Theory of Semiotics*, Bloomington and London, 1976, pp. 58–66.

133   Phyllis Trible, *God and the Rhetoric of Sexuality*, Philadelphia, 1978, p. 16.

134   Roland Barthes, *S/Z*, trans. Richard Miller, London, 1975, p. 94.

135   Frye, *The Great Code*, pp. 60–1.

136   Ibid., pp. 76–7, 137–8.

137   Culler, *Structuralist Poetics: Structuralism, Linguistics and the Study of Literature*, London, 1975.

138   Culler, *The Pursuit of Signs: Semiotics, Literature and Deconstruction*, London, 1981, p. 5.

139   Ibid., pp. 77–8.

140   T. S. Eliot, *Selected Essays*, p. 34.

141   See Wolfgang Iser, *The Implied Reader: Patterns of Communication in Prose Fiction from Bunyan to Beckett*, Baltimore, 1974; Hans Robert Jauss, 'Literary History as a Challenge to Literary Theory', in Ralph Cohen, ed., *New Directions in Literary History*, Baltimore, 1974; Harold Bloom, *The Anxiety of Influence: A Theory of Poetry*, New York, 1973; Norman Holland, *The Dynamics of Literary Response*, New Haven, 1968, and *5 Readers Reading*, New Haven, 1975; David Bleich, *Subjective Criticism*, Baltimore, 1978; Stanley Fish, *Is There a Text in This Class?*, Cambridge, Mass., 1980.

142   Jacques Lacan, *The Language of the Self: The Function of Language in Psychoanalysis*, trans. with notes and commentary by Anthony Wilden, Baltimore, 1968, pp. 39, 161–3.

143   Hans-Georg Gadamer, *Truth and Method*, trans. G. Bawden and W. G. Doepel, New York, 1982, p. 264.

144   Paul Ricoeur, *Interpretation Theory: Discourse and the Surplus of Meaning*, Fort Worth, Texas, 1976, p. 89.

145   Ricoeur, *Time and Narrative*, trans. Kathleen Mclaughlin and David Pellauer, 2 vols, Chicago, 1984–6, vol. I, pp. ix–x.

146   Ricoeur, *The Symbolism of Evil*, trans. Emerson Buchanan, Boston, Mass., 1969, p. 349.

2   ON READING THE BIBLE AS LITERATURE

Literary criticism of the Bible

All references to the Bible are to the Revised Standard Version unless otherwise stated.

1 Gerald Hammond, 'The Bible as Literature', Part I, *Critical Quarterly*, 25, no. 2 (1983) pp. 5–20 (q. p. 5). T. R. Henn's 'The Bible as Literature' in *Peake's Commentary on the Bible*, ed. M. Black and H. H. Rowley, expanded into *The Bible as Literature*, New York, 1970, deplores those who read the Bible for its aesthetic qualities without reference to its truth.

2 Robert Alter, *The Art of Biblical Narrative*, London, 1981, pp. 18–19.

3 Erich Auerbach, *Mimesis: The Representation of Reality in Western Literature*, Garden City, NY, 1957.

4 Northrop Frye, *The Great Code*, London, [1982] 1983, p. xv.

5 Alter, *The Art of Biblical Narrative*, pp. 16–17.

6 Paul Ricoeur, *The Symbolism of Evil*, trans. Emerson Buchanan, Boston, Mass., 1969, p. 350.

7 William Beardslee, *Literary Criticism of the New Testament*, Philadelphia, 1969, p. 13.

8 Norman R. Petersen, 'Literary Criticism in Biblical Studies', in Richard Spencer, ed., *Orientation by Disorientation*, Pittsburgh, 1980, pp. 25–51 (q. p. 37).

9 See Hans W. Frei, *The Eclipse of Biblical Narrative: A Study in Eighteenth and Nineteenth-Century Hermeneutics*, New Haven and London, 1974.

10 See John Barton, *Reading the Old Testament: Method in Biblical Study*, London, 1984.

11 James Barr, 'Reading the Bible as Literature', *Bulletin of the John Rylands University Library*, 56 no. 1 (1973) pp. 10–33 (q. p. 21). One of the chapters of Barr's *The Bible in the Modern World*, London, 1973, pp. 53–74, also discusses 'The Bible as Literature'.

12 Robert Davidson and A. R. C. Leaney, eds, *Biblical Criticism*, vol 3 of *The Pelican Guide to Modern Theology*, Harmondsworth, 1970, p. 92.

13 Norman C. Habel, *Literary Criticism of the Old Testament*, Philadelphia, 1971, pp. 1–15.

14 Petersen, 'Literary Criticism', pp. 26–7; see also his *Literary Criticism for New Testament Critics*, Philadelphia, 1978.

15 Barton, *Reading*, pp. 24–5.

16 Stephen Neill, *The Interpretation of the New Testament 1861-1961*, Oxford, [1963] 1966, pp. 240–1.

17 Ibid., pp. 244–5.

18 R. E. Clements, *A Century of Old Testament Study*, [1970] 1983, pp. 99–100.

19 Barton, *Reading*, p. 36.

20 Ibid., p. 52.

21　B. S. Childs, *Introduction to the Old Testament as Scripture*, Philadelphia, 1979, p. 74.

22　Stanley Fish, *Is There a Text in This Class?*, Cambridge, Mass., 1980.

23　David Clines, 'Methods in Old Testament Study', in John Rogerson, ed., *Beginning Old Testament Study*, London, 1983, pp. 35–7.

24　Neill, *Interpretation*, p. 242.

25　Alter, *The Art of Biblical Narrative*, p. 16. That book, incidentally, is Edwin M. Good's *Irony in the Old Testament*, Philadelphia, 1965.

26　Norman Perrin, 'The Interpretation of the Gospel of Mark', *Interpretation*, 30 (1976) p. 115.

27　Stephen Prickett, 'Poetry and Prophecy: Bishop Lowth and the Hebrew Scriptures in Eighteenth-Century England', in David Jasper, ed., *Images*, pp. 81–103; 'Towards a Rediscovery of the Bible: The Problem of the Still Small Voice', in Michael Wadsworth, ed., *Ways of Reading the Bible*, Brighton, 1981, pp. 105–17. Lowth's lectures were published in Latin in 1753 and in English in 1787.

28　S. T. Coleridge, *Confessions of an Inquiring Spirit*, London, [1840] 1971, p. 13.

29　C. S. Lewis, quoted in James Barr, 'Reading the Bible as Literature', p. 13.

30　T. S. Eliot, *Selected Essays*, p. 390.

31　Austin Farrer, *The Glass of Vision*, Glasgow, 1948, pp. 108–10.

32　Ibid., pp. 136–8.

33　Helen Gardner, *The Business of Criticism*, Oxford, 1959, pp. 101–2.

34　Auerbach, *Mimesis*, pp. 6–12.

35　Ibid., pp. 35–8.

36　Amos N. Wilder, *Early Christian Rhetoric: The Language of the Gospel*, London, 1964, p. 10.

37　Ibid., pp. 34–44, 81–2 and 133–4.

38　Beardslee, *Literary Criticism*, p. 56.

39　Funk, *Language, Hermeneutic and Word of God: The Problem of Language in the New Testament and Contemporary Theology*, New York and London, 1966, pp. 195.

40　Ibid., pp. 148–9.

41　Dan Otto Via, Jr, *The Parables: Their Literary and Existential Dimension*, Philadelphia, 1967.

42　See Edmund Leach, *Genesis as Myth and Other Essays*, London, 1969; Leach and Alan Aycock, *Structuralist Interpretations of Biblical Myths*, Cambridge, 1983.

43 Dan Otto Via, 'Editor's Foreword' to Daniel Patte's *What Is Structuralist Exegesis?*, Philadelphia, 1976, pp. iii-iv.
44 See Jonathan Culler, *Structuralist Poetics*, London, 1975, esp. ch. 9, 'Poetics of the Novel'.
45 Dan Otto Via, ed., *Semiology and Parables: An Exploration of the Possibilities Offered by Structuralism for Exegesis*, Pittsburgh, 1976, pp. 1–27.
46 The conference proceedings, which originally appeared under the title *Analyse structurale et exégèse biblique*, Neuchâtel, 1971, have been translated by Alfred Johnson as *Structuralist Analysis and Biblical Exegesis*, Pittsburgh, 1974. Barthes' essay, 'The Struggle with the Angel', can be found in his *Image – Music – Text*, London, 1977, pp. 125–41 (q. pp. 140–1).
47 Hammond, 'The Bible', p. 13.
48 Roland Barthes, 'The Structuralist Analysis of a Narrative from Acts X-XI', in Alfred Johnson, ed., *Structuralism and Biblical Hermeneutics*, Pittsburgh, 1979, p. 120.
49 Louis Marin, 'A Structural Analysis Essay of Acts 10:1–11:18', in Johnson, *Structuralism*, pp. 147–78.
50 See Louis Marin, 'Les Femmes au tombeau', *Langages*, 22 (1971), pp. 39–50, discussed by Robert A. Spivey in 'Structuralism and Biblical Studies: The Uninvited Guest', *Interpretation*, 28 (1974), pp. 133–64. This whole issue was given to the discussion of structuralist analysis of the Bible, as were the first two issues of *Semeia* (1974) and the supplement to *Vetus Testamentum* 22 (1972).
51 Paul Ricoeur, *Biblical Hermeneutics*, supplement to *Semeia*, 4 (1975), pp. 30 and 51.
52 Ibid., pp. 54–63.
53 Frank Kermode, *The Genesis of Secrecy: On the Interpretation of Narrative*, Cambridge, Mass., 1979, p. x. For a fuller discussion of the way in which midrash brings out the 'open' character of a text see Geoffrey Hartman and Sanford Budick, eds, *Midrash and Literature*, New Haven and London, 1986.
54 Kermode, *Genesis*, pp. 89–99.
55 Frye, *The Great Code*, pp. 169–72.
56 Petersen, 'Literary Criticism', p. 39.
57 Herbert Schneidau, *Sacred Discontent: The Bible and Western Tradition*, Berkeley, 1976, pp. 4–12.
58 John Dominic Crossan, 'Waking the Bible', *Interpretation* 32 (1978), pp. 269–85.
59 John Dominic Crossan, *In Parables: The Challenge of the Historical Jesus*, New York, 1973, p. 10.
60 Crossan, *The Dark Interval: Towards a Theology of Story*, Niles, Ill., 1975, pp. 121–2.

61   Ibid., pp. 73–6.
62   Ibid., pp. 93–5.
63   Lynn Poland, *Literary Criticism and Biblical Hermeneutics: A Critique of Formalist Approaches*, Chico, Calif., 1985, pp. 108 and 118–20, quoting from Crossan's *Finding Is the First Act*, Philadelphia, 1979, and *Cliffs of Fall*, New York, 1980. For further exploration of *Derrida and Biblical Studies*, see *Semeia*, 23 (1982).
64   Alter, *The Art of Biblical Narrative*, pp. 35, 67–9 and 115–26.
65   Ibid., pp. 132–48.
66   Ibid., pp. 51–62.
67   Robert Alter, *The Art of Biblical Poetry*, New York, 1985, pp. 9–24. Alter takes T. H. Robinson, *The Poetry of the Old Testament*, London, 1947, as a standard exposition of traditional views of parallelism. Among more recent considerations of the subject he cites James L. Kugel, *The Idea of Biblical Poetry*, New Haven and London, 1981, and Ruth apRoberts, 'Old Testament Poetry: The Translatable Structure', *PMLA*, 92 (1977), pp. 987–1004.
68   Alter, *The Art of Biblical Poetry*, p. 110.
69   Charles Williams, *War in Heaven*, London, [1930] 1962, p. 24.
70   Alter, *The Art of Biblical Poetry*, p. 205.
71   Dan Jacobson, *The Story of the Stories: The Chosen People and Its God*, London, 1982, pp. 89 and 125.

The readability of Genesis

72   Norman C. Habel, *Literary Criticism*, p. 26.
73   John C. L. Gibson, *Genesis*, 2 vols, Edinburgh and Philadelphia, 1981–2, vol. I, pp. 125–6.
74   Barthes, *Image – Music – Text*, pp. 131–2.
75   Alan Aycock, 'The Fate of Lot's Wife: Structural Mediation in Biblical Mythology' in Leach and Aycock, *Structuralist Interpretations*, pp. 113–19.
76   Gibson, *Genesis*, vol. II, pp. 290–9.
77   Dan Jacobson, *The Story of the Stories*, p. 131; *The Rape of Tamar*, London, 1970.
78   Alter, *The Art of Biblical Narrative*, p. 29.
79   See Wolfgang Iser, *The Implied Reader*, which finds an increasing indeterminacy and a more active role for the reader in the development of the modern novel.
80   Alan Aycock, 'The Mark of Cain', in Leach and Aycock, *Structuralist Interpretations*, pp. 120–7.

81 Auerbach, *Mimesis*, pp. 6–9.
82 Alter, *The Art of Biblical Narrative*, pp. 107–11.
83 Ibid., p. 165.
84 Ibid., p. 140.
85 Ibid., p. 175.
86 George W. Coats, 'Redactional Unity in Genesis 37–50', *JBL*, 93 (1974), pp. 15–21 (q. p. 21).
87 Hugh C. White, 'The Joseph Story: A Narrative which "Consumes" Its Content', *Semeia*, 31 (1985), pp. 49–69 (q. p. 57).

The meanings of Mark's story

88 Werner H. Kelber, *Mark's Story of Jesus*, Philadelphia, 1979, p. 16.
89 Norman Perrin, *The New Testament: An Introduction*, New York, 1974, p. 143.
90 D. E. Nineham, *Saint Mark*, Harmondsworth, 1963, p. 35.
91 See G. N. Stanton, *Jesus of Nazareth in New Testament Preaching*, Cambridge, 1974; C. H. Talbert, *What is a Gospel? The Genre of the Canonical Gospels*, London, 1978.
92 James M. Robinson and Herbert Koester, *Trajectories through Early Christianity*, Philadelphia, 1971.
93 B. H. M. G. M. Standaert, *L'évangile selon Marc: composition et genre littéraire*, Nijmegen, 1978.
94 Willi Marxsen, *Der Evangelist Markus*, Göttingen, 1956.
95 Kelber, *Mark's Story*.
96 Perrin, 'The Interpretation of the Gospel of Mark', *Interpretation*, 30 (1976) p. 116, quoting K. L. Schmidt.
97 David Rhoads and Donald Michie, *Mark as Story: An Introduction to the Narrative of a Gospel*, Philadelphia, 1982, p. 6.
98 Ernest Best, *Mark: The Gospel as Story*, Edinburgh, 1983, pp. 94 and 145.
99 Norman R. Petersen, ' "Point of View" in Mark's Narrative', *Semeia*, 12 (1978), pp. 97–121.
100 Best, *Mark*, p. 118.
101 Kermode, *The Genesis of Secrecy*, pp. 68 and 115.
102 Ibid., pp. 127–9.
103 Rhoads and Michie, *Mark as Story*, p. 54.
104 Ibid., p. 62.
105 Kelber, *Mark's Story*, pp. 32–41.
106 Kermode, *The Genesis of Secrecy*, pp. 49–73.
107 Kelber, *Mark's Story*, p. 90.
108 Alec McCowan, *Personal Mark*, London, 1985, p. 62.
109 Ibid., p. 101.

110   R. C. Tannehill, 'The Disciples in Mark: The Function of a Narrative Role', *Journal of Religion*, 57 (1977), pp. 386–405; cp. J. D. Hawkin, 'The Incomprehension of the Disciples in the Marcan Redaction', *JBL*, 91 (1972), pp. 491–500.

111   McCowan, *Personal Mark*, pp. 14, 33 and 210.

112   The only other New Testament uses of the word 'Abba' are in Galatians 4:6 and Romans 8:15. Michael Clévenot, *Materialist Approaches to the Bible*, trans. William J. Nottingham, Maryknoll, NY, 1985, pp. 111–14. Clévenot popularizes the position advocated more fully by Fernando Belo in *A Materialist Reading of the Gospel of Mark*, trans. Matthew J. O'Connell, Maryknoll, NY, 1981.

113   Nineham, *Saint Mark*, p. 439.

114   Kermode, *The Genesis of Secrecy*, pp. 67–8.

115   Norman R. Petersen, 'When is the End not the End? Literary Reflections on the Ending of Mark's Narrative', *Interpretation*, 34 (1980), pp. 151–66 (q. pp. 160–2).

116   Best, *Mark*, p. 73.

3   NARRATIVE THEOLOGY: THE STORIES OF FAITH

Narrative, myth and history

1   William G. Doty, 'The Stories of Our Time', in James B. Wiggins, ed., *Religion as Story*, New York, 1975, p. 94.

2   Gabriel Fackré, 'Narrative Theology: An Overview', *Interpretation*, 37, no. 4 (1983) pp. 340–52; this whole issue was given to 'Narrative Theology', while *Modern Theology*, 2, no. 2 (1986) is on 'Theology, Truth and Narrative'.

3   Michael Goldberg, 'Exodus 1: 13–14', also *Interpretation*, 37 (1983), p. 94.

4   Quoted in Robert Lee Wolff, *Gains and Losses: Novels of Faith and Doubt in Victorian England*, New York, 1977, frontispiece.

5   Sir Philip Sidney, *A Defence of Poetry*, ed. J. A. Van Dorsten, London, 1966, pp. 25–38.

6   Aristotle, 'On the Art of Poetry', in *Classical Literary Criticism*, trans. T. S. Dorsch, Harmondsworth, 1965, pp. 43–4.

7   Amos Wilder, 'Story and Story-World', *Interpretation*, 37 (1983), pp. 353–64 (q. pp. 362 and 354–5).

8   Michel Foucault, 'Nietzsche, Genealogy, History', in *Language, Counter-Memory, Practice*, ed. and trans. Donald F. Bouchard, and Sherry Simon, pp. 156–7.

9 George Stroup, *The Promise of Narrative Theology*, Atlanta, 1981, p. 71. He compiled 'A Bibliographical Critique' of texts employing the terms 'story' and 'narrative' in *Theology Today*, 32 (1975), pp. 133–43. See also Harald Weinrich, 'Narrative Theology', *Concilium*, 51, no. 9 (1973), pp. 84–96.

10 H. Richard Niebuhr, *The Meaning of Revelation*, New York, 1941, p. 35.

11 Stroup, *Promise*, p. 17.

12 Stephen Crites, 'The Narrative Quality of Experience', *Journal of the American Academy of Religion*, 39 (1971), pp. 291–311 (q. pp. 295–6).

13 Frank Kermode, *The Sense of an Ending: Studies in the Theory of Fiction*, New York, 1969, pp. 39 and 43.

14 John Dominic Crossan, *The Dark Interval: Towards a Theology of Story*, Niles, Ill., 1975, pp. 128–9. These terms, as Crossan himself acknowledges, derive from Sheldon Sacks, *Fiction and the Shape of Belief*, Chicago and London, [1964] 1980.

15 John B. Cobb, Jr, 'A Theology of Story: Crossan and Beardslee', in Richard Spencer, ed., *Orientation by Disorientation*, Pittsburgh, 1980, p. 158.

16 Maurice Wiles, 'Myth in Theology', in John Hick, ed., *The Myth of God Incarnate*, London, 1977, pp. 148–66.

17 Aristotle, 'On the Art of Poetry', pp. 41–2.

18 These distinctions are clearly expounded in Seymour Chatman, *Story and Discourse: Narrative Structure in Fiction and Film*, Cornell, 1978.

19 Ibid., p. 48.

20 Paul Ricoeur, *Time and Narrative*, trans. Kathleen Mclaughlin and David Pellauer, 2 vols, Chicago, 1984–6, vol. I, pp. 3–30; cp. Crites, 'Narrative Quality', pp. 298–9.

21 James W. McClendon, Jr, *Theology as Biography*, Nashville, 1974.

22 Sam Keen and Anne Valley Fox, *Telling Your Story*, Garden City, NY, 1973.

23 Sam Keen, quoted in William Beardslee, *Literary Criticism of The New Testament*, Philadelphia, 1969, p. ix.

24 David A. Stewart, *Theology and Personal Story*, Ph. D. thesis at San Francisco Theological Seminary, San Anselmo, California, 1982.

25 Fackré, 'Narrative Theology', p. 349. He cites a number of black and feminist theologians.

26 Roland Barthes, 'Introduction to the Structural Analysis of Narratives', in *Image – Music – Text*, London, 1977, pp. 79 and 121.

27   Victor Turner, *Drama, Fields and Metaphors*, Ithaca, NY, 1975, pp. 248–9.

28   Gordon H. Bower, 'Experiments in Story Understanding and Recall', *Quarterly Journal of Experimental Psychology*, 28 (1976), pp. 511–34, quoted by Stephen Sykes in 'The Grammar of Narrative and Making Sense of Life', *Anglican Theological Review*, 67, no. 2 (1985), pp. 117–26.

29   Stephen Sykes, 'The Role of Story in the Christian Religion: An Hypothesis', *Literature and Theology*, 1 (1987), pp. 19–26 (q. p. 24). See in the same issue an essay by Wesley A. Kort on 'Narrative Theology', pp. 27–38.

30   Stephen Sykes, 'Story and Eucharist', *Interpretation*, 37 (1983), pp. 365–72.

31   Sykes, 'The Role of Story', referring to Dietrich Ritschl and H. O. Jones, *'Story' als Rohmaterial der Theologie*, Munich, 1976, and *Zur Logik der Theologie*, Munich, 1984.

32   See Jonathan Culler, *Structuralist Poetics: Structuralism, Linguistics and the Study of Literature*, London, 1975, p. 219.

33   W. J. Hollenweger, 'Karl Barth as a Narrative Theologian', foreword to David Ford, *Barth and God's Story*, Munich, 1981, pp. 6–8.

34   Ford, ibid., p. 24, quoting Karl Barth, *Church Dogmatics*, Edinburgh, 1936–69, I i 362 and 321.

35   Ford, ibid., pp. 20–2 and 52.

36   James Barr, 'Revelation Through History in the Old Testament and in Modern Theology', *Interpretation*, 17, no. 2 (1963); 'The Concepts of History and Revelation', in *Old and New in Interpretation*, New York, 1966; 'Story and History in Biblical Theology', *Journal of Religion*, 56, no. 1 (1976), pp. 1–17.

37   Gerhard von Rad, *Old Testament Theology*, 2 vols, New York, 1962 and 1965; Oscar Cullmann, *Christ and Time*, Philadelphia, 1964; Ernest Wright, *God Who Acts*, London, 1952.

38   Wolfhart Pannenberg, ed., *Revelation as History*, London, 1969, p. 4.

39   Niebuhr, *The Meaning of Revelation*, p. 44.

40   Hayden White, 'The Structure of Historical Narrative', *Clio*, 1 (1972), pp. 52; 'The Value of Narrativity in the Representation of Reality', *Critical Inquiry* 7 (1980–1) pp. 5–14; 'The Question of Narrative in Contemporary Historical Theory', *History and Theory*, 23, no. 1 (1984), pp. 1–33; cp. *Metahistory: The Historical Imagination in Nineteenth-Century Europe*, Baltimore and London, 1973.

41   Robert Scholes and Robert Kellog, *The Nature of Narrative*, New York, 1966, p. 211.

42 'Editor's Note: On Narrative', *Critical Inquiry* 7 (1980–1) p. 2.
43 Ricoeur, *Time and Narrative*, vol. I, pp. 95–105, discussing the work of Marc Bloch and Fernand Braudel.
44 Ibid., pp. 143–4, quoting Arthur C. Danto, *Analytic Philosophy of History*, Cambridge, 1965, p. 11.
45 Ibid., pp. 149–54, summarizing W. S. Gallie, *Philosophy and Historical Understanding*, New York, 1968.
46 Hayden White, *The Tropics of Discourse*, Baltimore and London, 1978, p. 82.
47 Ricoeur, *Time and Narrative*, vol. I, pp. 175–8.
48 Lionel Trilling, *Sincerity and Authenticity*, London, 1974, p. 138.
49 See C. A. Patrides, *The Grand Design of God: The Literary Form of the Christian View of History*, London, 1972; D. Forbes, *The Liberal Anglican View of History*, Cambridge, 1952; Gillian Beer, *Darwin's Plots*, London, 1983.
50 Pierre Teilhard de Chardin, *The Phenomenon of Man*, trans. Bernard Wall, London, 1959.
51 Cobb, 'A Theology of Story', pp. 157–9.

Religious Autobiography: writing God and the self

52 James Olney, *Metaphors of Self: The Meaning of Autobiography*, Princeton, 1972, p. vii.
53 Ibid., pp. 30–1, 105 and 108; the phrase 'mythic statements', of course, is taken from Jung while the last quotation is from Ernst Cassirer, *Essay on Man*, New York, 1944, p. 221.
54 Mark C. Taylor, *Erring: A Post-Modern A/theology*, Chicago, 1984, pp. 44–5.
55 Roland Barthes, *Roland Barthes by Roland Barthes*, trans. Richard Howard, London, 1977, p. 56.
56 Jean Starobinski, 'The Style of Autobiography', in Seymour Chatman, ed., *Literary Style: A Symposium*, London and New York, 1971, pp. 285–94 (q. p. 287).
57 Samuel Taylor Coleridge, *Biographia Literaria*, London, [1817] 1956, p. 167.
58 For a fuller explanation of the origin of these terms in linguistics and their adoption by literary theory see David Lodge, *The Modes of Modern Writing*, London, 1977.
59 Pelican Freud Library, trans. James Strachey, ed. Angela Richards, vol. IX, 'Case Histories II', p. 240.
60 Roy Pascal, *Design and Truth in Autobiography*, London, 1960, p. 19.

61 Ibid., p. 117; see Michael Sprinker, 'Fictions of the Self: The End of Autobiography', in James Olney, ed., *Autobiography: Essays Theoretical and Critical*, Princeton, 1980, pp. 321–42, for further exploration of Freud's 'reticence'.

62 Saint Augustine, *Confessions*, trans. R. S. Pine-Coffin, Harmondsworth, 1961, pp. 215–16.

63 Taylor, *Erring*, p. 45.

64 William James, *The Varieties of Religious Experience*, London and Glasgow, [1902] 1960, pp. 43–5.

65 Sprinker, 'Fictions of the Self', p. 325.

66 Peter Brown, *Augustine of Hippo: A Biography*, London, 1967, pp. 159–79; Brown himself refers to P. Courcelle, *Les confessions de S. Augustin dans la tradition littéraire*, Paris, 1963.

67 Sallie McFague, *Speaking in Parables: A Study in Metaphor and Theology*, Philadelphia, 1975, pp. 158–61.

68 John O'Meara, *The Young Augustine*, London and New York, [1954] 1980, pp. 182–3.

69 Augustine, *Confessions*, pp. 166–78.

70 Harold Bloom, *The Anxiety of Influence*, New York, 1973.

71 Augustine, *Confessions*, pp. 186–7.

72 Ibid., p. 208.

73 Starobinski, 'The Style of Autobiography', p. 290.

74 Augustine, *Confessions*, p. 267.

75 Louis A. Renza, 'The Veto of the Imagination: A Theory of Autobiography', in Olney, *Autobiography*, pp. 268–95 (q. p. 277).

76 James, *Varieties*, pp. 176–8.

77 For a critical summary of these see David Burrell, 'Reading *The Confessions* of Augustine: An Exercise in Theological Understanding', *Journal of Religion*, 50 (1970), pp. 327–51.

78 Augustine, *Confessions*, pp. 164–5.

79 Ibid., pp. 170–5.

80 Ibid., pp. 223–4.

81 Ibid., p. 233.

82 Ibid., pp. 237 and 293.

83 Starobinski, 'The Style of Autobiography', p. 288.

84 Burrell, 'Reading *The Confessions*', p. 332.

85 Augustine, *Confessions*, pp. 21–3.

86 Ibid., p. 88; cp. p. 104.

87 Ibid., p. 133.

88 Ibid., p. 304; cp. pp. 108 and 115.

89 Ibid., p. 111.

90 Brown, *Augustine of Hippo*, p. 168.

91 Augustine, *Confessions*, p. 188.

92 Ibid., pp. 211–13.

93 Pascal, *Design and Truth*, pp. 25 and 186.
94 Stephen Medcalf, ed., *The Later Middle Ages*, London, 1981, pp. 120–3.
95 *The Book of Margery Kempe*, trans. with an introd. by Barry Windeatt, Harmondsworth, 1985, pp. 103–4.
96 Ibid., p. 144.
97 Ibid., p. 155.
98 Ibid., pp. 176 and 187.
99 Ibid., p. 214.
100 Ibid., pp. 228–49.
101 Medcalf, *Later Middle Ages*, pp. 114–15.
102 James, *Varieties*, pp. 302–5.
103 Medcalf, *Later Middle Ages*, p. 118.
104 *Kempe*, p. 83.
105 Ibid., p. 182; for more about the textual 'background' to *The Book of Margery Kempe* see pp. 15–22.
106 Ibid., p. 78; cp. James, *Varieties*, p. 39.
107 Ibid., pp. 41–3.
108 Paul Delaney, *British Autobiography in the Seventeenth Century*, London and New York, 1969, p. 36.
109 Roger Sharrock, *John Bunyan*, London, 1954, pp. 56–7.
110 John Bunyan, *Grace Abounding to the Chief of Sinners*, ed. Roger Sharrock, Oxford, [1666] 1962, p. xxxi.
111 Ibid., p. 14.
112 Ibid., p. 27.
113 Ibid., p. 33.
114 Ibid., p. 50.
115 James, *Varieties*, pp. 163, 175 and 191–3.
116 Sharrock, *John Bunyan*, pp. 57–8.
117 Delaney, *British Autobiography*, pp. 34–5.
118 Bunyan, *Grace Abounding*, p. 2.
119 Ibid., p. 21.
120 Ibid., pp. 64–82.
121 Delaney, *British Autobiography*, pp. 95–7.
122 Bunyan, *Grace Abounding*, pp. 52–3.
123 Thomas Carlyle, *Sartor Resartus*, London, [1833–4] 1908, p. 127.
124 Pascal, *Design and Truth*, ch. 3.
125 *The Confessions of Jean-Jacques Rousseau*, trans. J. M. Glen, Baltimore, 1953, p. 7.
126 John Henry Newman, *Apologia pro Vita Sua*, Everyman edn, London, [1864] n. d., p. 31.
127 Ibid., p. 29.
128 Ibid., p. 186.

129　Ibid., p. 164.
130　Ibid., p. 215.
131　Wilfrid Ward, *The Life of John Henry Newman, Based on His Private Journals and Correspondence*, 2 vols, London, 1912, vol. I, pp. 534–613; see also A. O. J. Cockshut, *The Art of Autobiography in Nineteenth and Twentieth-Century England*, London, 1984.
132　John Henry Newman, *Autobiographical Writings*, ed. Henry Tristram, London, 1956, p. 5.
133　John Henry Newman, *Historical Sketches*, 3 vols, London, 1872–3, vol. III, p. 227.
134　Newman, *Apologia*, pp. 120–1.
135　O'Meara, *The Young Augustine*, pp. 160–9.

Realism in the novel: from metaphysics to metafiction

136　Auguste Comte, *System of Positive Polity*, trans. J. H. Bridges and others, 4 vols, London, [1851–4] 1875–7, vol. I, pp. 44–5; see *Oxford English Dictionary*, Oxford, [1931] 1961, pp. 1152–3.
137　Colin McCabe, *James Joyce and the Revolution of the Word*, London, 1978, p. 15.
138　Georg Lukács, *The Theory of the Novel*, trans. Anna Bostock, London, 1971 [1920], pp. 86–8.
139　Edwards, *Towards a Christian Poetics*, pp. 76–7.
140　Lukács, *Theory of the Novel*, p. 11 (from the preface of 1962).
141　Ibid., pp. 29–30.
142　Georg Lukács, *Writer and Critic and Other Essays*, ed. Arthur E. Kahn, New York, 1971, pp. 42–3.
143　Georg Lukács, *Studies in European Realism*, trans. Edith Bone, London, 1972 [1950].
144　Ibid., pp. 13–18.
145　Ibid., pp. 152–3.
146　Sheldon Sacks, *Fiction and the Shape of Belief*, pp. 264–5.
147　Ibid., pp. 8, 14 and 54.
148　Ian Watt, *The Rise of the Novel*, London, 1957.
149　Patricia Meyer Spacks, *Imagining a Self: Autobiography and Novel in Eighteenth-Century England*, Cambridge, Mass., and London, 1976, p. 29.
150　Henry Fielding, *Tom Jones*, Harmondsworth, [1749] 1966, p. 363.
151　Laurence Sterne, *Tristram Shandy*, New York, [1760–7] 1967, p. 384.

152 Ibid, p. 302.

153 Margaret Maison, *Search Your Soul, Eustace: Victorian Religious Novels*, London and New York, 1961; Robert Lee Wolff, *Gains and Losses: Novels of Faith and Doubt in Victorian England*, London, 1977.

154 Kathleen Tillotson, *Novels of the 1840's*, Oxford, 1954, pp. 116–17.

155 Thomas Pinney, ed., *Essays of George Eliot*, New York and London, 1963, p. 310.

156 Ibid., p. 123.

157 George Eliot, *Adam Bede*, New York, [1858] 1966, pp. 140–2.

158 Gordon Haight, ed., *George Eliot Letters*, 9 vols, New Haven and London, 1954 and 1978, vol. IV, pp. 300–1; U. C. Knoepflmacher, '*Middlemarch*: An Avuncular View', *NCF* 30 (1975), pp. 53–81.

159 *George Eliot Letters*, vol. III, pp. 382 and 371.

160 George Eliot, *Silas Marner*, Harmondsworth, [1861] 1967, p. 51.

161 Ludwig Feuerbach, *The Essence of Christianity*, trans. George Eliot, New York, [1854] 1957, p. 188.

162 Eliot, *Silas Marner*, p. 127.

163 David Friedrich Strauss, *The Life of Jesus Critically Examined*, trans. George Eliot, London, 1973 [1846], p. 88.

164 Eliot, *Silas Marner*, p. 128.

165 Strauss, *Life of Jesus*, pp. 39–92.

166 Eliot, *Silas Marner*, pp. 139–40 and 226; cp. Joseph Wiesenfarth, 'Demythologizing *Silas Marner*', *ELH* 37 (1970) pp. 226–44.

167 Eliot, *Silas Marner*, pp. 80–1.

168 Ibid., pp. 163–4.

169 Ibid., pp. 190–1.

170 John Philip Crouch, *George Eliot in France: A French Appraisal of George Eliot's Writings, 1858–1960*, Chapel Hill, 1967, pp. 86–105; Owen Chadwick, *The Secularization of the European Mind in the Nineteenth Century*, Cambridge, 1975, pp. 244–9.

171 Chadwick, *Secularization*, p. 246.

172 Leo Tolstoy, *Anna Karenina*, trans. Rosemary Edmonds, Harmondsworth, 1973 [1874–6], p. 853.

173 T. G. S. Cain, *Tolstoy*, London, 1977, pp. 129–31.

174 Fedor Dostoyevsky, *The Brothers Karamazov*, trans. Constance Garnett, 2 vols, London, 1927 [1880], vol. I, pp. 241–70.

175 Mikhail Bakhtin, *Problems of Dostoevsky's Poetics*, ed. and trans. Caryl Emerson, Minneapolis, 1984, pp. 6–7.

176 Terry Eagleton, 'Lawrence', in Ian Gregor and Walter Stein, eds, *The Prose for God*, London, 1973, pp. 86–100.

177 E. M. Forster, *A Passage to India*, Harmondsworth, [1924] 1979, p. 272.
178 Iris Murdoch, *The Nice and the Good*, London, [1968] 1977, p. 125.
179 Iris Murdoch, *The Good Apprentice*, London, 1985, p. 52.
180 Ibid., pp. 77, 140 and 445.
181 Iris Murdoch, *The Fire and the Sun: Why Plato Banished the Artists*, Oxford, 1977, pp. 87–8; cp. Elizabeth Dipple, *Iris Murdoch: Work for the Spirit*, London, 1982, esp. ch. 2, 'Reality and Realism'.
182 Iris Murdoch, *Nuns and Soldiers*, London, 1980, p. 66.
183 Ibid., pp. 291–3.
184 Christopher Sykes, *Evelyn Waugh: A Biography*, Harmondsworth, 1977, p. 450.
185 Evelyn Waugh, *Helena*, Harmondsworth, 1950, p. 128.
186 David Lodge, *Working with Structuralism*, London, 1981, p. 123.
187 Donat Gallagher, ed., *Evelyn Waugh: A Little Order*, London, 1977, p. 148.
188 Ibid., p. 32.
189 Evelyn Waugh, *Brideshead Revisited*, Harmondsworth, [1945] 1951, p. 83; cp. the revised edition, Harmondsworth, [1960] 1962, p. 83.
190 Ibid., p. 140.
191 Ibid., pp. 272–9.
192 Ibid. (1962 edn), p. 7.
193 Ian Littlewood, *The Writings of Evelyn Waugh*, Oxford, 1983, p. 159.
194 François Mauriac, quoted in Georg M. A. Gaston, *The Pursuit of Salvation: A Critical Guide to the Novels of Graham Greene*, Troy, NY, 1984, p. 44.
195 Graham Greene, *The End of the Affair*, Harmondsworth, [1951] 1962, pp. 7 and 35–6.
196 Ibid., p. 69.
197 Ibid., pp. 111–12.
198 Frank Kermode, 'The House of Fiction: Interviews with Seven English Novelists', *Partisan Review*, 30 (1963), p. 67.
199 Lodge, *Working with Structuralism*, p. 111.
200 Graham Greene, Letter to Dr Michel Lechat at the front of *A Burnt-Out Case*, Harmondsworth, [1960] 1963.
201 Flannery O'Connor, *Mystery and Manners: Occasional Prose*, ed. Sally and Robert Fitzgerald, New York, 1969, pp. 40–1 and 124.
202 Flannery O'Connor, 'The Fiction Writer and His Country' in Granville Hicks, ed., *The Living Novel: A Symposium*, New York, [1957] 1962, pp. 162–3.

203 Flannery O'Connor, *Everything That Rises Must Converge*, London, [1955, 1960] 1969, p. 148.
204 Flannery O'Connor, *Wise Blood*, London, [1952] 1968, 'Author's Note'.
205 Ibid., pp. 54–5 and 105.
206 Flannery O'Connor, *The Violent Bear It Away*, London, [1955] 1965, p. 113.
207 Patricia Waugh, *Metafiction: The Theory and Practice of Self-Conscious Fiction*, London, 1984.
208 Kurt Vonnegut, *Cat's Cradle*, Harmondsworth, [1963] 1965, p. 109.
209 Ibid., p. 177.
210 Ibid., p. 9.
211 Ibid., p. 160.
212 Ibid., p. 179.

4 METAPHORICAL THEOLOGY: THE POETRY OF FAITH

The dynamics of metaphor: metaphysical wit

1 Ramsey, *Religious Language*, p. 107; see Owen Barfield, 'The Meaning of the Word "Literal" ', in L. C. Knights and Basil Cottle, eds, *Metaphor and Symbol*, London, 1960, pp. 48–57.
2 Roman Jakobson, quoted in Terry Eagleton, *Literary Theory: An Introduction*, Oxford, 1983, p. 8.
3 Aristotle, 'On the Art of Poetry', in *Classical Literary Criticism*, trans. T. S. Dorsch, Harmondsworth, 1965, pp. 61–5.
4 Terence Hawkes, *Structuralism and Semiotics*, London, 1977, pp. 77–9; cp. David Lodge, *The Modes of Modern Writing*, London, 1977, pp. 74–8.
5 See Janet Soskice, *Metaphor and Religious Language*, Oxford, 1985, pp. 24–7 and 77–9; the positions she attacks are represented by A. J. Ayer, *Language, Truth and Logic*, London, 1936, J. L. Austin, *How to Do Things with Words*, Oxford, 1962, John Searle, *Speech Acts*, Cambridge, 1969, and Colin Turbayne, *The Myth of Metaphor*, New Haven, 1962.
6 Max Black, *Models and Metaphors: Studies in Language and Philosophy*, Ithaca, NY, 1962, pp. 35–47.
7 Stephen Prickett, *Words and 'The Word': Language, Poetics and Biblical Interpretation*, Cambridge, 1986, pp. 221–2; see Douglas Berggren, 'The Use and Abuse of Metaphor', *Review of Metaphysics*, 16 (1962–3), pp. 237–58 and 450–72; Berggren himself

draws on W. Bedell Stanford, *Greek Metaphor: Studies in Theory and Practice*, Oxford, 1936.

8   Philip Wheelwright, *Metaphor and Reality*, Bloomington, 1962.
9   Paul Ricoeur, *The Rule of Metaphor*, Toronto, 1977, pp. 221–4 and 255–6.
10 Northrop Frye, *The Great Code*, London, [1982] 1983, pp. 54–5.
11 Edmund Ryden, 'Aquinas on the Metaphorical Expression of Theological Truth', *Heythrop Journal*, 27 (1986), pp. 409–19.
12 Sallie McFague, *Metaphorical Theology: Models of God in Religious Language*, London, [1982] 1983, pp. 9 and 169–73; cp. Phyllis Trible, *God and the Rhetoric of Sexuality*, Philadelphia, 1978.
13 Soskice, *Metaphor and Religious Language*, pp. 95–6.
14 Philip Wheelwright, *The Burning Fountain: A Study in the Language of Symbolism*, Bloomington, [1954] 1968, p. 120.
15 Mark Searle, 'Liturgy and Metaphor', *Notre Dame Journal of English*, 14 (1981), pp. 185–206 (q.p. 201).
16 *Poems of Gerard Manley Hopkins*, ed. W. H. Gardner and N. H. Mackenzie, 4th edn, London, 1967, pp. 53–4.
17 *The Sermons and Devotional Writings of Gerard Manley Hopkins*, ed. Christopher Devlin, London, 1959, p. 197.
18 Hans Urs von Balthasar, *The Glory of the Lord: A Theological Aesthetics*, 7 vols, Edinburgh, 1982, III 391.
19 Alexander Pope, 'An Essay in Criticism', in *The Poems of Alexander Pope*, ed. John Butt, London, 1965, p. 153.
20 Samuel Johnson, *Lives of the English Poets*, 2 vols, London, [1779, 1781] 1952, I 13–14 and 36.
21 *The Metaphysical Poets*, ed. Helen Gardner, Harmondsworth, 1957, p. 208.
22 Helen Gardner, *Religion and Literature*, London, [1971] 1983, pp. 171–94; cp. Louis Martz, *The Poetry of Meditation*, London, 1954.
23 *The Poems of George Herbert*, ed. F. E. Hutchinson, London, 1961, p. 44.
24 See A. D. Nuttall, *Overheard by God: Fiction and Prayer in Herbert, Milton, Dante and St John*, London, 1980.

Symbol and sacrament: the Romantic imagination

25 Paul Ricoeur, *Interpretation Theory*, Fort Worth, Texas, 1976, p. 61.
26 Wheelwright, *The Burning Fountain*, p. 6, quoting Mary Anita Ewer, *A Survey of Mystical Symbolism*, London, 1933.

27 Karl Rahner, 'The Theory of Symbol', in *Theological Investigations*, 10 vols, London, 1974, vol. IV, pp. 221–52; cp. Joseph H. P. Wong, 'Karl Rahner's Christology of Symbol and Three Models of Christology', *Heythrop Journal*, 27 (1986), pp. 1–25.

28 Paul Ricoeur, *The Symbolism of Evil*, Boston, Mass., 1969, pp. 15 and 350; cp. William York Tindall, *The Literary Symbol*, Bloomington, 1955, pp. 13 and 22.

29 Paul Tillich, *The Dynamics of Faith*, London, 1957, pp. 42–3.

30 Tillich, *The Shaking of the Foundations*, London, 1949, p. 86.

31 Tillich, *The Protestant Era*, Chicago, 1948, p. xxiii.

32 Mircea Eliade, *Images and Symbols: Studies in Religious Symbolism*, London, 1961, p. 18.

33 Thomas Fawcett, *The Symbolic Language of Religion*, London, 1970, p. 22.

34 Eliade, *Images and Symbols*, p. 162.

35 'The Dream of the Rood', trans. Michael Alexander, in Donald Davie, ed., *New Oxford Book of Christian Verse*, Oxford, 1981, pp. 1–4.

36 See 'Poems on the Passion' in *Medieval English Verse*, trans. Brian Stone, Harmondsworth, 1964, pp. 33–41.

37 George Chapman, 'A Hymn to Our Saviour on the Cross', in Peter Levi, ed., *Penguin Book of English Christian Verse*, Harmondsworth, 1984, p. 58.

38 *John Donne: The Complete English Poems*, ed. A. J. Smith, Harmondsworth, 1971, p. 330.

39 *The English Hymnal*, no. 107 and 'Explanatory Notes'; *Hymns Ancient and Modern*, no. 116.

40 *The English Hymnal*, no. 96.

41 Siegfried Sassoon, 'The Redeemer', in *Selected Poems*, London, 1968, p. 16.

42 C. Day Lewis, 'Introduction' to *The Collected Poems of Wilfred Owen*, London, 1963, p. 23; for a number of First World War poems which focus upon the symbolic figure of Christ see *Poetry of the Great War*, ed. Dominic Hibberd and John Onions, London and Basingstoke, 1986.

43 Edith Sitwell, 'Still Falls the Rain', in Levi, ed., *English Christian Verse*, p. 293.

44 Edward Schillebeeckx, *Christ the Sacrament of the Encounter with God*, London, [1963] 1985, pp. 92–4.

45 Searle, 'Liturgy and Metaphor', pp. 189–90.

46 John Henry Newman, *Lectures on the Present Position of Catholics in England*, London, [1851], no. 6, 'Prejudice the Life of the Protestant View', pp. 27–8.

47 F. W. Dillistone, *Christianity and Symbolism*, London, 1955, pp. 183–7.

48 Eliade, *Images and Symbols*, pp. 153–8.

49 *Pope John Sunday Missal: A Treasury of Catholic Spirituality*, ed. Michael Buckley, Leigh-on-Sea, Essex, 1978, pp. 317–50.

50 William Blake, 'Auguries of Innocence', in *Blake: The Complete Poems*, ed. W. H. Stevenson, London, 1971, p. 585.

51 'The Marriage of Heaven and Hell', Ibid., pp. 105 and 112.

52 William Wordsworth, 'Tintern Abbey', in *Wordsworth: Poetry and Prose*, ed. W. M. Merchant, London, 1969, p. 153.

53 Stephen Prickett, *Romanticism and Religion: The Tradition of Coleridge and Wordsworth in the Victorian Church*, Cambridge, 1976, p. 109.

54 Wordsworth, *The Prelude*, ed. J. C. Maxwell, Harmondsworth, 1971, p. 108 (1805–6 version, Book III, line 129).

55 Ibid., pp. 238–40 (Book VI, lines 534–6 and 568–72).

56 Ibid., pp. 514–6 (Book XIII, lines 68–73; 1850 version, XIV, 76).

57 Harold Bloom, *The Visionary Company: A Reading of English Romantic Poetry*, London, 1962, p. 159. For a fuller and more sympathetic recognition of Wordsworth's religious beliefs see J. R. Watson, *Wordsworth's Vital Soul: The Sacred and Profane in Wordsworth's Poetry*, London and Basingstoke, 1982.

58 Wordsworth, *The Prelude*, p. 504 (XII, 301–5).

59 Prickett, *Words and 'The Word'*, pp. 105–23.

60 Ibid., p. 146, quoting *The Correspondence of G. M. Hopkins and R. W. Dixon*, ed. C. C. Abbott, Oxford, 1935, pp. 147–8.

61 G. M. Hopkins, 'Pied Beauty' and 'As Kingfishers Catch Fire', *Poems*, pp. 69 and 90.

62 S. T. Coleridge, *Lay Sermons*, ed. R. J. White, Princeton, [1816–7] 1972, p. 80; cp. David Jasper, 'Some Romantic Theories on Religious Symbolic Language', *Heythrop Journal*, 28 (1987), pp. 31–9.

63 Thomas Carlyle, *Sartor Resartus*, London [1833–4] 1908, pp. 165–9.

64 Ibid., p. 198. See M. H. Abrams, *Natural Supernaturalism: Tradition and Revolution in Romantic Literature*, London, 1971, for a comprehensive study of the Romantic attempt to locate God in the natural world.

65 Richard Ellmann, 'Introduction' to Arthur Symons, *The Symbolist Movement in Literature*, New York, [1899] 1918, p. vii.

66 Ibid., pp. 1–5.

67 Tindall, *The Literary Symbol*, p. 44.

68 W. B. Yeats, *Autobiographies*, London, 1955, p. 279.

69 Yeats, 'The Symbolism of Poetry', in *Essays and Introductions*, New York, 1968, pp. 162–3.

70 Peter Ackroyd, *T. S. Eliot*, London, 1984, pp. 33–4.

71 *The Complete Poems and Plays of T. S. Eliot*, London, 1969, p. 37.
72 Michael Edwards, *Towards a Christian Poetics*, London, 1984, pp. 106 and 116.
73 Eliade, *Images and Symbols*, p. 176.
74 Eliot, *Complete Poems*, pp. 61–80.
75 Ibid., p. 175.
76 Ibid., p. 196.

Paradox and ambiguity: the modern dilemma

77 Wheelwright, *The Burning Fountain*, p. 29.
78 John Henry Newman, *University Sermons: Fifteen Sermons Preached before the University of Oxford, 1826–43*, ed. D. M. MacKinnon and J. D. Holmes, London, [1843] 1970.
79 Cleanth Brooks, 'The Language of Paradox', reprinted from his book *The Well-Wrought Urn*, in David Lodge, ed., *Twentieth-Century Literary Criticism*, London, 1972, p. 297.
80 Stephen Prickett, *Words and 'The Word'*, p. 188; see John Wisdom, *Paradox and Discovery*, Oxford, 1965.
81 William Empson, *Seven Types of Ambiguity*, London, [1930] 1947, pp. 1–3 and 234–5.
82 Ruth Page, *Ambiguity and the Presence of God*, London, 1985, pp. 11–13.
83 John Macquarrie, *God-Talk: An Examination of the Language and Logic of Theology*, London, 1967, pp. 123–46.
84 Quoted by Bernard Williams in his unsympathetic account of 'Tertullian's Paradox' in Antony Flew and Alasdair MacIntyre, eds, *New Essays in Philosophical Theology*, London, 1955, pp. 41–2.
85 Ninian Smart, *The Philosophy of Religion*, New York, 1970, pp. 41–2.
86 Erasmus, *Praise of Folly*, trans. Betty Radice, Harmondsworth, 1971, pp. 154 and 198.
87 Martin Luther, *A Commentary on St Paul's Epistle to the Galatians*, London, 1953, p. 269.
88 Eliot, *Selected Essays*, London, [1932] 1934, p. 416.
89 Blaise Pascal, *Pensées*, ed. Louis Lafuma, trans. John Warrington, London, 1960, p. 10.
90 Ibid., pp. 14 and 20.
91 Ibid., pp. 31–2.
92 Ibid., p. 62.
93 Ibid., p. 65.
94 John Henry Newman, *Apologia pro Vita Sua*, Everyman edn, London, [1864] n.d., pp. 217–8.

95 Newman, 'The Pillar of the Cloud', in *Verses on Various Occasions*, London, [1868] 1890, pp. 156–7.

96 Hugh Ross Mackintosh, 'The Theology of Paradox: Søren Kierkegaard', in *Types of Modern Theology: Schleiermacher to Barth*, London, 1937, pp. 218–62.

97 Dante Alighieri, Epistola X to Can Grande, quoted in Frye, *The Great Code*, pp. 220–1, and Prickett, *Words and 'The Word'*, p. 157. I am indebted throughout my discussion of Dante to Prickett's chapter on 'The Paradoxes of Disconfirmation'.

98 Dante Alighieri, *Purgatorio*, Canto XXVII, lines 124–42, *The Divine Comedy*, trans. John D. Sinclair, 3 vols, New York, 1961, vol. II, pp. 356–7.

99 Ibid., Canto XXX, lines 1–75, vol. II, pp. 392–6.

100 Ibid., Canto XXXI, lines 121–3, vol. II, pp. 408–9.

101 Frye, *The Great Code*, p. 221, quoting Milton, *De Doctrina Christiana*, I xxx.

102 Alastair Fowler, 'Introduction' to his edition of *Paradise Lost*, London, 1965, p. 37.

103 William Blake, 'The Marriage of Heaven and Hell', *Complete Poems*, p. 107.

104 William Empson, *Milton's God*, London, 1961; for the opposite point of view see Dennis Richard Danielson, *Milton's Good God: A Study in Literary Theodicy*, Cambridge, 1982.

105 Robert Lowell, 'Waking Early Sunday Morning', quoted by Donald Davie in his 'Introduction' to *The New Oxford Book of Christian Verse*, p. xix.

106 Andrew Marvell, 'The Definition of Love', *The Complete Poems*, ed. Elizabeth S. Donno, Harmondsworth, 1972, p. 49.

107 Davie, *New Oxford Book of Christian Verse*, pp. xxv-xxvii.

108 Hopkins, *Poems*, p. 69.

109 Empson, *Seven Types of Ambiguity*, p. 225.

110 Ted Hughes, *Crow*, London, 1970, pp. 17–18.

111 Ibid., p. 57.

112 Geoffrey Hill, *For the Unfallen*, London, 1959, p. 39.

113 Hill, 'Lachrimae: I. Lachrimae Verae', in *Tenebrae*, London, 1978; see Christopher Ricks, '*Tenebrae* and at-one-ment', in Peter Robinson, ed., *Geoffrey Hill: Essays on His Work*, Milton Keynes, 1985, pp. 62–85, to which I am also indebted for the following quotations from Hill.

114 *Viewpoints: Poets in Conversation with John Haffenden*, London, 1981, p. 89.

115 Hill, *The Lords of Limit: Essays on Literature and Ideas*, London, 1984, p. 2.

116 Ricks, *'Tenebrae'*, pp. 64–7.
117 R. S. Thomas, 'Kierkegaard', *Selected Poems, 1964–1968*, Newcastle upon Tyne, [1973] 1986, p. 86.
118 Ibid., p. 43.
119 Ibid., p. 44.
120 R. S. Thomas, ed., *Penguin Book of Religious Verse*, Harmondsworth, 1963.
121 R. S. Thomas, *Later Poems, 1972–1982*, London, 1983, pp. 23 and 95.
122 Ibid., p. 111.
123 R. S. Thomas, *Experimenting with an Amen*, London, 1986, p. 31.
124 Ibid., p. 53.
125 Ibid., p. 52.
126 Thomas, *Later Poems*, p. 118; see D. Z. Phillips, *R. S. Thomas: Poet of the Hidden God*, London, 1986.

5 THEOLOGY AND DRAMA: ACTS OF FAITH AND DOUBT

Liturgical drama: from the mass to the mystery plays

1 Alexander Schmemann, *Introduction to Liturgical Theology*, trans. Asheleigh E. Moorhouse, Leighton Buzzard, [1966] 1975, pp. 14 and 141.
2 John A. T. Robinson, *Honest to God*, London, 1963, p. 89.
3 I. R. Thompson, 'The Other Liturgical Revolution', in Brian Morris, *Ritual Murder: Essays in Liturgical Reform*, Manchester, 1980, pp. 154–62.
4 Schmemann, *Introduction*, pp. 18 and 138–40.
5 D. H. Lawrence, *The Rainbow*, Harmondsworth, [1915] 1949, p. 280.
6 Hamish F. G. Swanston, 'Icon and Word', in Ian Gregor and Walter Stein, eds, *The Prose for God*, London, 1973, pp. 163–4.
7 Ibid., p. 163.
8 Jürgen Moltmann, 'The Liberating Feast', *Concilium* n.s. 2, no. 10 (1974) on 'Liturgy', pp. 74–84.
9 A. Stewart Todd, 'Movement and Drama in Worship' in R. C. D. Jasper, ed., *Getting the Liturgy Right*, London, 1982, pp. 56–62.
10 *The Alternative Service Book: A Commentary*, by the Liturgical Commission of the Church of England, London, 1980, p. 167.
11 *Vatican Council II: The Conciliar and Post-Conciliar Documents*, ed. Austin Flannery, O. P., 2 vols, Collegeville, Minn., 1975, vol. I, pp. 12 and 35.

12   A. H. Couratin, 'Liturgy', in *Historical Theology*, ed. J. Danielou, John Kent and Couratin, vol. II of the *Pelican Guide to Modern Theology*, Harmondsworth, 1969, p. 224.

13   Ibid., pp. 225–7.

14   See Jane Harrison, *Ancient Art and Ritual*, London, 1913, Gilbert Murray, *Five Stages of Greek Religion*, Oxford, 1925, and F. M. Cornford, *The Origin of Attic Comedy*, Cambridge, 1934.

15   O. B. Hardison, Jr, *Christian Rite and Christian Drama in the Middle Ages*, Baltimore, 1965, pp. 36–7.

16   Jerome Taylor, 'Critics, Mutations, and Historians of Medieval English Drama' in *Medieval English Drama: Essays Critical and Contextual*, ed. Taylor and Alan H. Nelson, Chicago, 1972, p. 9.

17   Hardison, *Christian Rite*, p. 43.

18   Ibid., pp. 38 and 78–9.

19   Ibid., pp. 44–6.

20   Ibid., p. 55.

21   Ibid., pp. 59 and 62.

22   Ibid., p. viii.

23   David Bevington, *Medieval Drama*, Chicago, 1975, p. 9.

24   Rosemary Woolf, *The English Mystery Plays*, Berkeley and Los Angeles, 1972, pp. 5–7.

25   Bevington, *Medieval Drama*, pp. 14–15.

26   Ibid., p. 16.

27   Woolf, *English Mystery Plays*, p. 7.

28   Ibid., pp. 20–1.

29   Bevington, *Medieval Drama*, pp. 12–13; Richard Axton plays down the dramatic elements in these ceremonies in his *European Drama of the Early Middle Ages*, London, 1974, pp. 62–4, pointing to the absence of an audience and of complete impersonation.

30   Ibid., pp. 21–4.

31   Ibid., pp. 27–8; for a fuller discussion of this play in its monastic, liturgical and musical context see George B. Bryan, *Ethelwold and Medieval Music-Drama at Winchester*, Berne, 1981.

32   Ibid., pp. 34–5 and 42–4.

33   Axton, *European Drama*, pp. 70 and 171–2.

34   Ibid., pp. 206–8.

35   A. M. Kinghorn, *Medieval Drama*, London, 1968, ch. 5, 'Realism in the Middle Ages'.

36   A. P. Rossiter, *English Drama from Early Times to the Elizabethans*, London, 1950, pp. 69–71.

37 Stanley J. Kahrl, *Traditions of Medieval English Drama*, London, 1974, pp. 75–82.

38 W. H. Auden, *Collected Longer Poems*, London, 1968, p. 149.

39 Erich Auerbach, *Mimesis: The Representation of Reality in Western Literature*, Garden City, NY, 1957, p. 138.

40 Kahrl, *Traditions*, pp. 84–91.

41 *The York Plays*, ed. Richard Beadle, London, 1982, pp. 315–22.

42 V. A. Kolvé, *The Play Called Corpus Christi*, London, 1966, pp. 27–31.

43 Kahrl, *Traditions*, p. 64.

44 Kolvé, *The Play*, p. 119; cp. the chapter on 'Figura' in Erich Auerbach, *Scenes from the Drama of European Literature*, trans. Ralph Manheim, New York, 1959.

45 Ibid., p. 84.

46 Ibid., p. 48.

47 Taylor and Nelson, *Medieval English Drama*, p. 150; but see Woolf, *English Mystery Plays*, pp. 68–75, for some reservations about the cycles as specifically constructed for the feast of Corpus Christi.

Renaissance tragedy and Reformation theology

48 George Poulet, *Studies in Human Time*, trans. Eliott Coleman, Baltimore, 1956, p. 10.

49 Ernst Robert Curtius, *European Literature and the Latin Middle Ages*, trans. W. R. Trask, New York, 1953, p. 142.

50 John R. Elliott, Jr, 'The Sacrifice of Isaac as Comedy and Tragedy', in Taylor and Nelson, *Medieval English Drama*, pp. 157–76 (q. p. 173).

51 John Calvin, *Institutes of the Christian Religion*, trans. Ford Lewis Battles, 2 vols, London, 1960, I 700–1 (Book III, ch. vii, section 10).

52 Ibid., II 930–1 (III, xxi, 7).

53 Ibid., I 340 (II, v, 19).

54 Alan Sinfield, *Literature in Protestant England 1560–1660*, London, 1983, p. 5; cp. Jonathan Dollimore, *Radical Tragedy: Religion, Ideology and Power in the Drama of Shakespeare and His Contemporaries*, Brighton, 1984. I am indebted to these two books for references to Calvin and other Reformation theologians, though I come to very different conclusions.

55 Dollimore, *Radical Tragedy*, pp. 6–10; cp. James Kavanagh, 'Shakespeare in Ideology', in *Alternative Shakespeares*, ed. John Drakakis, London, 1985, pp. 144–65.

56 John Tinsley, 'Tragedy and Christian Beliefs', *Theology*, 85 (1982), pp. 98–106.

57 Adrian Poole, *Tragedy: Shakespeare and the Greek Example*, Oxford, 1987, pp. 1–3.

58 See Helen Gardner, *Religion and Literature*, London, [1971] 1983, esp. ch. 1, 'Concepts of Tragedy'.

59 For a survey of criticism see Max Bluestone, '*Libido Speculandi*: Doctrine and Dramaturgy in Contemporary Interpretations of Marlowe's *Doctor Faustus*', in N. Rabkin, ed., *Reinterpretations of Elizabethan Drama*, New York, 1969; see also the introduction to the Casebook on *Doctor Faustus*, ed. John D. Jump, London, 1969.

60 All references to *Dr. Faustus* are to the Revels Plays Edition, ed. John D. Jump, London, 1962.

61 Dollimore, *Radical Tragedy*, pp. 110–12.

62 Ibid., p. 110.

63 See Wilbur Sanders, *The Dramatist and the Received Idea*, Cambridge, 1968, esp. ch. 12, 'Marlowe and the Calvinist Doctrine of Reprobation'.

64 William Lawne, *An Abridgment of the Institution of Christian Religion*, trans. Christopher Fetherstone, Edinburgh, 1587, p. 222.

65 Calvin, *Institutes*, I 620 (III, iii, 24) and I 321 (II, v, 5).

66 Sinfield, *Literature in Protestant England*, p. 119.

67 Calvin, *Institutes*, I 231 (V, ii, 86).

68 *Marlowe's 'Doctor Faustus' 1604–1616*, Parallel Texts ed. W. W. Greg, Oxford, 1950, p. 285.

69 For a critical survey of 'Theologizing Analyses' and 'Secular Analyses' of Shakespeare see the first two chapters of R. M. Frye, *Shakespeare and Christian Doctrine*, Princeton, 1963; see also the first chapter of Ivor Morris, *Shakespeare's God: The Role of Religion in the Tragedies*, London, 1972. All references to Shakespeare's plays are to the Tudor Edition, *William Shakespeare: The Complete Works*, ed. Peter Alexander, London and Glasgow, 1951.

70 Frye, *Shakespeare and Christian Doctrine*, pp. 12 and 57.

71 Morris, *Shakespeare's God*, pp. 24–5 and 31.

72 Richard Hooker, *Works*, ed. John Keble, Oxford, 1863, vol. I, p. 223, quoted in Sanders, *The Dramatist*, p. 310, in a chapter on '*Macbeth* and the Theology of Evil'.

73 J. H. Jack, 'Macbeth, King James and the Bible', *English Literary History*, 22 (1955), pp. 176–93 (q.p. 176).

74 Gardner, *Religion and Literature*, pp. 85–6.

75 Jack, '*Macbeth*, King James and the Bible', p. 181.

76 *Calvin's Sermons on Job*, trans. A. Golding, London, 1573, pp. 29–35.

77 William R. Elton, *'King Lear' and the Gods*, San Marino, Calif., 1966.

78 A. C. Bradley, *Shakespearean Tragedy*, New York, [1904] 1955, p. 228.

79 But see the first chapter of Elton's *'King Lear' and the Gods* for a strong condemnation of the over-confident Christian readings popular earlier this century.

The theology of the absurd: Godotology

80 Arthur Adamov, *L'Aveu*, Paris, 1946, p. 45, translated and quoted by Martin Esslin in *The Theatre of the Absurd*, 3rd edn, Harmondsworth, [1961] 1983, p. 94.

81 Albert Camus, *The Myth of Sisyphus*, trans. Justin O'Brien, New York, 1961.

82 Esslin, *Theatre of the Absurd*, pp. 24–6.

83 Ibid., pp. 402 and 424.

84 Ibid., pp. 128–32.

85 Ibid., p. 152; see Eugene Ionesco, *Rhinoceros, The Chairs, The Lesson*, Harmondsworth, 1959.

86 Esslin, Ibid., p. 23.

87 Francis Doherty, *Samuel Beckett*, London, 1971, p. 89.

88 All references to *Waiting for Godot* are to the Faber edition, London, [1956] 1965. I am partially indebted to D. Z. Phillips's as yet unpublished Riddell Memorial Lectures delivered in Newcastle in November 1986 on 'God's Word and Our Words'.

89 For a summary of contemporary speculation over the name Godot see Melvin J. Friedman, 'Critic!', *Modern Drama*, 9 (1966), pp. 300–8. This number (no. 3) was devoted entirely to Beckett, including a section on 'Godotology'.

90 Doherty, *Samuel Beckett*, p. 89.

91 Robert E. Todd, 'Proust and Redemption in *Waiting for Godot*', *Modern Drama*, 10 (1967), pp. 175–81 (q. p. 178); see Samuel Beckett, *Proust*, London, 1931.

92 John J. Sheedy, 'The Comic Apocalypse of King Hamm', *Modern Drama*, 9 (1966), pp. 310–18; references in parentheses are to *Endgame*, London, 1958.

93 For discussion of the allusions to St John's Gospel and the Book of Revelation see Ruby Cohn, *Samuel Beckett: The Comic Gamut*, New Brunswick, 1962, pp. 231–2.

94 Samuel Beckett, *Fin de Partie*, Paris, 1957, pp. 103–5, translated and quoted in Esslin, *Theatre of the Absurd*, p. 72.

232 *Notes to pp. 187–199*

95 Jan Kott, *Shakespeare Our Contemporary*, trans. Boleslaw Taborski, London, [1965] 1967, p. 126.
96 Charles R. Lyons, 'Beckett's *Endgame*: An Anti-Myth Creation', *Modern Drama*, 7 (1964), pp. 204–9.
97 Samuel Beckett, *Happy Days*, London, 1963.
98 Samuel Beckett, *All That Fall*, London, 1957.
99 Linda Ben-Zvi, 'Samuel Beckett's Media Plays', *Modern Drama*, 28 (1985), pp. 22–37.
100 Samuel Beckett, *Eh Joe and Other Writings*, London, 1967.
101 Samuel Beckett, *Krapp's Last Tape and Embers*, London, 1959.
102 Peter Nichols, *Passion Play*, London, 1981, p. 60.
103 June Schlueter, 'Adultery is Next to Godliness: Dramatic Juxtaposition in Peter Nichols' *Passion Play*', *Modern Drama*, 24 (1981), pp. 540–5.
104 Peter Shaffer, *Three Plays*, Harmondsworth, 1976.
105 Tom Stoppard, *Jumpers*, London, 1972.
106 Keir Elam, 'After Magritte, after Carroll, after Wittgenstein: What Tom Stoppard's Tortoise Taught Us', *Modern Drama*, 27 (1984), pp. 169–85.

SELECT BIBLIOGRAPHY

A comprehensive bibliography for this subject would be a book in itself while simply to list the books referred to in the text would be to duplicate the notes. What follows will, I hope, be more useful: a select bibliography suggesting ways in which the questions raised in each of the chapters could be followed up in greater detail. I do not give references to books on individual writers, since any such selection would be entirely arbitrary.

JOURNALS

The major journals for the joint study of theology and literature are, in America *Religion and Literature* (formerly *The Notre Dame English Journal: A Journal of Religion in Literature*), *Christianity and Literature* and the *Journal of the American Academy of Religion*. In England only *Literature and Theology* is aimed specifically at the interaction of the two disciplines but among theological periodicals *Heythrop Journal, Religious Studies* and *Modern Theology* have shown a particular interest in literature. Of the many journals in Biblical Studies, *Semeia* is dedicated to exploring new critical approaches while *Interpretation* has devoted a number of special issues to such areas as structuralism and narrative theology. Among literary periodicals perhaps *PN Review* has shown most interest in theology, particularly the language of the Bible and liturgy. Specialist journals such as *Worship, Ritual Studies, The Novel, Modern Fiction Studies* and *Modern Drama* should obviously be consulted in these areas, as should those journals devoted to particular periods: *Mediaeval Studies, Renaissance Quarterly, Eighteenth-Century Studies, Victorian Studies,* and so on.

1   TOWARDS A POETICS OF FAITH

There is no obvious introduction to the joint study of theology and literature. A good survey and selection of major American contributions to the subject is provided in Giles Gunn, ed., *Literature and Religion* (New York, 1971). Nathan Scott's *Poetics of Belief* (Chapel Hill and London, 1985), John Coulson's *Religion and Imagination* (Oxford, 1981), Michael Edwards's *Towards a Christian Poetics* (London, 1984), Helen Gardner's *Religion and Literature* (London, 1971), William Lynch's *Images of Faith* (Notre Dame and London, 1973) and David Jasper's (ed.) *Images of Belief in Literature* (London, 1984) are all useful collections of essays on individual writers without aiming at being comprehensive or systematic. There is, of course, von Balthasar's monumental contribution to theological aesthetics, *The Glory of the Lord* (Edinburgh, 1982), while Gordon Kaufman and David Tracy consider *The Theological Imagination* (Philadelphia, 1981) and *The Analogical Imagination* (London, 1981) respectively.

For a philosophical analysis of religious language Ian Ramsey's work continues to provide a clear introduction (especially his short study of *Christian Discourse*, London, 1965), to be supplemented (and complicated) by the existentialist approach of John Macquarrie's *God-Talk* (London, 1967), the Heideggerian 'language of Being' in Robert Funk's *Language, Hermeneutic and Word of God* (New York and London, 1966), the structuralism of George Lindbeck's *The Nature of Doctrine* (London, 1984) and the deconstruction of Mark Taylor's *Erring* (Chicago, 1984). In the general area of hermeneutics I have found the work of Paul Ricoeur most valuable, with his introduction to *Interpretation Theory* (Fort Worth, Texas, 1976) a good place to start. Those totally unacquainted with literary theory can find recent trends clearly articulated in the work of Jonathan Culler, especially *Structuralist Poetics* (London, 1975), *The Pursuit of Signs* (London, 1981) and *On Deconstruction* (London, 1983).

2 LITERARY CRITICISM OF THE BIBLE

Clear introductions to literary criticism of the Bible are provided by William Beardslee's *Literary Criticism of the New Testament* (Philadelphia, 1969), Norman Petersen's *Literary Criticism for New Testament Critics* (Philadelphia, 1969), David Jasper's *The New Testament and the Literary Imagination* (London, 1987) and John Barton's *Reading the Old Testament* (London, 1984). A real sense of the excitement of this subject could be gained from Frank Kermode's *The Genesis of Secrecy* (Cambridge, Mass., 1979), Northrop Frye's *The Great Code* (London, [1982] 1983) and Robert Alter's two books on the Old Testament: *The Art of Biblical Narrative* (London, 1981) and *The Art of Biblical Poetry* (New York, 1985).

Daniel Patte asks (and answers) the basic question, *What is Structuralist Exegesis?* (Philadelphia, 1976), Dan Otto Via studies how it works in *Semiology and Parables* (Pittsburgh, 1976) and Alfred Johnson has translated some of the pioneering French essays in *Structuralist Analysis and Biblical Exegesis* (Pittsburgh, 1974). See also the special issues on the subject in *Interpretation*, 28 (1974), *Semeia*, 1–2 (1974) and *Vetus Testamentum*, 22 (1972). Herbert Schneidau's *Sacred Discontent* gives a clear indication of what deconstruction can do for (or to?) the Bible, which is further illustrated by the many volumes of John Dominic Crossan. See *Semeia* for special issues on deconstruction (vol. 23, 1982), feminist hermeneutics (vol. 28, 1983) and reader-response criticism (vol. 31, 1985). See Phyllis Trible, *Texts of Terror* (Philadelphia, 1981) and Letty M. Russell, ed., *Feminist Interpretation of the Bible* (Oxford, 1985) for further exploration of feminist biblical criticism.

3 NARRATIVE THEOLOGY

George Stroup's *The Promise of Narrative Theology* (Atlanta, 1981) gives a solid, bibliographically helpful, introduction to the varieties of narrative theology, which is made more exciting by Crossan's *The Dark Interval: Towards a Theology of Story* (Niles, Ill., 1975). See also the special issues of *Interpretation* (vol. 37, no. 4, 1983) and *Modern Theology* (vol. 2, no. 2, 1986). The clearest account of modern narrative theory is probably Seymour Chatman's *Story and Discourse* (Cornell, 1978), the most profound Ricoeur's *Time and Narrative* (Chicago, 1984–6), though this is definitely *not* the place to start.

James Olney's collection of essays on *Autobiography* (Princeton, 1980) includes a wide range of possible approaches to this subject, including psychoanalytic and structuralist. For a sound historical basis to the autobiographies of different periods see Stephen J. Greenblatt's *Renaissance Self-Fashioning* (Chicago, 1980), Paul Delaney's *British Autobiography in the Seventeenth Century* (London and New York, 1969), Patricia Spacks's *Imagining a Self: Autobiography and Novel in Eighteenth-Century England* (Cambridge, Mass., and London, 1976) and A. O. J. Cockshut, *The Art of Autobiography in Nineteenth and Twentieth-Century England* (London, 1984). Sallie McFague's *Speaking in Parables* (Philadelphia, 1975) also considers a number of modern religious autobiographies.

Sheldon Sacks's *Fiction and the Shape of Belief* (Chicago and London, [1964] 1980) and Ian Watt's *The Rise of the Novel* (London, 1957) provide a good introduction to religious novels of the eighteenth century while Margaret Maison's *Search Your Soul, Eustace* (London and New York, 1961) and Robert Lee Wolff's *Gains and Losses* (New York, 1977) provide comprehensive surveys of Victorian religious fiction. See also Michael Wheeler's survey of *English Fiction of the Victorian Period 1830–1900* (London, 1985), with its useful bibliographies. For an introduction to theology in the modern novel see Nathan Scott, *Craters of the Spirit: Studies in the Modern Novel* (Washington, 1968) and Robert Detweiler's survey of the 'Theological Trends of Post-Modern Fiction', *Journal of the American Academy of Religion*, 44 (1976), pp. 225–37.

4   METAPHORICAL THEOLOGY

Sallie McFague's *Metaphorical Theology* (London, [1982] 1983), Paul Ricoeur's *The Rule of Metaphor* (Toronto, 1977) and Janet Soskice's *Metaphor and Religious Language* (Oxford, 1985) provide the most systematic theoretical introductions to this area. For more practical but wide-ranging studies of religious poetry see David Daiches's *God and the Poets* (Oxford, 1984) and A. D. Nuttall, *Overheard by God* (London, 1980). Donald Davie's *New Oxford Book of Christian Verse* (Oxford, 1981), Peter Levi's *Penguin Book of English Christian Verse* (Harmondsworth, 1984) and R. S. Thomas's *Penguin Book of Religious Verse* (Harmondsworth, 1963) are the best of many anthologies.

M. H. Abrams's *Natural Supernaturalism* (London, 1971) is the classic study of Romantic symbolism, while Edmund Wilson's *Axel's Castle* (London and New York, 1936) remains the standard introduction to the Symbolists as such. Of Mircea Eliade's many books on religious symbolism *Images and Symbols* (London, 1961) is perhaps the best introduction to the subject. William Empson's *Seven Types of Ambiguity* (London, [1930] 1947), Cleanth Brooks's *The Well-Wrought Urn* (New York, 1947) and W. K. Wimsatt's *The Verbal Icon* (Lexington, 1954) show 'close' reading of poetic and theological ambiguity in New Critical practice. Stephen Prickett's *Words and 'The Word'* (Cambridge, 1986) includes an illuminating discussion of paradox.

5   THEOLOGY AND DRAMA

See Alexander Schmemann's *Introduction to Liturgical Theology* (Leighton Buzzard, [1966] 1975) for an Orthodox introduction to that subject. Eric Bentley has written a number of lively general introductions to drama, including *The Life of the Drama* (London, 1966). See also Keir Elam, *The Semiotics of Theatre and Drama*

(London, 1980). The best introduction to *Medieval Drama* is David Bevington's book of that title (Chicago, 1975), which provides an interesting selection of plays with translations and commentary.

To counterbalance the radical post-structuralist accounts of Renaissance tragedy provided by Dollimore and Sinfield it would be worth consulting A. D. Nuttall's *The New Mimesis: Shakespeare and the Representation of Reality* (London, 1983). For a radical Marxist view of French tragedy and its relation to ideology (especially Jansenism) see Lucien Goldmann, *The Hidden God* (London, 1964). Northrop Frye's *Anatomy of Criticism* (Princeton, 1957) and *A Natural Perspective* (New York, 1965) would be the obvious points from which to begin a study of Shakespearean comedy in relation to theology. Martin Esslin's *The Theatre of the Absurd* (Harmondsworth, [1961] 1983) was responsible for this whole concept. See the annual bibliographies in *Modern Drama* for the many other contributions to the subject.

INDEX

absurd, theatre of, 12
Acts of the Apostles, 52
Adamov, Arthur, 187
aesthetics, 3
Alter, Robert, 41, 56–8, 71
Althusser, Louis, 15
Amalarius, Bishop of Metz, 167–9
ambiguity, 152–62
Andrewes, Lancelot, 150
Angela of Foligno, 102
Annales, School of, 91
Anselm, St, 132
Apocrypha, 53
Aquinas, Thomas, 2, 8, 14, 131–2
Arians, 18–19
Aristotle, 22, 83, 84, 86, 129
Arnold, Matthew, 32
Arrabal, Fernando, 189
Articles, the Thirty-Nine, 19, 177
Athanasius, 153
atonement, 17
Auden, W. H. 6, 173
Auerbach, Erich, 42, 48, 68, 110, 173
Augustine, St, of Hippo, 2, 11, 87, 94, 95–100, 109–10, 143–4, 153, 185
Aurelius, Marcus, 95
Austen, Jane, 87, 113, 114
Austin, J. L., 19
autobiography, 11, 92–110
Ayer, A. J., 17

Bakhtin, Mikhail, 119
Balthasar, Hans Urs von, 2–3, 136
Balzac, Honoré de, 36, 112
baptism, 89, 144–5, 164
Barnabus, Gospel of, 141
Barr, James, 90
Barth, Karl, 2, 8, 21, 26, 90
Barthes, Roland, 4, 36–7, 51–2, 93
Barton, John, 44
Baxter, Richard, 104
Beardslee, William, 8, 49
Beckett, Samuel, 12, 188, 189–97, 199
Bennett, Tony, 15
Berlin, Isaiah, 5
Bèze, Théodore de, 176
biblical theology, 46
Black, Max, 13, 130–1
Blake, William, 7, 130, 146, 158
Bleich, David, 39
Bloom Harold, 39, 96, 147
Bonaventura, St, 102
Bonhoeffer, Dietrich, 8
Bradley, A. C., 187
Braithwaite, R. B., 23
Brecht, Bertold, 177
Bridget, St, of Sweden, 102
Brooks, Cleanth, 34, 153
Buddhism, 120
Bultmann, Rudolf, 8, 26–8, 49
Bunyan, John, 11, 94, 102–6, 182
Burney, Fanny, 114
Burrow, Isaac, 113